A Physician on the Nile

Letter from the General Editor

The Library of Arabic Literature makes available Arabic editions and English translations of significant works of Arabic literature, with an emphasis on the seventh to nineteenth centuries. The Library of Arabic Literature thus includes texts from the pre-Islamic era to the cusp of the modern period, and encompasses a wide range of genres, including poetry, poetics, fiction, religion, philosophy, law, science, travel writing, history, and historiography.

Books in the series are edited and translated by internationally recognized scholars. They are published in parallel-text and English-only editions in both print and electronic formats. PDFs of Arabic editions are available for free download. The Library of Arabic Literature also publishes distinct scholarly editions with critical apparatus.

The Library encourages scholars to produce authoritative Arabic editions, accompanied by modern, lucid English translations, with the ultimate goal of introducing Arabic's rich literary heritage to a general audience of readers as well as to scholars and students.

The publications of the Library of Arabic Literature are generously supported by Tamkeen under the NYU Abu Dhabi Research Institute Award G1003 and are published by NYU Press.

Philip F. Kennedy
General Editor, Library of Arabic Literature

About this Paperback

This paperback edition differs in a few respects from its dual-language hardcover predecessor. Because of the compact trim size the pagination has changed. Material that referred to the Arabic edition has been updated to reflect the English-only format, and other material has been corrected and updated where appropriate. For information about the Arabic edition on which this English translation is based and about how the LAL Arabic text was established, readers are referred to the hardcover.

A Physician on the Nile

A Description of Egypt and Journal of the Famine Years

BY

ʿAbd al-Laṭīf al-Baghdādī

TRANSLATED BY

Tim Mackintosh-Smith

FOREWORD BY

Mansoura Ez-Eldin

VOLUME EDITOR

Shawkat M. Toorawa

NEW YORK UNIVERSITY PRESS
New York

NEW YORK UNIVERSITY PRESS
New York

Library of Congress Cataloging-in-Publication Data

Names: 'Abd al-Laṭīf al-Baghdādī, Muwaffaq al-Dīn, 1162–1231, author. | Mackintosh-Smith, Tim, 1961– translator. | 'Izz al-Dīn, Manṣūrah, writer of foreword. | Horta, Paulo Lemos, writer of afterword. | Toorawa, Shawkat M., editor.
Title: A physician on the Nile : a description of Egypt and journal of the famine years / by 'Abd al-Laṭīf al-Baghdādī ; translated by Tim Mackintosh-Smith ; foreword by Mansoura Ez-Eldin ; afterword by Paulo Lemos Horta ; volume editor Shawkat M. Toorawa.
Other titles: Kitāb al-Ifādah wa-l-i'tibār fī l-umūr al-mushāhadah wa-l-ḥawādith al-mu'āyanah bi-arḍ Miṣr. English
Description: New York : New York University Press, 2022. | Series: Library of Arabic Literature | Includes bibliographical references and index. | Summary: "A Physician on the Nile begins as a description of everyday life in Egypt at the turn of the seventh/thirteenth century, before becoming a harrowing account of famine and pestilence"— Provided by publisher.
Identifiers: LCCN 2022018705 | ISBN 9781479820078 (paperback) | ISBN 9781479820054 (ebook) | ISBN 9781479820085 (ebook)
Subjects: LCSH: Natural history—Egypt—Pre-Linnean works. | Famines—Egypt—History—13th century. | Egypt—Description and travel—Early works to 1800. | Egypt—History—640-1250.
Classification: LCC DT51 .S12813 2022 | DDC 916.204/2—dc23/eng/20220429
LC record available at https://lccn.loc.gov/2022018705

Series design and composition by Nicole Hayward
Typeset in Adobe Text

Manufactured in the United States of America

10 9 8 7 6 5 4 3 2 1

For Habiba
provider of mulūkhiyyah *and wisdom*
with thanks and love

and

in memory of Leslie Valentine Grinsell, O.B.E., F.S.A. (1907–1995)
connoisseur of pyramids and tumuli
teacher of the ancient characters

Contents

Foreword

MANSOURA EZ-ELDIN

Islamic history abounds with accounts of scholars who journeyed in search of knowledge and experience. One reason for this is that Islam encourages travel for the purpose of acquiring knowledge. A close connection between travel and the quest for knowledge is drawn in many Qurʾanic verses and prophetic hadiths, such as "Whoever travels a path in search of knowledge, God will ease a path to paradise for him." Unsurprisingly, travel literature flourished in Islamic societies as travelers recorded their observations and experiences in order to share what they had learned.

This is the model the scholar ʿAbd al-Laṭīf al-Baghdādī followed when he journeyed Muslim lands in search of knowledge, experience, and patronage. There is something in his book, *A Physician on the Nile* (or *The Book of Edification and Admonition*, to translate its Arabic title), however, that sets him apart from other travelers. It is a work that resists categorization, and it would be reductive to restrict it to the genre of travel literature. What is more, the author recorded his observations and eye-witnessing of events with one, and perhaps only one, reader in mind, the Abbasid caliph al-Nāṣir li-dīn Allāh. This unique account—in fact, a letter addressed to a specific reader—comes to us across the centuries and invites us to reflect on its trajectory through time and on its survival, rescued from the oblivion into which many other works fell, including some by this same author.

To write specifically for the caliph, God's representative on earth, is to hone all your talents and to aspire to the highest degree of accuracy and clarity of vision. And to write for a caliph like al-Nāṣir li-dīn Allāh, who inherited an empire in decline and sought to regain the lost glory of his predecessors, means that your writing carries a whiff of prophetic mission; it means that you are the caliph's ally or aide in his quasi-sacred undertaking. It is therefore only natural that Iraq, the seat of the Abbasid Caliphate, be the standard by which ʿAbd al-Laṭīf al-Baghdādī measures everything he witnessed in Egypt. When he sees a boat that the Egyptians call the *ʿushayrī*, for example, he compares it to the *shabbārah* of the Tigris (§1.5.10). Elsewhere, he writes:

> "that the Copts in Egypt are the counterparts of the Nabateans in Iraq, that Memphis is the counterpart of Babylon, and that the Romans and the Caesars in Egypt are the counterparts of the Persians and the Kisrās in Iraq; also that Alexandria is the counterpart of al-Madāʾin, and Fusṭāt that of Baghdad. Today all these people and places come under the aegis of Islam, and are embraced by the mission of the Abbasid Caliphate" (§1.4.77).

From the beginning, the author invites his readers to anticipate the marvelous and the strange, calling it a "a land of wondrous monuments and strange stories . . ." (§1.1.1). With those words he stresses the importance of his book, for what good is a book presented to God's caliph if it doesn't encompass the strange and wondrous? In addition to his intent to awe and amaze, he is set on providing edification and admonition (in that order). This combination of the wondrous with the beneficial and edifying reminded me, in spite of myself, of *A Thousand and One Nights*. I found myself drawing parallels, seeing ʿAbd al-Laṭīf al-Baghdādī as a Scheherazade of sorts, and the caliph al-Nāṣir li-dīn Allāh as an importuned Shahriyar. As I read and reread the book, I kept thinking that its stories and events, especially the eyewitness account of the famine and the plague, are best captured by the following iconic phrase from *A Thousand and One Nights* about stories: "so strange that if you were to carve it with a needle in the corner of the eyes, it would be a warning to the wise."

Al-Baghdādī views Egypt and Egyptians through the lens of the other. Impressively, this doesn't undermine the objectivity of his perspective. He never falls into the trap of exoticized fabrications, nor does he sacrifice truth for shock effect. He is not a peddler of fictions or a contriver of marvels, but rather a scholar who happened to be in Egypt at a tumultuous time, one of strife, desolation, and terror. This endows the record of his experiences with great historical importance, conveyed with levelheaded clarity of vision and meticulousness even when he recounts some of the strangest and most revolting horrors.

What particularly distinguishes *A Physician on the Nile* from other works on medieval Egypt is the scientific perspective coupled with a personal take, which is rare in pre-modern writing and ahead of its time. From the jolter fish to crocodiles and skinks, al-Baghdādī leaves no aspect of Egypt without comment: plants, animals, topography, architecture, cuisine. In some parts we feel as if we are reading the work of a contemporary writer turning to science and reason to assess the things he comes across and witnesses. He views monuments with the interest and respect they deserve and believes that they "remind one of the fate of past peoples and recall the end that befell them" (§1.4.57). For him, the value of most of the things we encounter lies in the lessons we can extract from them and the knowledge and wisdom they can offer us.

If his imagination does sometimes stretch, as we see in his suggestion that the banana is kin to the date palm and that it is a hybrid produced from taro and date stones, his speculations are nevertheless couched in the language of science, inviting us, through his comparison, to notice the similarities between seemingly different plants. He uses a similarly rational and deliberate tone when he narrates horrors such as cannibalism and corpses left to rot in the streets. And yet *A Physician on the Nile* reminds us of other texts that similarly describe Egypt and whose authors commented on some of the same aspects as does al-Baghdādī.

Safarnāme (*The Book of Travels*) by the Persian poet and traveler Nasir Khusraw and *Sūrat al-arḍ* (*The Configuration of the Earth*) by Ibn Ḥawqal came to mind when I read *A Physician on the Nile*. Nasir Khusraw's book, written a century and half before al-Baghdādī's, paints a very different picture of Egypt under Fatimid rule. It is a picture of a land of such luxury and prosperity that Nasir Khusraw writes: "The houses were so clean and opulent that you'd think they were built with precious stones instead of plaster, brick, and rock." His descriptions of wealth are a stark comparison to al-Baghdādī's portrait of Egypt as a wasteland of famine and plague.

But some things don't change with time. Both Nasir Khusraw and al-Baghdādī describe the practice of despoiling and looting of Egyptian antiquities, even though the two authors have different attitudes about this. Al-Baghdādī, who is clearly aware of the cultural and civilizational value of these antiquities, condemns it decisively, whereas Nasir Khusraw merely mentions it in the context of "seekers" who comb the Egyptian hills in search of buried treasures and then pay a fifth of their finds to the Sultan.

Certain plants and animals unique to Egypt draw the attention of all three authors, among them the garden of ʿAyn Shams and the balsam plant. On the balsam al-Baghdadī provides the most detail, saying, "it is only found in Egypt, at ʿAyn Shams, in an enclosed reserve approximately seven *faddāns* in area" (§1.2.9). He goes on to describe the plant in detail, including the methods of harvesting its gum and the extraction of its oil. Al-Baghdādī distinguishes between two varieties of the plant: oil-bearing balsam which doesn't produce fruit and wild male balsam that bears fruit but produces no oil. He cites Galen's statement that the finest balsam oil comes from Palestine, and the lowest grade from Egypt. He also quotes Nicolaus Damascenus to the effect that Levantine balsam is sweet-scented in all its parts, and Ibn Samajūn's statement that in his time balsam oil was only found in Egypt.

Of the same plant Nasir Khusraw writes: "The Sultan had a garden two *farsakhs* away from Cairo called 'Ayn Shams. . . . The garden had balsam trees. It is said that the Sultan's ancestors brought the seed from the west and planted them in this garden. Balsam is not found anywhere else and is unknown in the west." He offers a more personal observation on the plant and passes on reports about the historical origins of the garden and balsam's presence in Egypt, but has little to say about the plant's natural properties and uses. Ibn Ḥawqal, on the other hand, provides only a succinct overview, noting that "in 'Ayn Shams near Fustat, you find a stick-like plant called balsam from which oil is extracted. It is found nowhere else. People eat the bark of the stem which has a pleasant taste; it is spicy, and its tips are sweet."

Part One of the book is dedicated to these close observations of Egypt's plant and animal life, but even in its first chapter, he offers us a foreshadowing of the horrors to come in Part Two. To prepare his reader for the accounts of plague and death, he mentions that in Egypt, "high humidity accelerates putrefaction, and [. . .] rats and mice proliferate" (§1.1.10). Through such narrative techniques, al-Baghdādī masterfully weaves the threads of his book. Armed with his encyclopedic knowledge, he impresses and intrigues his readers and keeps them holding their breath.

If al-Baghdādī's text is a keen observer's portrait of Egypt encompassing both the marvelous and the horrific, its significance does not lie in its content alone. Rather, it rests primarily in the author's approach and skill in presenting his ideas and narrating his observations. Like Scheherazade, he knows when to elaborate, when to be brief, and when to hold back. As he modestly states at one point, "If we were to set out to recount in detail everything we caught sight of and heard tell, we would surely be suspected of exaggeration, or would babble on too long" (§2.2.15).

For three months I read and reread this book, and with every reading I became more convinced that books are of two kinds. There are books that we read, and perhaps enjoy, without becoming involved or invested. And there are books which draw us in—we live in them, and they live in us. *A Physician on the Nile* is such a book.

Mansoura Ez-Eldin
Cairo, Egypt
Translated by Huda Fakhreddine

واعــلم أنّ للعلم عقبة وعرفًا ينادي على صاحبه ونورًا وضياءً يشرق عليه ويدلّ عليه
. . . كمن يمشي بمشعل في ليل مدلهـم

Keep this in mind: knowledge leaves a trail, a trace of scent that leads to its possessor; it sheds a brightness, too, a brilliance that both illuminates and reveals its bearer . . . as when someone walks with a firebrand in a dark night.

ʿABD AL-LAṬĪF AL-BAGHDĀDĪ[1]

Acknowledgments

Apart from the obvious debt of gratitude to ʿAbd al-Laṭīf al-Baghdādī for writing this book in the first place, I must record my thanks to the guardian angels who preserved the only known copy of it through centuries of sackings in Aleppo—and to those who have preserved me, while working on it, through the vicissitudes of current history in the Yemeni capital, Sanaa. As you will learn from the Introduction, the manuscript seems to have spent many years under a curse—one that plagued the attempts to edit and translate it of no fewer than four of Oxford University's Laudian Professors of Arabic. There were times when I wondered—as my house rocked to the thunder of high explosives—whether that curse had returned to haunt me, too.

In the end, though, this strange book has been a blessing, a relief from the conflict outside my window, and—though part of it describes great suffering in great detail—an unexpected consolation. So I am grateful to the editorial board of the Library of Arabic Literature for giving me the opportunity to work on it at such a time, for bearing with the restrictions that events have placed on me, and for understanding, encouraging, sympathizing with, and supporting me in every way possible. Philip Kennedy and Shawkat Toorawa, in particular, have been earthly guardians, and I cannot thank them enough.

Further thanks are due to Shawkat, for electronically furnishing me with texts and, as my Project Editor, for slimming down my overfed endnotes and putting a spring in the step of my statelier prose; to Chip Rossetti, for assiduous communications; to Wiam El-Tamami, Alia Soliman, and Stuart Brown, for their thoughtful editing of proofs; and to Lucie M. Taylor, for invaluable logistical support. I am grateful also to Alasdair Watson of the Bodleian Library, Oxford, current guardian of the manuscript, for sending such a fine digital scan of it and, eventually, introducing me to the original.

Of my predecessors, my debt to Antoine Isaac Silvestre de Sacy will be apparent in many notes, not least those where ʿAbd al-Laṭīf's quotations from Greek authors are located in the original works. The good baron (as he deservedly became, at Napoleon's command) was a human search engine.

Of my contemporaries, I am particularly indebted to Habiba Ahmed Mohamed Al-Sayfi, born and raised in the shadow of Qāʾit Bāy's majestic Cairene mausoleum-mosque. She has kindly answered queries about modern manners and customs. It was also Habiba who introduced me to the real Cairo—including the pleasures of semi-rotten mullet and "old cheese"—and this volume is jointly dedicated to her in token of thanks.

And then there is my Sanʿani family: Abdulwahhab, Umm Mohammed, Ashwaq, Shaima, Mohammed, Shatha, Ruqayyah, and Ghayda. Not only have they kept their home and their hearts wide open through difficult and dangerous times; we have also wandered together through the curious and often dark byways of this book. I thank them for the light they have shed on the text, seeing it with fresh eyes, and for the light they continue to bring into my life.

Sanaa, July 2019—Kuala Lumpur, August 2020

Introduction

This book is a report on Egypt, written there in 600/1204 by ʿAbd al-Laṭīf al-Baghdādī for the Abbasid caliph in Iraq, and entitled in the original, *Kitāb al-Ifādah wa-l-iʿtibār fī l-umūr al-mushāhadah wa-l-ḥawādith al-muʿāyanah bi-arḍ Miṣr* (*The Book of Edification and Admonition: Things Eye-Witnessed and Events Personally Observed in the Land of Egypt*[2]). It begins as a descriptive geography but goes much further and becomes as a contemporary biographer of the author put it—"a book that stupefies the intellect,"[3] that is, "a book that blows the mind."

The book is divided into two parts. The first, the "Edification," covers general topography, then proceeds to plants, trees, and animals. It then turns into a pioneering work of Egyptology. Among his other credentials, ʿAbd al-Laṭīf was a physician; this inspired and informed his observations, both anatomical and esthetic, on pharaonic sculpture, mummies, and other antiquities. He looked hard at things, and didn't mind getting his hands dirty: in order to correct a possible error in an anatomical work by Galen, for example, he studied two thousand human jawbones in a necropolis. He was also an early and ardent champion of archeological conservation who accused monument robbers of "the heights of avarice and the depths of rascality" (§1.4.39). The long chapter on antiquities is followed by a shorter one on contemporary buildings and boats, then a chapter on food, including a detailed but easy-to-follow recipe for a sultanic picnic pie (try it at home, if you have a large enough oven: it contains not a mere four-and-twenty blackbirds, but no fewer than ninety fowl of various sorts, plus the odd three or four sheep).

All edifying indeed. But then comes the "mind-blowing" Part Two, the "Admonition"—a horrifying account of the famine and plague that afflicted Egypt in 597–98/1200–2. ʿAbd al-Laṭīf was a clinical spectator and a ruthless reporter, and he knew that his first-hand depictions of starvation and cannibalism, of a society in moral free fall, "gave the truest information and made the most striking impression" (§0.2). Here he is, for example, observing the remains of famine victims heaped up in a hollow known as "Pharaoh's Pickle Bowl" (§2.3.33):

> And when we looked down into [it] . . . we saw the skulls—white, black, dark brown, stacked on top of each other in layers. So numerous were they, and piled so high, that they had completely hidden all the other bones and might have been heads without bodies. To an onlooker, they resembled a newly cut crop of watermelons, heaped together at the harvest. I saw them again, some days later, when the sun had scorched the flesh off them and they had turned white; this time, they seemed to me like ostrich eggs piled up.

Once seen, not easily forgotten—like the skulls in *The Killing Fields*.

From Aristotle to Infinity: the Life and Work of ʿAbd al-Laṭīf al-Baghdādī

Who was this man, peering into a pit of hell with an all-seeing eye—and an all-searching mind that sought to make sense of novelty, beauty, and tragedy? We are fortunate to have a good account of ʿAbd al-Laṭīf's life in a biographical dictionary of physicians by Ibn Abī Uṣaybiʿah (d. 668/1270), who knew him personally; ʿAbd al-Laṭīf was a close friend of the biographer's grandfather, and the teacher of his father.[4] In fact we are doubly fortunate: not only does the biography include a long list of ʿAbd al-Laṭīf's works, and a selection of his memorable sayings (one of them quoted as the epigraph to this book); it also includes an extract from ʿAbd al-Laṭīf's own memoirs. As the biography–autobiography has been translated and annotated,[5] what follows here is only an outline of ʿAbd al-Laṭīf's life, including a few salient dates.[6]

ʿAbd al-Laṭīf ibn Yūsuf ibn Muḥammad al-Baghdādī, also surnamed Ibn al-Labbād ("Son of the Feltmaker/-seller"), was born in Baghdad into a family of scholars, originally from Mosul, in Rabīʿ al-Awwal 557/March 1162. He had a rather miserable-sounding childhood: he says he "knew no fun or games," but instead was crammed with lessons. In his youth, a charismatic wandering scholar and alchemist called al-Nāʾilī (fl. after 525/1131) turned up in Baghdad; ʿAbd al-Laṭīf fell under the man's influence, but was eventually to renounce alchemy as nonsense. A more lasting formative experience (mentioned in another surviving fragment of autobiography[7]) came about when, having fallen ill, ʿAbd al-Laṭīf diagnosed and treated himself using al-Rāzī's (d. 313/925 or 323/935) encyclopedic medical work, *The Comprehensive Book on Medicine* (*al-Ḥāwī fī l-ṭibb*). The success of the treatment sparked off a fascination with medicine that was to endure, grow, and gain him fame. At around the same time, he also developed a deep and lasting interest in philosophy.

Baghdad may have been the seat of a caliphate that at least nominally reigned over the Sunni Muslim world, but it was far from being an intellectual center. In his mid-twenties, therefore, like so many keen young scholars, ʿAbd al-Laṭīf set off in search of knowledge, contacts, and patronage. Arriving in Damascus in 586/1190, he found himself in a new and vigorous polity, the Ayyubid sultanate of Syria and Egypt. Its founder and ruler, Saladin (d. 589/1193), was famous as a warrior fighting the Franks, but the great man's magnetism (and money) were attracting scholarly as well as military talent. ʿAbd al-Laṭīf made for the sultan himself, and found him encamped at ʿAkkah (Acre); there, the young man made an impression on Saladin's learned secretary and adviser, al-Qāḍī al-Fāḍil

(d. 596/1200). The latter wrote him a letter of introduction to an influential contact in Cairo. A door opened.

Arriving in the Egyptian capital, ʿAbd al-Laṭīf hobnobbed with intellectuals, including the celebrated Jewish physician and thinker Moses Maimonides (d. 601/1204). The biggest influence on the young scholar, however, was a philosopher called al-Shāriʿī (d. 598/1201),[8] who steered him away from the sophistries of more recent Arabic thinking, and back to what ʿAbd al-Laṭīf regarded as a pristine Aristotelianism. In that other surviving autobiographical fragment, we learn that al-Shāriʿī was, in effect, ʿAbd al-Laṭīf's guru: "his speech and his doubts remained in my heart like something which gnaws away inside"; he was, in short, "the perfect master."[9]

Returning to the Levant in 588/1192, ʿAbd al-Laṭīf caught up again with Saladin in Jerusalem, where the princely patron awarded him a monthly allowance of thirty dinars. When ʿAbd al-Laṭīf moved on to Damascus, the sum was upped by Saladin's sons to 100 dinars—ten times the usual stipend of a professor of law.[10] This pleasing amount continued to be paid after Saladin's death in 589/1193.

With the great man gone, however, a game of musical thrones began within the Ayyubid family. Saladin's son, al-Malik al-ʿAzīz, emerged as the ruler of Egypt; when, in 592/1196, he went to take his seat, ʿAbd al-Laṭīf traveled in the prince's entourage. Back in Cairo, our author fell into a busy schedule, holding Qurʾan classes at the great mosque–academy of al-Azhar, teaching medicine, and writing—including "ghosting" at least one title for the young sultan. Al-ʿAzīz, however, died in 595/1198. There was a new and bloody round of the inter-Ayyubid struggle, but eventually, in 596/1200, Saladin's brother al-ʿĀdil managed to plant himself firmly on both the main thrones of the realm, in Syria and Egypt.

Soon after, in 597–98/1200–2, came the devastating Egyptian famine and plague described so vividly in the coming pages. ʿAbd al-Laṭīf had already been working on a big volume on Egypt and its history, largely compiled from earlier sources; he now realized that his first-person observations of the country and its catastrophe could be the material for a shorter book—this one—that would be uniquely "striking [in] impression." He finished it *in situ*, in Cairo, at some time in Shaʿban–Ramadan 600/May 1204. Shortly after, he moved to Jerusalem, where he continued teaching and writing; he also worked on a final version of this book, now lost. What we have here is by no means a rough copy, but it is a text still in motion, still growing, and particularly in its second, unsettling part. It loses nothing by this; rather, the "Admonition" gains in immediacy. We are there in the editing suite, as it were, watching the rushes.

From Jerusalem ʿAbd al-Laṭīf moved to Damascus, then to Aleppo, teaching, practicing medicine, and writing on medical matters. This time the Levantine sojourn was long: before, he had kept ahead of the years by frequent changes of scene; now they caught up with him. Ibn Abī Uṣaybiʿah, meeting him in Damascus, described him as "a thin, elderly man, of medium height, sweet-voiced and expressive."[11]

ʿAbd al-Laṭīf's travels, however, were not yet over, nor was his search for patronage. He was to move on again, after 616/1220, to Erzincan in eastern Anatolia, where once more he taught, wrote, and attached himself to the local ruler, Dāwud ibn Bahrām. As with al-ʿAzīz, the attachment involved at least one ghost-writing job. Following a regime change in Erzincan in 625/1228, ʿAbd al-Laṭīf headed back for the Levant, settling again in Aleppo in 626/1229.

But there was still one journey to be made. It had two destinations: the first was God's representative on earth, the second His house in Mecca. For ʿAbd al-Laṭīf had decided to go on the Pilgrimage, and to travel via his native Baghdad, from which he had been absent for nearly half a century. There, he intended to present some of his choicest works to the current Abbasid caliph, al-Mustanṣir—titles that doubtless included the most recent version of this book. After all, in the copy we have, he had written on the first page of his intention "to present it to the ruling authority and leader of the age" (§0.2), the caliph.[12] It has been suggested, quite plausibly,[13] that ʿAbd al-Laṭīf was angling for a teaching job at the caliph's Mustanṣiriyyah law college, then under construction in Baghdad (and still extant today in that mother-city of vicissitudes). That would have been only natural.

Did ʿAbd al-Laṭīf, and this text, reach that first destination, the caliph? No one knows. It was soon after arriving in the city of his birth that he fell ill and died, on 12 Muharram 629/9 November 1231. He was survived by a son, Sharaf al-Dīn Yūsuf, and by a multifarious corpus of writings. Few of them are extant; none of them, however, could have been more extraordinary than this book.

ʿAbd al-Laṭīf was remembered with fondness by many. The memories, however, were not unmixed. One contemporary, Ibn al-Qifṭī (d. 646/1248), attacked him for his "pretensions to learning . . . like a blind man groping his way but claiming to be sharp-sighted." He added that everyone nicknamed ʿAbd al-Laṭīf "al-Muṭajjin," the Frying-Pan-Man; the precise implications of this are unclear, but the word has a faintly ridiculous ring in Arabic, and perhaps a touch of the English "potboiler."[14] Ibn al-Qifṭī seems to have been a less than amiable character himself: according to a verse rhyming with his name, "They all agree he's mean and shifty."[15] That said, it seems ʿAbd al-Laṭīf himself had attacked a friend of Ibn al-Qifṭī as no less than a "damned devil."[16]

ʿAbd al-Laṭīf himself was no angel; he could clearly rub people up the wrong way. His aversions—to alchemists, to tomb-robbers, to officials "devoid of foresight" (§1.4.4) and others who had committed "wanton and puerile vandalism" (§1.4.28)—are strong, and strongly expressed. Even the admiring Ibn Abī Uṣaybiʿah admitted that "on occasion, he could—God have mercy on him—go too far in what he said, because of the high opinion he had of himself; he would detract from the achievements of the scholars of his own time, and of very many earlier scholars too."[17]

We can only judge him by the trail of knowledge that he left behind—his surviving works. When we do, what comes across is, admittedly, a sometimes spiky character, but with an acute, humane, and ever-curious mind, one that probed a vast body of interests. In the catalogue of ʿAbd al-Laṭīf's compositions, there are 173 titles, of which fifty-three are on medicine and forty-eight on philosophy; sixteen of this total are known to be extant, plus a collection of eleven short treatises that are not on that main list.[18] Among the losses are not only the big book on the history of Egypt, alluded to several times in the present work, but titles on a whole gamut of topics, "from rhetoric to rhubarb and from Aristotle to infinity."[19]

The Eye Atop the Pyramid: The Historical Context of the Book

Other than the lost larger book about Egypt and his own memoirs, none of ʿAbd al-Laṭīf's titles deals overtly with history, whether ancient or recent. At the same time, the context of events past and current shaped not only his life, as we have seen, but also gave a structure to this book. We should examine that context a little more closely.

ʿAbd al-Laṭīf came from a great city fallen on hard times. The traveler Ibn Jubayr, visiting Baghdad in 580/1184 when the young ʿAbd al-Laṭīf was still pursuing his studies there, was underwhelmed: "Of this ancient city, even if it remains the seat of the Abbasid caliphate . . . most of the traces are gone, and nothing of it remains but its famous name."[20] A few years later, ʿAbd al-Laṭīf forsook this hollow heart of Islamic civilization and, as we have seen, placed himself at the new center of events, the lands ruled by Saladin. His timing, though, was off. Within only a few years, Saladin was dead, and the Ayyubid center itself suddenly looked less solid. "The sons of Saladin," one commentator says, "were incapable of doing anything but amuse themselves or wrangle among themselves."[21] As a contemporary—ʿAbd al-Laṭīf's first patron and Saladin's confidant, al-Qāḍī al-Fāḍil—described this stage of the Ayyubids' history, "they had united and flourished, but then disunited and perished."[22] The commotion at the Ayyubid center—Egypt and the Levant, the pivot between Mashriq and Maghrib, the East and West of the Arabic-Islamic world—did keep ʿAbd al-Laṭīf in pocket and on his toes, as he moved around in search of patrons. It did not supply much spiritual stability.

In compensation, ʿAbd al-Laṭīf looked back to al-Nāṣir (r. 575–622/1180–1225), the Abbasid caliph in Baghdad. The caliphate had long ceased to wield its old physical power; but the institution had a rich residue of spiritual and moral force, and—especially when viewed from amid the undignified wranglings of Ayyubid princes—al-Nāṣir's office was hallowed by time and tradition. After all, he had 450 years of dynastic history behind him; the Ayyubid family tree looked as if it might wither in the second generation. Moreover, al-Nāṣir had sensed that the time was ripe for an Abbasid revival, and—blessed by the longest reign of any of the Baghdad caliphs—had begun to re-establish himself as both the spiritual cynosure of Sunni Islam, and the recognized mediator between the human and the divine. This is the foundation of ʿAbd al-Laṭīf's preface (§§0.2–3), the basis on which this book is built. Elsewhere, ʿAbd al-Laṭīf was more specific about the caliphate's reinvigorated role, following centuries of decline: al-Nāṣir, he says, "filled hearts with that awe of the caliphate that had died with the death of al-Muʿtaṣim"[23]—that is, in 227/842, over a third of a millennium earlier.

In practice, then, although the caliph was short on military might, he was armed with "awe"—moral might, and spiritual mana. And if he could not impose rule by arms, he could at least enjoy a control of sorts through intelligence. Thus ʿAbd al-Laṭīf says in his preface, "My aim in offering him this book is that no news of his territories, however remote, should be concealed from the sublime corpus of his knowledge, and that nothing be hidden from him regarding the conditions of his subjects, however distant" (§0.2). Along with the overt, there was also clandestine intelligence-gathering. Al-Nāṣir had spies operating throughout his nominal realm,[24] and was even said to have monopolized the swiftest channels of communication, by ordering the extermination of all carrier pigeons other than his own.[25]

In short, then, ʿAbd al-Laṭīf, by observing Egypt, was serving the caliph—and, since the caliph mediated with the divine, he was also, by extension, serving God. This book is thus an act of faith.[26]

But its preface provides the basis for something else, too. Moderate though the book is in size, it contains (or perhaps is contained within) a model of history on the grand scale. We read on the opening page that the Abbasid caliph al-Nāṣir is "supreme governor of the people of the world by the exercise among them of the commands and prohibitions of God the Exalted" (§0.2). Well, perhaps in theory, in Sunni thinking; but the thinking had been wishful at best for centuries. Later, however, ʿAbd al-Laṭīf's centerpiece chapter on monuments builds up to a conclusion which, if it cannot give substance to the wish, at least gives it striking and elegant form (§1.4.77, emphasis added):

> You must . . . be aware that the Copts in Egypt are the counterparts of the Nabataeans in Iraq, that Memphis is the counterpart of Babylon, and that the Romans and the Caesars in Egypt are the counterparts of the Persians and the Kisrās [the Sasanid Persian emperors] in Iraq; also that Alexandria is the counterpart of al-Madāʾin [the old Persian capital], and Fustat [the first Arab capital of Egypt] that of Baghdad. *Today, all these peoples and places come under the aegis of Islam, and are embraced by the mission of the Abbasid caliphate.*

Those few lines are a reduction of ʿAbd al-Laṭīf's historical and political thinking—a scale model, in effect, of a pyramid. Just as a pyramid is "a tapering form that rises from a square base and culminates at a point . . . . Its center of gravity lies at its midpoint . . ." (§1.4.7), so too does that vast basis of pasts, places, and peoples—Pharaonic, Babylonian, Hellenistic, Persian, Roman—taper upwards through time to culminate in "today," Islam, and the Abbasid caliph. By squaring the Egyptian past with the Mesopotamian, then by triangulating those pasts with the present, ʿAbd al-Laṭīf pyramidizes history: time and space, history and geography, cultures and empires are all consummated at one point—now—and placed at the Abbasid apex and center of gravity. For ʿAbd al-Laṭīf, al-Nāṣir, controling his virtual realm through the eyes of his spies and the observations of ʿAbd al-Laṭīf himself, was like the all-seeing eye atop the pyramid on the United States one-dollar bill.

*

It was only a hologram of power. And the lovingly projected structure was fated to collapse within a generation of ʿAbd al-Laṭīf's death. Already—but in the late sixth to early seventh/early thirteenth century as yet unseen, even from the caliph's lofty viewpoint—the might of the Mongols was building, 4,500 miles to the east. In time, ʿAbd al-Laṭīf himself was to feel the thunder of their approach: hearing news of the Mongols' first depredations in the lands of Islam, he called it "a tale to devour all tales, an account that rolls into oblivion all accounts, a history to make one forget all histories."[27] Though he would not live to see their devastation, in 656/1258, of his native city and of his beautiful, monumental Abbasid history, one senses from those words that he felt it coming. Prescient also was his feeling that, even if al-Nāṣir had "filled people's hearts with that awe of the caliphate that had died with the death of al-Muʿtaṣim," yet, as he continues, "the awe died once more with al-Nāṣir."[28]

But ʿAbd al-Laṭīf was also part of another, more durable history.

Promethean Fire: the Intellectual and Literary Background to the Book

Looking at the plethora of subjects on which he wrote, there seems to be something of the "Renaissance man" about ʿAbd al-Laṭīf, as there is about other polymaths from an Arabic cultural background. This is partly because the European renaissance was a continuation of something already current in the Arabic-Islamic sphere, an intellectual movement that preserved the learning of the classical Mediterranean world and its wide Hellenistic hinterland. That culture had never died; rather, it had gone traveling, and it was to come back to Europe the richer.

ʿAbd al-Laṭīf thus sometimes comes across as Leonardo-like, with his interest in mechanics (§1.4.27), his positing of a robot (§1.4.52), and his fascination with harmonious proportion (§1.4.22). Then again, that last concern looks back, too, to the fourth/tenth century and the Brethren of Purity, an intellectual wing of the Ismāʿīlī movement, who wrote on the moral value of proportion;[29] and the whole subject goes back in turn to the Pythagoreans, and their belief in number and proportion as the organizing principles of the cosmos.

From this it should be clear that "Renaissance" is indeed a misleading word. The intellectual tradition to which ʿAbd al-Laṭīf belonged had never needed rebirth; or, to extend the metaphor from the epigraph of this book, the torch of knowledge had merely been passed from hand to hand. ʿAbd al-Laṭīf had received the Promethean fire from his Greek and Hellenistic forerunners. As he himself put it, "Be aware that knowledge moves from nation to nation and from land to land."[30]

ʿAbd al-Laṭīf places himself overtly in this intellectual relay. Looking for historical references to the pyramids, for example, he goes first to the sacred scriptures, the Torah and the Qurʾan, and then to Greek authorities—Aristotle, Alexander of Aphrodisias, and Galen (§1.4.76). For ʿAbd al-Laṭīf, the continuum of knowledge begins with God and His revealed books, and continues on earth with the great Classical philosophers and scientists of Hellenism. Elsewhere, he relays information from the pharmacologist Dioscorides, the physician Hippocrates, the geographer and astronomer Claudius Ptolemy, the botanist Nicolaus of Damascus, and the little-known veterinarian Anatolius of Beirut.

ʿAbd al-Laṭīf may not have been aware of the two great ancient writers on Egypt, Herodotus and Hecataeus, but he was their unwitting heir. For Herodotus, Egypt was the most marvelous land on earth[31]—as it was for ʿAbd al-Laṭīf, who saw at Abusir alone "more marvels than this book could possibly contain" (§1.4.71). Again for Herodotus, the Nile was uniquely contrary in its habit of rising in midsummer[32]—as it was for ʿAbd al-Laṭīf, for whom a particularly unusual aspect of the Nile was that "it rises at the time when all other rivers decrease" (§1.1.3). Like Herodotus, the fourth-century BC Hecataeus visited the land of the Nile and—in his *Aegyptiaca*, perhaps the earliest known work of description devoted to the country—enthused about all things Egyptian.

'Abd al-Laṭīf is the beneficiary of all of these Classical writers and thinkers; but he also inherited a longstanding Arabic legacy. Written Arabic accounts of Egypt supposedly began with 'Amr ibn al-'Āṣ's (d. 42/663) short but poetic report to the caliph 'Umar, the Prophet Muḥammad's second successor. "Give me such a description of Egypt and its current circumstances," the caliph wrote to 'Amr, the Arab conqueror of Egypt, "that would make me think I was actually there." The reply, about a land of "tawny plains, rolling blue waters, black clay, a brocade of green" is impressionistic; but, being a report to a caliph from a loyal subject, it is the lineal ancestor of this book.[33]

Subsequently, descriptive geographers, historians, and travelers added to the knowledge of Egypt and its antiquities available to Arabic readers. As 'Abd al-Laṭīf says, the pyramids in particular were "already so extensively discussed, described, and surveyed by so many" (§1.4.2). Indiana Jones-style tales of boobytrapped ancient tombs were told with relish; writers like al-Mas'ūdī provided soberer accounts of pharaonica.[34]

'Abd al-Laṭīf does not belong to the sensational school of Egyptology; then again, he is not exactly sober, either. For what is new and different in this book—and seldom if ever bettered—is his esthetic response to antiquities. They are not merely wonders to be rubbernecked at, or repositories of earthly treasure to be pillaged for their contents, but—as he enthuses, in a rare flight of rhyming prose—"the utmost accomplishment man could achieve, and the most perfect embellishment stone could receive" (§1.4.44). For one thing, 'Abd al-Laṭīf sees the monuments as the key to understanding another people who carried the torch of science: the true treasure to be gained, by reflecting upon antiquities rather than ransacking them, is knowledge of their creators' "noble intellects ... pure minds ... and enlightened souls" (§1.4.6).

For another thing, the Egyptian antiquities are beautiful in themselves, especially the "idols," whose harmonious proportions and anatomical precision inspired ʿAbd al-Laṭīf's most intense enthusiasm. As a Muslim reacting to figurative art, he is at the opposite end of the spectrum to iconoclasts old and new. He would have been scandalized by two eighth/fourteenth-century acts of vandalism—the destruction of the celebrated Saite monolithic Green Chamber at Memphis, and the literal defacing of the Sphinx;[35] he would have been no less appalled by the spectacle of zealots blowing up the Buddhas of Bamiyan or sledgehammering Assyrian sculpture in our own not always enlightened millennium. Just as he belonged to a republic of learning that had no borders, geographical or temporal, he could respond with enthusiasm to the art of a culture that was at least superficially distant from his own aniconic, Islamic milieu.

ʿAbd al-Laṭīf, however, was an exceptional case, a connoisseur long before the term was invented. The sort of cool rapture with which he writes of the Sphinx's features and their proportions, for example, would not be heard again until the arrival of the French. ʿAbd al-Laṭīf, contemplating "Old Father Dread"—as Arabic calls the Sphinx—sees it as "handsomely, indeed admirably portrayed, with a touch of elegance and beauty about the features, as if a smile were playing across them" and wonders at "how the sculptor ... was able to follow the rules of harmonious proportion in the figure's features, given that they are so enormous" (§§1.4.21–22). Compare that with Vivant Denon's response to the Sphinx, almost exactly six hundred years on: "Colossal though its proportions may be, its lines are as supple as they are pure; the expression of the face is gentle, graceful, and tranquil .... The mouth ... has a softness to its movement and a fineness in its execution which are truly admirable; it is the depiction of flesh, and of life itself."[36] It might be ʿAbd al-Laṭīf rephrasing his own words, but it is in fact an artist and archeologist of the French revolutionary era speaking.

Personal, close-up observation is the basis of ʿAbd al-Laṭīf's whole method: he is an arch-proponent of autopsy—in its original sense of "seeing for oneself" (although, for a medical man and anatomist like ʿAbd al-Laṭīf, who examined corpses, the usual modern sense of the word is appropriate too). Of those ancient authorities listed earlier, it is Aristotle who provides ʿAbd al-Laṭīf's methodology. For both of them, *phainomena/aḥwāl*, "appearances, observable states," are the essential raw material of knowledge.[37] But ʿAbd al-Laṭīf's insistence on looking, particularly in order to understand the past, comes also from repeated divine promptings: «Do they not travel through the land,» the Qurʾan asks, «and see what sort of end came to those before them?»[38] These promptings were heard by the earliest descriptive geographers writing in Arabic in the third–fourth/ninth–tenth century, for whom *ʿiyān*—autopsy—was paramount.[39] A derivative of the word, *muʿāyanah*, "autopsized," and its near-synonym *mushāhadah*, "eye-witnessed," appear in the Arabic title of this book: they stare out, challenging the reader to look with the writer, before the first page is even turned.

The practice of looking, in all its aspects, is the basis of a truly scientific approach. It was a habit that rubbed off on at least some of ʿAbd al-Laṭīf's many students; one of them, al-Ṣūrī, is on record as always taking a painter with him when going out botanizing, to draw plants at different stages of their development.[40] That sounds "modern"; so too does ʿAbd al-Laṭīf's own careful observation and analysis of Nile water samples (§2.1.10–12). "Modern," also, is the way in which repeated, regular observation leads to theory, as in ʿAbd al-Laṭīf's idea of building up a data bank on the Nile, to give early warning of potential disasters (§2.1.15). Careful collection of data is what meteorologists and climate-change scientists do today, only with computers instead of reed pens.

ʿAbd al-Laṭīf is thus both an autopsist and an empiricist, someone who can form "a hypothesis constructed on the basis of evidence observed" (§1.2.20). It doesn't matter that his hypotheses can sometimes be wrong—that, for example, we know no one could have planted a date stone in a taro corm and grown a banana. You can be wrong and still be scientific, as he is in his marshaling of the data on those plants, and in his refusal to come to a dogmatic conclusion on the relationship between them (§§1.2.15–28). As Karl Popper put it, it is "not the *verifiability* but the *falsifiability* of a [scientific] system" that matters.[41] Again, ʿAbd al-Laṭīf tries to correct another possible error of the venerable Galen—his description of the human sacrum—and half succeeds, then admits in a marginal afterthought, "I am not . . . certain of this, however . . ." (§2.3.32). By saying that, he is admitting his own falsifiability (as well as Galen's). Certainty is pre-scientific; it is ʿAbd al-Laṭīf's doubt that makes him scientific.

From the Sublime to the Pit: ʿAbd al-Laṭīf's panoptic gaze

With the author's historical and intellectual background in mind, it is now time to look at his book with fresh eyes.

ʿAbd al-Laṭīf's preface is, admittedly, high-flown. Professor White, no doubt with a sniff about "Oriental hyperbole"—perhaps with a brow wrinkled by the difficulty of translating some of its phrases—omitted it from both his editions (of 1789 and 1800). But you have to write high when your dedicatee is the caliph. Besides, the preface prepares the ground for that pyramid of history, the great transparent structure (though more Louvre than Giza) which both contains the book and illuminates it.

Once past the preface, however, ʿAbd al-Laṭīf's prose is mostly low-flown, and nearly always perfectly lucid. In addition to his other interests, ʿAbd al-Laṭīf was a scholar of Arabic and the author of works on grammar, syntax, and rhetoric. That does not always guarantee lucidity, but he also had an organized mind: a close look at the manuscript reveals, for example, that the four benefits of preserving ancient monuments (§1.4.57) are numbered above the line ا, ب, ج, د, the equivalent of *a, b, c, d*. And ʿAbd al-Laṭīf uses four distinct punctuation marks, plus carets to indicate the placing of inserted matter; his paragraphing may be sporadic, but it is a help.

Just occasionally, ʿAbd al-Laṭīf's language can be obscure, as if the shadow of his words cannot quite keep up with the firelight of his ideas. Sometimes he is willfully technical, as when his eye tracks slowly and in great detail—and in a crescendo of anatomical terms—down the torso of a colossus (§1.4.42). But sometimes, too, he can be sublime, as in his microcosmic glimpse of creation, which begins in "the internal parts and cavities of living beings" and ends in a hymn of praise to their Maker (§1.4.51–53). It is at points like this that his prose is briefly transcendent. If there is anything in English remotely like it, it is perhaps only the writing of the seventeenth-century physician–metaphysician–antiquarian Sir Thomas Browne, another close observer of the natural world and debunker of misconceptions, who, like ʿAbd al-Laṭīf, transports the reader from pharaohs and pyramids to "the extasie of being ever."[42]

And then, in the second part of the book, ʿAbd al-Laṭīf takes us from earthly wonders and heavenly sublimity to Pharaoh's Pickle Bowl, that pit of hell. As Ibn Abī Uṣaybiʿah noted, it was enough to turn one's brain.[43] Even six and a half centuries later, minds were still being blown; near the end of a two-page note on historical accounts of cannibalism, Sir Henry Yule, who was Victorian but no prude, wrote, "Probably, however, nothing of the kind in history equals what Abdallatif, a sober and scientific physician, describes as having occurred before his own eyes . . . . The horrid details fill a chapter of some length, *and we need not quote from them*."[44] It is one of the most disturbing things ever written. Even today, in an age desensitized by the moving image—by footage of emaciated fellow-humans and mass graves from Dachau to Ethiopia, from Cambodia to Srebrenica—ʿAbd al-Laṭīf's mere words still shock.

Alberto Manguel has justly said that "books merely allow us to remember what we have never suffered and have never known. The suffering itself belongs only to the victims. Every reader is, in this sense, an outsider."[45] Except that the deliberate plainness of the telling, not just a coolness but a cold-bloodedness, makes ʿAbd al-Laṭīf's account unusually immediate. Even eight centuries are not a comfortable distance. We are *not* outsiders: these are human beings like us, and we are watching them, in close-up, doing terrible things to each other. We find ourselves "eye to eye with the heads of five small children, stewed in a single pot with high-grade spices" (§2.2.18). By subtitling the book "an eyewitness account," ʿAbd al-Laṭīf is saying: not only have you been challenged to look with the author; you have also been warned.

But if the reportage of the second part (the "Admonition") is ruthless, it is not voyeuristic. When we read in Sacy's translation of "détestable barbarie,"[46] the phrase jumps out as an interpolation. The Arabic says, simply, "the habit" (i.e., of cannibalism; §2.2.8). And, strangely, the detachment, the deliberate lack of moral judgement, the avoidance of sensational adjectives, all affirm the humanity not only of the observer but also of the victims (and where hunger drives men and women mad, the perpetrators are themselves also victims, of a monstrous, gnawing necessity). Given this humanity under the harrow, perhaps most shocking of all are not the actual scenes of cannibalism, but the two instances when its perpetrators are said to have lost that last link with us—their human nature (§§2.2.7, 2.2.14).[47]

Surprisingly, perhaps, where there is humanity there is also comedy, even among the horror. The humor is black, inevitably: but it is hard not to smile at the tale of the third doctor and his precipitous exit, jellified, from a window (§2.2.10). That said, one smiles as much from relief as amusement. And, in any case, well-written comedy is a deadly serious matter.

It is all the stuff of nightmares; but it had to be written down for there to be any hope of redemption. To quote Alberto Manguel again, "an inspired writer can tell the unspeakable and lend a shape to the unthinkable, so that evil loses some of its numinous quality and stands reduced to a few memorable words."[48] Or, to return again to ʿAbd al-Laṭīf's own simile, quoted as the epigraph to this book, when you walk on a dark night with the torch of knowledge, you will reveal the horror that lies hidden—but you will also cast out the darkness that hides it.

*

No other writer described the famine so unflinchingly. There are brief confirmations that it took place, for example in al-Maqrīzī (d. 845/1442), as we shall see below, and in other slightly later chroniclers of Egypt, such as Ibn Taghrībirdī (d. 874/1470).[49] But no one else dwells on it; no other writer was so close to it and, besides, history seldom cares about the *fuqarā'*, the "paupers"—the seventh and last class of society[50] and the principal victims. (Donning my historian's hat, I admit that it is easy to ignore them. I am writing this in the middle of war and famine. The war I can't ignore: things go bang, my house shakes, my windows shatter, people whom I know are killed. The famine I might not notice. Hunger is a quiet murderer; one does not know the sort of people whom it kills.)

For the most poignant evidence in support of ʿAbd al-Laṭīf's record, we have to look beyond official accounts—to the Geniza, the sprawling collection of ephemera from the ancient synagogue of Old Cairo and the most precious wastepaper basket in history. Shlomo Dov Goitein, who devoted himself to studying the documents, estimates that over half of the Jewish population in Old Cairo was wiped out in the famine.[51] Even before the worst of it had struck, a letter found in the Geniza, written near the beginning of 597/in the fall of 1200 from a seemingly well-off Jewish Alexandrian to a friend in the capital, already sounded desperate:

> Alexandria is in great trouble.... People eat up one another. This catastrophe came upon the population quite suddenly, may God grant relief in his mercy. [I] was able to purchase only three *irdabb*s [of wheat] and most of it has already been consumed. May I ask you to get the wheat under all circumstances. Your servant is [like one] of your family. May I never miss you.[52]

*

How do all these apparently ill-assorted bits of the book fit together—flora and pharaonica, picnic pies and cannibalism? Of course, in Egypt, the Nile links time and geography together: ʿAbd al-Laṭīf's detailed description of the river and its habits provides the transition from the immutable Egypt of Part One into the chaotic present of Part Two. But ʿAbd al-Laṭīf also stitches his material together in subtler ways. For example, peering closely at a hillock of ancient human remains at al-Maqs, he finds that "the quantity of earth in it was almost less than the quantity of the dead" (§2.3.26). A couple of pages on, speaking of the remains of the famine victims around the Pickle Bowl, he notes that "the dead had taken over the hillocks hereabouts so completely that they . . . almost exceeded in quantity the dust of those hummocks" (§2.3.33). The unstated message is this: that what took millennia to happen at the first place happened at the second place in months. What is more, those recent dead have decayed at an untimely rate: the ancient corpses "looked better preserved than the remains of the people who perished in the year 597 [1200–1]" (§1.4.71). The past is embalmed; the present rots.

ʿAbd al-Laṭīf, as both an observer of current events—of history in the raw—and as a historian, knows that time flows in different ways: sometimes deep and slow, sometimes in cataracts. Like the fourth/tenth-century poet, al-Mutanabbī (and for that matter the fourteenth/twentieth-century traveler Dean Moriarty, of Kerouac's *On the Road*), ʿAbd al-Laṭīf can say, "I have come to know all about time."[53]

But something else holds it all together, and that is ʿAbd al-Laṭīf's sweeping gaze, which pans from *al-tharā* to *al-thurayyā*—to use the proverbial Arabic poles of reference—from the earth to the Pleiades, from dust to stardust; or, to use two of his own extremes, from the fug and dung of chicken factories to the highest esthetics of pharaonic sculpture. The panoptic view swings, as ever, between his own two poles of reference: Aristotle, for whom nothing in creation is too “ignoble” to be contemplated and analyzed (§1.4.50), and God, “Whose unity is affirmed in [His creation’s] plurality” (§1.4.53).

That last phrase is what gives order to ʿAbd al-Laṭīf’s apparent eclecticism: by looking at the many, we might catch a glimpse of the One. The looking, like the writing, is an act of faith.

The Tale of a Text

The biography of ʿAbd al-Laṭīf by Ibn Abī Uṣaybiʿah states that he finished writing this book in Jerusalem on 10 Shaʿban 603/12 March 1207.[54] The manuscript copy that we have—the only one known to exist—is, however, dated Ramadan 600/May 1204. It is thus a work in progress. (Sometimes ʿAbd al-Laṭīf’s works could take a long time to progress: a treatise on palm trees, begun in Egypt in 599/1202–3, was only given its final polishing twenty-six years later in Erzincan.[55]) It also bears the marks of an evolving text: marginalia as well as interlinear inserts and alternatives.

The markings look like live authorial intervention. As I read the manuscript, I feel that I am looking over ʿAbd al-Laṭīf’s shoulder not only as he writes, but as he thinks. I am, of course, making an assumption—that it is in his hand, and not that of a scribe. And there, at the very end, it declares that it was indeed “written in the hand of its author . . .” (§2.3.41); except that next to the phrase, in the margin, is a note, *qūbila*, “checked”—that is, against an earlier copy. The word raised doubts in the minds of my predecessors White, Paulus, and Silvestre de Sacy, as to whether the manuscript *is* actually in ʿAbd al-Laṭīf’s hand.[56] For them, it was the sort of comment a professional copyist would add, transcribing from a master copy (including, dutifully, the colophon that says the author wrote it himself). And yet there is nothing in the sense of that word, “checked, collated,” to suggest why a busy author like ʿAbd al-Laṭīf should not write it as a note to himself. All it implies is that an earlier draft had been made, and that the present copy had been compared with that earlier version. There was as yet no “master” for a professional copyist to reproduce.

It is certainly possible that ʿAbd al-Laṭīf had an amanuensis who made this fair (but not final) copy of an earlier draft. But one piece of evidence seems to prove that the manuscript is an autograph (that is, in the author's hand): another manuscript, preserved in Bursa, containing a collection of ʿAbd al-Laṭīf's treatises, annotated with corrections. S.M. Stern, who studied the Bursa manuscript carefully, was absolutely certain that the annotations are ʿAbd al-Laṭīf's own,[57] and they do seem to be by the same writer as this book. Stern himself had no doubts.

I will maintain a little scientific caution. As ʿAbd al-Laṭīf himself admitted, while analyzing not script but skeletons: "I am not . . . certain" (§2.3.32). Nevertheless, I feel that, in our manuscript, another triangle is complete—one made by the witnessing eye, analyzing mind, *and* recording hand.

*

The fate of any other copies that might have existed is unknown. If a finished version did ever make it to the caliph in Baghdad, then almost certainly, like the other books in the caliphal library, "it was lost with those books which Hulagu, the ruler of the Tatars [the Mongols], threw into the Tigris."[58] All we can do is look for the "specter" of the elusive text as it haunts other works that do survive.

ʿAbd al-Laṭīf's book may, for example, have inspired a short passage on the famine that mentions the kidnapping of physicians visiting the sick (the jellified doctor mentioned above was one who got away). This passage appears in more than one seventh/thirteenth-century history.[59] More notably, al-Maqrīzī's short study of famines in Egypt, from the past up to his own day (the early ninth/fifteenth century), includes information given in ʿAbd al-Laṭīf's account.[60] Not only are the tales of cannibalism briefly confirmed; specific details also crop up again, such as the execution by burning of thirty women (cf. §2.2.7), and the price of a bull for plowing rising to seventy dinars (cf. §2.2.33).

Other data given by al-Maqrīzī are different, however. The price of a measure of wheat is said to have reached eight dinars, while

ʿAbd al-Laṭīf (§2.2.35) says five, and the sultan to have contributed to the costs of 220,000 funerals, rather than ʿAbd al-Laṭīf's 111,000 (§2.3.9). But perhaps most significantly, the present book is mentioned by title neither in this treatise, nor in the same author's huge descriptive work on Egypt, usually known as *Al-Maqrīzī's City Quarters* (*al-Khiṭaṭ al-Maqrīziyyah*). The latter, often referred to in my endnotes, sums up most of what had been written in Arabic on Egypt, and preserves much that would have been lost. It is not remiss about naming its sources; it cites ʿAbd al-Laṭīf's autobiography several times, and includes four generations of ancestors when giving his name.[61] On this book, however—and, for that matter, on the lost longer book on Egypt that ʿAbd al-Laṭīf wrote—it is silent.

Not much can be deduced from all this, except to say that the sort of stories ʿAbd al-Laṭīf tells, and even some of the detailed information he records, were doing the rounds in the centuries after he wrote this account. Then again, the material would almost certainly have been public knowledge, and not just confined to his pages. That defenestrated doctor is the stuff of urban anecdote.

We do, however, have some definite sightings of this present book in someone else's work—a case not just of reading and recycling, but of plunder and plagiarism. The unacknowledged borrowings were made by Nāṣir al-Dīn Shāfiʿ ibn ʿAlī (649–730/1251–1330), a scholar and bibliophile originally from Palestine who moved to Egypt.[62] In his *Marvels of Architecture* (*Kitāb ʿAjāʾib al-bunyān*), he uses quite substantial passages of ʿAbd al-Laṭīf's material on the Sphinx and the pyramids almost verbatim, merely tweaking phrases; for example, ʿAbd al-Laṭīf's "I asked" becomes an impersonal "it was asked."[63] *The Marvels of Architecture* seems also to be lost (one is tempted to say, *Serves it right*), but a number of passages, including these borrowings, are preserved by al-Maqrīzī. The latter attributed them to Shāfiʿ ibn ʿAlī, and was clearly unaware of their ultimate origin.

It seems likely, therefore, that ʿAbd al-Laṭīf's two works on Egypt—the present book, and the longer one to which he often refers—had either slipped out of circulation at some point in the seventh to eighth/thirteenth to fourteenth centuries; or, perhaps, that they had never been circulated. We are extremely fortunate that this single known manuscript has survived.

*

The manuscript was to have an eventful history. After ʿAbd al-Laṭīf's death, his books, presumably including this one, were sold in Aleppo.[64] That seems to be where it stayed, surviving the Mongol sacks by Hulagu (fresh from his Baghdad blood- and book-bath) in the seventh/thirteenth century, and by Timur at the end of the following century. At any rate, Aleppo was where it came to light again, more than two hundred years after Timur, when it was bought by the Arabist Edward Pococke, chaplain to the English "Turkey Merchants" in that city. Appointed first Laudian Professor of Arabic at Oxford University, Pococke took ʿAbd al-Laṭīf to England in 1636, together with the many other manuscripts he had collected. ʿAbd al-Laṭīf himself might not have disapproved: it was, after all, only another case of knowledge moving "from nation to nation and from land to land."[65]

Once in England, however, the manuscript seemed to fall under a curse.[66] According to one account, Pococke eventually began work late in life on a printed edition, but an "omnipotent" bishop commandeered the Arabic fonts at the University Press for another project, "which so vexed the good old man, Dr Pocock [*sic*], y^{t} he could never be prevail'd to go any further."[67] It seems likelier, though, that Pococke was simply too busy to work on the manuscript (he was Professor of Hebrew as well as of Arabic) and that it was the good old man's son, Edward Pococke the Younger, who had started work on the printed version, as well as on a Latin translation. In this version of events, it was the son who abandoned the printing on his father's death in 1691. The younger man had expected to inherit his father's Hebrew professorship; it went to another candidate, and he pulled the work (titled *Abdollatiphi Historiæ Ægypti Compendium*) from the press "upon a disgust at his being disappointed."[68]

For most of the following century, the manuscript had no better luck. Thomas Hyde, the second Laudian Professor of Arabic, began his own Latin version and commentary, and even planned plates; he died in 1703, mid-project. In 1746, another incumbent of the Laudian chair, Thomas Hunt, decided to have a go, and advertised for subscribers: a total of two signed up, and the project was abandoned again. Yet another Laudian Professor, Joseph White, worked on an Arabic edition in the 1780s. At last, all seemed to go smoothly—until, when it was at proof stage, the curse struck again: White had last-minute reservations (apparently about the book's typography rather than its contents), and decided not to release it.

No one, it seemed, would be edified or admonished. But then the book's fortunes took a turn for the better. A German colleague, H. E. G. Paulus, persuaded White to let him publish the already typeset text (*Abdollatiphi Compendium Memorabilium Aegypti*) in Tübingen in 1789; from this, a rushed German translation was made by S. F. G. Wahl (*Abd-allatif's, eines arabischen Arztes: Denkwürdigkeiten Egyptens*). White later brought out an updated Arabic version in Oxford in 1800, with a Latin translation on facing pages.[69] But the curse had not quite run its course. White meant to do an English translation, entitled *Aegyptiaca*, but only an introductory volume ever came out.[70]

It took the greatest Arabist of the age to scotch the lingering ill luck. Silvestre de Sacy's annotated French translation, *Relation de l'Égypte*, is a *tour de force*; it was a product of the golden age of French Egyptology, itself inspired by Napoleon's invasion of Egypt in 1798. (Napoleon, the dedicatee of the volume, would raise Sacy to a barony.) The translation itself is sometimes rather loose and, as we have seen, inclined to make interpolations that are as judgmental as they are explanatory. Any shortcomings, though, are more than made up for by Sacy's notes. They are monumentally copious: the gloss on the *labakh* tree, for example, is a full twenty-five pages long—and it still can't decide exactly what a *labakh* was (and neither can I).[71]

ʿAbd al-Laṭīf, however, would still have to wait another century and a half to become known to an anglophone readership. The English translation by Judge K. Hafuth Zand and Mr. and Mrs. John A. Videan, published as *The Eastern Key* in 1965, often follows the French master with poodle-like loyalty; it does sometimes slip the leash and correct an error in Sacy's version,[72] but is more likely to bark up the wrong tree.[73] In diametric opposition to Sacy, however, the commentary is almost non-existent. There is, however, one extraordinary aspect to *The Eastern Key*, unparalleled in the history of translation and confirming Robert Irwin's view that "translation is like a séance with the dead."[74] For Zand and the Videans, it was *literally* a séance with the dead.

The West in the early twentieth century had seen a growth in the popularity of spiritualism, the idea that it is possible to communicate with departed souls. The trend accelerated with the Great War, and the resulting massive loss of human life—and of traditional faith. It was around this time that ʿAbd al-Laṭīf became known in spiritualist as well as Orientalist circles; he was even the subject of a book entitled *Healing Through the Spirit Agency: by the great Persian [sic] physician Abduhl Latif, "the man of Baghdad", and information concerning the life hereafter of the deepest interest to all inquirers and students of psychic phenomena.*[75] He was—perhaps still is—regarded as "a Universal Master who leads and directs a band of workers on and around the earth."[76] Here is Ivy E. Videan, in cold print, in her introduction to *The Eastern Key*:

> Our first meeting with ʿAbd al-Latīf was in August, 1957, when he spoke to my husband and to me during a conversation with a sensitive, Mrs. Ray Welch, in London. Since then we have had very many long talks with him, through Mrs. Welch and also through Mr. Jim Hutchings. It was not unexpected, therefore, that he should tell us in 1960 that he wished my husband to make a photographic copy of the Bodleian manuscript of the Kitāb al-ifādah for presentation to the British Museum in London, where it would

> be more easily accessible to a wider public. ʿAbd al-Laṭīf promised to prepare the way for the accomplishment of this plan, adding later that he would send a translator from Baghdad.[77]

That translator—Mr. Zand—was necessary to the undertaking, as the Videans do not appear to have actually known the language of the original (not necessarily an impediment: think, for one, of Proust translating Ruskin). Just as necessary was M. le baron Silvestre de Sacy, though it seems he did not intervene from beyond the grave. ʿAbd al-Laṭīf, however, was involved in the project throughout. It all makes Madam Arcati and *Blithe Spirit* seem frightfully low-brow.

I boast no endnotes credited to "al-Baghdādī, personal communication." That said, there are moments, when you live and work closely with a text, in which the present is revealed for what it is—merely the latest layer in a mound of lives. At such times there is no absolute past or present; only continuum.[78]

In the end, ʿAbd al-Laṭīf needs no medium other than his own words. He comes across from the other side loud and clear, a man of sturdy opinions and lively enthusiasms. He is no feeble ectoplasm, but an enlightened soul if ever there was one, a firebrand on a dark night.

*

Can ʿAbd al-Laṭīf illuminate anything for us today, and for readers to come? We know a lot more about the Egyptian past than he could have done. "The ancient characters that no one understands," (§1.4.13)—the hieroglyphic ones—are now an open book; mummies, subjected to the indignity of magnetic resonance scanners, have revealed their inmost secrets. But, as well as his meditations on the ancient dead and their monuments, ʿAbd al-Laṭīf also records the deeds and voices of the latter-day dead, those hungry ghosts. Both he, the doctor, and they, the sufferers, bear witness: to the need to think historically about the future as much as the past, for prognosis as much as diagnosis.

ʿAbd al-Laṭīf described an Egypt that had gone awry. It was not only the Nile that was behaving strangely; the book draws to a close with a series of ominous happenings, both major (epidemic disease, earthquake) and minor (a dignified gentleman runs amok, a baby is born with two heads). Just as crisis had become a "natural temperament" (§2.3.2), so the temperament of nature itself seemed unbalanced.

We live in a time when the temperament not just of a river and a land, but of the entire global climate, is increasingly unbalanced; when epidemic becomes pandemic in a few short months. Only rarely do we have the evidence of the past to warn us of what happens when things go out of kilter; historians are so often deaf to the poor, the usual victims of catastrophe, that we seldom hear the most urgent warnings, let alone heed them. So when the past speaks, as it does here, in the voices of the victims, we should listen—and then the dead who people these pages may not have died in vain.

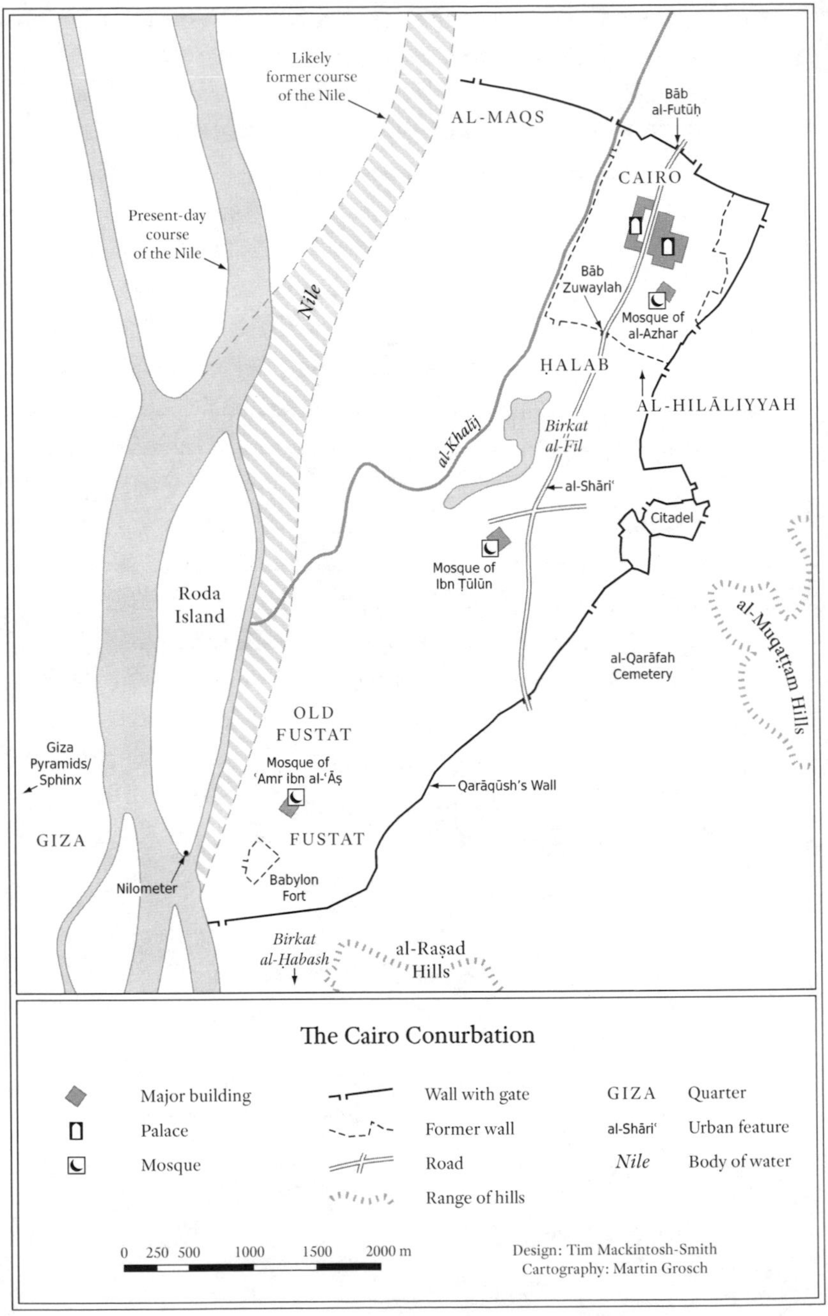
Likely former course of the Nile
AL-MAQS
Bāb al-Futūḥ
CAIRO
Present-day course of the Nile
Nile
Bāb Zuwaylah
Mosque of al-Azhar
ḤALAB
AL-HILĀLIYYAH
Birkat al-Fīl
al-Khalīj
al-Shāriʿ
Citadel
Mosque of Ibn Ṭūlūn
Roda Island
al-Muqaṭṭam Hills
al-Qarāfah Cemetery
OLD FUSTAT
Giza Pyramids/ Sphinx
Mosque of ʿAmr ibn al-ʿĀṣ
Qarāqūsh's Wall
GIZA
FUSTAT
Nilometer
Babylon Fort
Birkat al-Ḥabash
al-Raṣad Hills
Major building
Palace
Mosque
Wall with gate
Former wall
Road
Range of hills
GIZA Quarter
al-Shāriʿ Urban feature
Nile Body of water
0 250 500 1000 1500 2000 m
Design: Tim Mackintosh-Smith
Cartography: Martin Grosch

The Cairo Conurbation

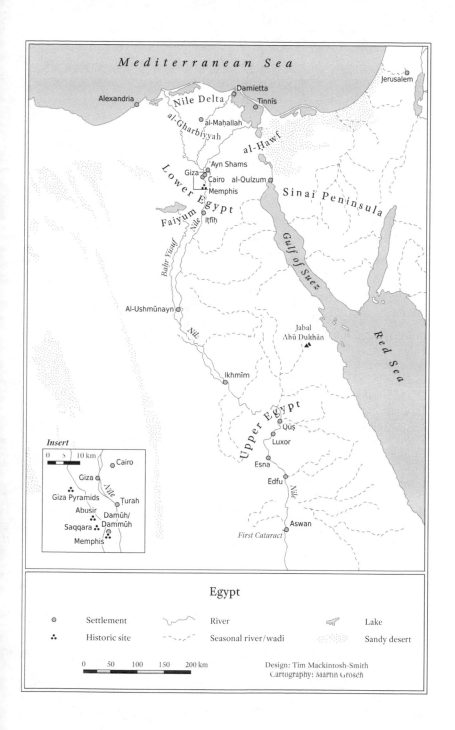

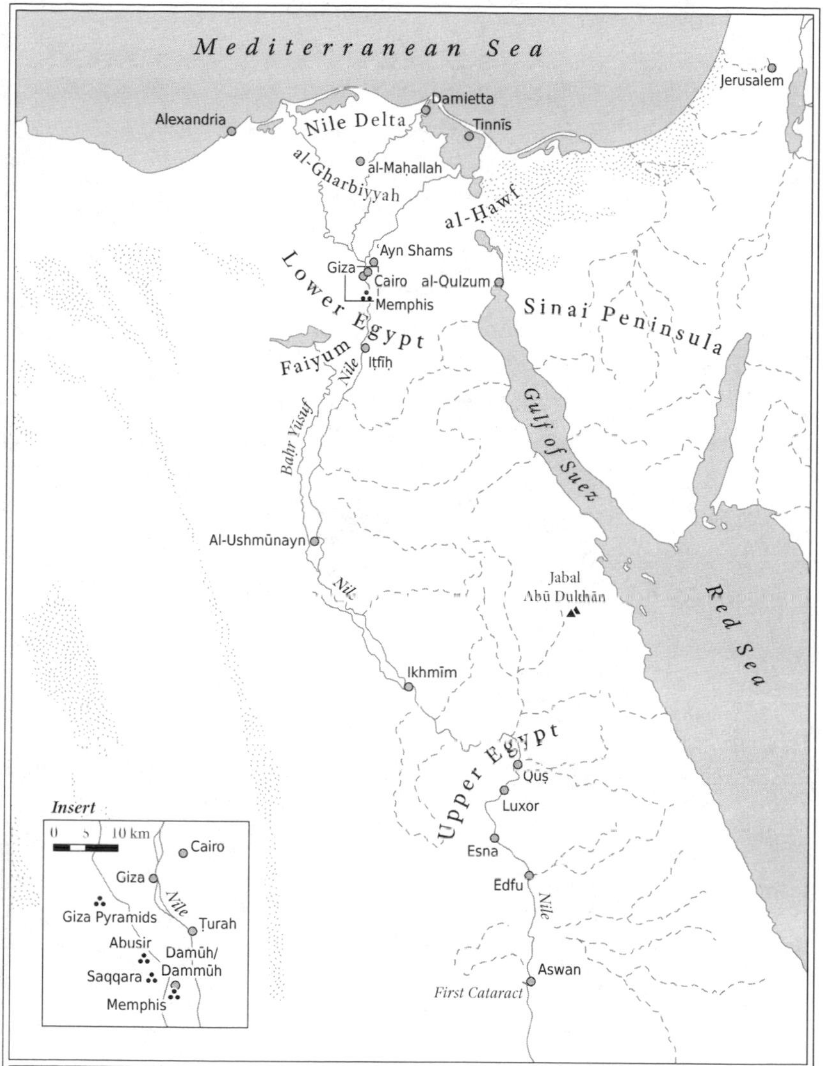

Egypt

Settlement
Historic site
River
Seasonal river/wadi
Lake
Sandy desert

0 50 100 150 200 km

Design: Tim Mackintosh-Smith
Cartography: Martin Grosch

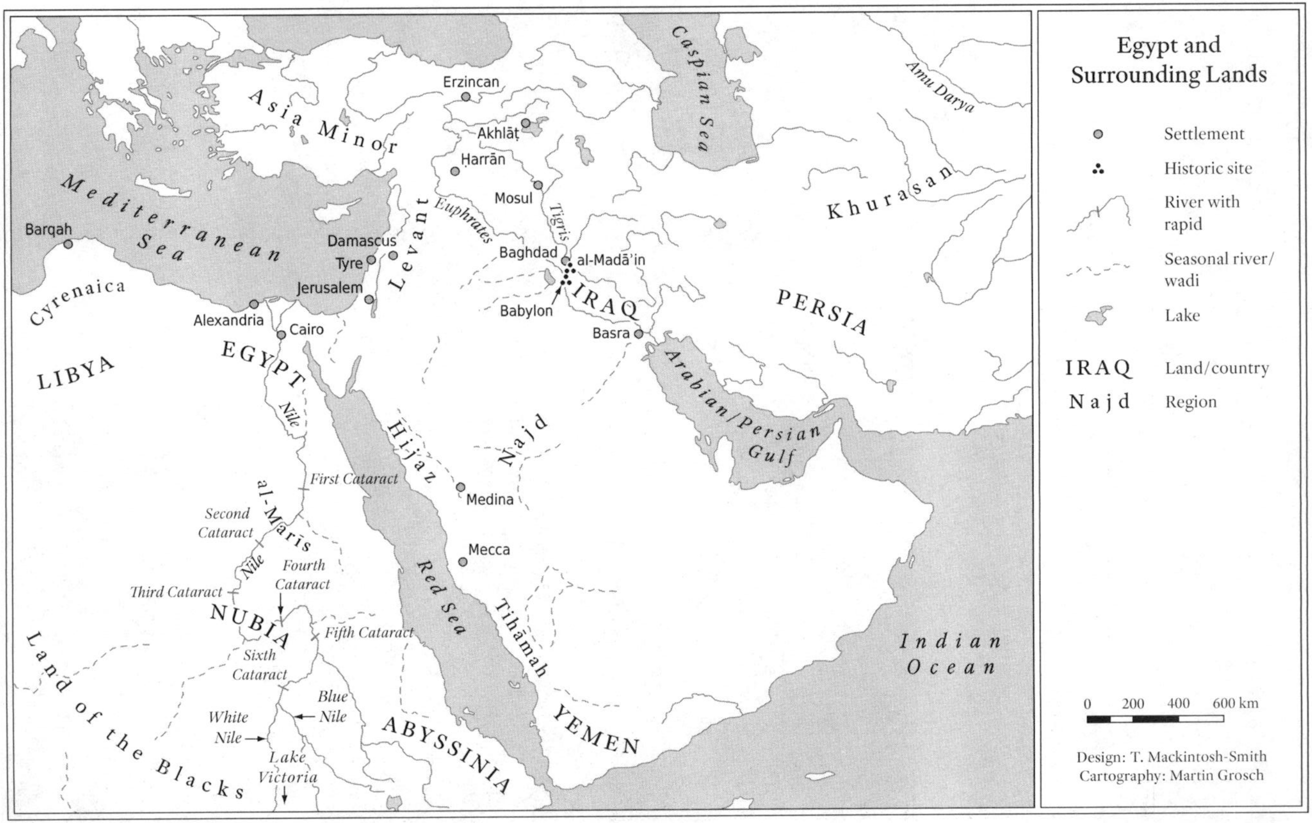

Egypt and Surrounding Lands
Settlement
Historic site
River with rapid
Seasonal river/wadi
Lake
IRAQ
Land/country
Najd
Region
0
200
400
600 km
Design: T. Mackintosh-Smith
Cartography: Martin Grosch
Caspian Sea
Amu Darya
Khurasan
PERSIA
Asia Minor
Erzincan
Akhlāṭ
Ḥarrān
Mosul
Tigris
Euphrates
Baghdad
al-Madā'in
Babylon
IRAQ
Basra
Arabian/Persian Gulf
Mediterranean Sea
Barqah
Cyrenaica
Damascus
Tyre
Levant
Jerusalem
Alexandria
Cairo
LIBYA
EGYPT
Nile
Hijaz
Najd
Medina
Mecca
Red Sea
Tihāmah
YEMEN
Indian Ocean
First Cataract
al-Marīs
Second Cataract
Nile
Fourth Cataract
Third Cataract
NUBIA
Fifth Cataract
Sixth Cataract
Blue Nile
White Nile
Lake Victoria
ABYSSINIA
Land of the Blacks

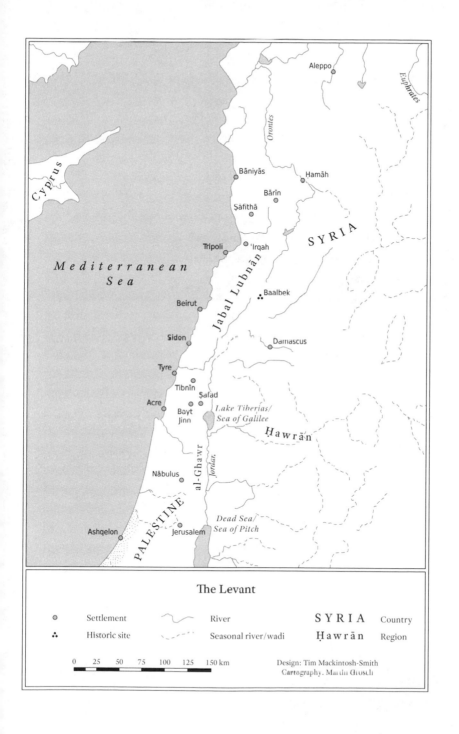

The Levant

Settlement · Historic site · River · Seasonal river/wadi · SYRIA Country · Ḥawrān Region

0 25 50 75 100 125 150 km

Design: Tim Mackintosh-Smith
Cartography: Martin Grosch

Note on the Text

Getting the basic meaning right has not always been easy, given the range of subject matter in the book. What, for example, is the *sās* with which you insulate an egg incubator? It is not in any of the standard dictionaries. What, precisely, is the "button of the heart"? Here the dictionaries do help, defining it as a small bone which supports that organ—except that the bone in question seems to be a figment of someone's (probably Galen's) imagination. The nearest thing is probably the xiphoid process or metasternum.

Apropos bones and processes, it has been said that a translator is like an anatomist, not a taxidermist.[79] My approach (and I hope ʿAbd al-Laṭīf the anatomist would approve) is to take the meaning apart from the inside, and expose it to view as literally and lucidly as possible. Having said that, there are a few places—notably the striking opening of the second chapter in Part Two—where I believe that literalness would kill the original. Most other instances where I depart from the literal are those where ʿAbd al-Laṭīf has used *sajʿ*—rhyming and rhythmic prose. In contrast to many of his contemporaries, he employs it sparingly; it is thus all the more arresting when he does use it. I therefore usually try to echo it: it should stand out in the translation, as it does in the original. (To give an example, the scant irrigation provided by an insufficient rise in the Nile is likened, in §2.2.32, to "a token touch at most, like some dream visit from the river's ghost.")

Translations from the Qurʾan are my own.

Appendix: The Egyptian Calendar

In addition to the Islamic lunar calendar, ʿAbd al-Laṭīf uses two different solar calendars—the Coptic and, occasionally, the Syriac or "Syro-Macedonian." He does so because the lunar Islamic months are not in step with the solar year, by which the rise of the Nile and most agricultural activities are timed. The table below shows the Coptic months, first in their arabicized versions and then in standard modern transliterations, together with their starting dates in the Julian calendar ("Old Style" dating, used in western Europe before the Gregorian adjustments to the calendar that began in the sixteenth century) and their approximate Syro-Macedonian and Julian/Gregorian equivalents.

Coptic (arabicized)	**Coptic (standard)**	**Begins**	**Syro-Macedonian**	**Julian/Gregorian**
Ṭūbah	Tōbe	27 Dec.	Kānūn al-thānī	January
Amshīr	Mshir	26 Jan.	Shubāṭ	February
Barmahāt	Paremhat	25 Feb.	Ādhār	March
Barmūdah	Parmoute	27 Mar.	Nīsān	April
Bashans	Pashons	26 Apr.	Ayyār	May
Ba'ūnah	Paōne	26 May	Ḥazīrān	June
Abīb	Epep	25 Jun.	Tammūz	July
Misrā	Mesōre	25 Jul.	Āb	August
[Nasī']	Epagomenai	24 Aug.	*(an intercalary period of 5/6 days)*	
Tūt	Thoout	29 Aug.	Aylūl	September
Bābah	Paape	28 Sep.	Tishrīn al-awwal	October
[Hātūr]	Hatōr	28 Oct.	Tishrīn al-thānī	November
[Kīhak]	Kiahk	27 Nov.	Kānūn al-awwal	December

Notes to the Introduction

1 Al-Baghdādī, *Kitāb al-Ifādah wa-l-iʿtibār* (1403/1983), 159; cf. Martini Bonadeo, *ʿAbd al-Laṭīf al-Baġdādī's Philosophical Journey*, 142.

2 To give a more literal translation of the subtitle than that in §0.1.

3 Quoted in al-Baghdādī, *Kitāb al-Ifādah* (1403/1983), 153.

4 Ibn Abī Uṣaybiʿah, *ʿUyūn al-anbāʾ fī ṭabaqāt al-aṭibbāʾ* , s.v. "ʿAbd al-Laṭīf"; the entry is reprinted in al-Baghdādī, *Kitāb al-Ifādah* (1403/1983), 141–65, and in al-Baghdādī, *Riḥlat ʿAbd al-Laṭīf al-Baghdādī fī Miṣr*, 36–52.

5 In English, Martini Bonadeo, *Philosophical Journey*, 111–43; in French, al-Baghdādī, *Relation de l'Égypte*, 457–94. A detailed and fascinating commentary appears in the articles by Shawkat Toorawa, cited below.

6 Cf. the chronology in Toorawa, "Travel in the medieval Islamic world: the importance of patronage, as illustrated by ʿAbd al-Latif al-Baghdadi (d. 629/1231) (and other littérateurs)," 63–65.

7 From ʿAbd al-Laṭīf's *Kitāb al-Naṣīḥatayn*, quoted in Martini Bonadeo, *Philosophical Journey*, 175.

8 Identified in Toorawa, "A Portrait of ʿAbd al-Laṭīf al-Baghdādī's Education and Instruction," 105.

9 *Kitāb al-Naṣīḥatayn*, translated in Martini Bonadeo, *Philosophical Journey*, 179.

10 Makdisi, quoted in Toorawa, "Travel," 61.

11 Translation from Toorawa, "Portrait," 107 n. 103.

12 The dedicatee of this version is al-Mustanṣir's late grandfather, al-Nāṣir, who had died in 622/1225.

13 Makdisi, quoted in Martini Bonadeo, *Philosophical Journey*, 139 n. 152.

14 Al-Baghdādī, *Kitāb al-Ifādah* (1403/1983), 166–67; cf. Martini Bonadeo, *Philosophical Journey*, 108 n. 3. Regarding "al-Muṭajjin," the letters *ṭ* and *j* are supposed not to occur together in chaste Arabic words. My suggestion of "potboiler" is partly inspired by a nickname of a former president of Yemen, who, owing to an alleged fondness for consumption, was known as "ʿAlī Maqlā," "ʿAlī Fry Pot."

15 Al-Baghdādī, *Kitāb al-Ifādah* (1403/1983), 168; a rather loose translation, but I wanted to find at least an approximate rhyme.

16 Martini Bonadeo, *Philosophical Journey*, 151–52.

17 Al-Baghdādī, *Kitāb al-Ifādah* (1403/1983), 142.

18 Martini Bonadeo, *Philosophical Journey*, 197–200.

19 Mackintosh-Smith, *Ghost Writer*, 5.

20 Translated in Mackintosh-Smith, *Arabs: A 3,000-Year History of Peoples, Tribes and Empires*, 363.

21 *Encyclopaedia of Islam, Second Edition*, s.v. "Ayyūbids"(Cl. Cahen).

22 Translated in Mackintosh-Smith, *Arabs*, 285.

23 Al-Baghdādī, *Kitāb al-Ifādah* (1403/1983), 111.

24 ʿAbd al-Laṭīf quoted in al-Baghdādī, *Kitāb al-Ifādah* (1403/1983), 108–9.

25 *Encyclopaedia of Islam*, s.v. "al-Nāṣir" (J. R. Blackburn).

26 Cf. n. 7 to the text.

27 Translated in Mackintosh-Smith, *Arabs*, 365; cf. al-Baghdādī, *Kitāb al-Ifādah* (1403/1983), 136.

28 Al-Baghdādī, *Kitāb al-Ifādah* (1403/1983), 111.

29 Irwin, *The Alhambra*, 110.

30 Al-Baghdādī, *Kitāb al-Ifādah* (1403/1983), 159.

31 Herodotus, *The Histories*, §2.25.

32 Herodotus, *The Histories*, §2.25.

33 Quoted in al-Harawī, *Kitāb al-Ishārāt ilā maʿrifat al-ziyārāt*, 51–52.

34 Quoted in al-Maqrīzī, *Khiṭaṭ*, 1:40–41.

35 See, respectively, "Green Chamber" in the Glossary, and n. 108 to the text.

36 Quoted in al-Baghdādī, *Relation*, 225 n. 38.

37 Cf. Hornblower and Spawforth, *The Oxford Classical Dictionary*, 167 section 15.

38 Q Rūm 30:9. Though only one of many such verses, it seems to have some special relevance to Egypt: on a visit to Luxor, ʿAbd al-Laṭīf's near contemporary al-Harawī, a noted guidebook writer and graffiti artist, wrote the text on the chest of a colossus (*Kitāb al-Ishārāt*, 44).

39 Miquel, *La géographie humaine du monde musulman jusqu'au milieu du 11è siècle*, 1, chapter 8.

40 *Encyclopaedia of Islam*, s.v. "Nabāt" (R. Kruk).

41 Popper, *The Logic of Scientific Discovery*, 1959, chap. 1, section 6.

42 Browne, *The Voyce of the World*, 158.

43 See al-Baghdādī, *Kitāb al-Ifādah* (1403/1983), 153.

44 Yule, *The Travels of Marco Polo*, 1:313; italics added.

45 Manguel, *The Library at Night*, 247.

46 Al-Baghdādī, *Relation*, 364; al-Baghdādī, *Eastern Key*, 229 has the copycat "detestable barbarism."

47 The short paragraph §2.2.27 does seem to give vent to moral outrage. But ʿAbd al-Laṭīf's reaction is one of surprise at people's ignorance of divine law, rather than anger at their innate wickedness.

48 Manguel, *A Reader on Reading*, 247.

49 Quoted in al-Baghdādī, *Riḥlat ʿAbd al-Laṭīf*, 10.

50 See n. 224 to the text.

51 Goitein, *Mediterranean Society*, 2:141.

52 Goitein, *Mediterranean Society*, 4:239.

53 Quoted in Irwin, *Night and Horses and the Desert*, 221.

54 Al-Baghdādī, *Kitāb al-Ifādah* (1403/1983), 162.

55 Al-Baghdādī, *Kitāb al-Ifādah* (1403/1983), 164.

56 Al-Baghdādī, *Kitāb al-Ifādah* (1403/1983), xvi–xvii and 453–54 n. 69.

57 Stern, "A Collection of Treatises by ʿAbd al-Laṭīf al-Baghdādī," 56 and plates II–V.

58 Ibn Khaldūn, *The Muqaddimah*, 261.

59 Those of Sibṭ Ibn al-Jawzī and Abū Shāmah, recycled in the later Ibn Taghrībirdī, who is quoted in turn in al-Baghdādī, *Riḥlat ʿAbd al-Laṭīf*, 10.

60 Al-Maqrīzī, "Le Traité des famines de Maqrīzī," 29–32.

61 Al-Maqrīzī, *Khiṭaṭ*, 1:115.

62 Ibn Ḥajar, *Al-Durar al-kāminah*, 2:184–86.

63 Al-Maqrīzī, *Khiṭaṭ*, 1:120–21.

64 Al-Baghdādī, *Kitāb al-Ifādah* (1983), 167.

65 Al-Baghdādī, *Kitāb al-Ifādah* (1983), 159; cf. p. xxi, above.

66 Cf. Kratchkovsky, *Al-Adab al-jughrāfī al-ʿArabī*, 346.

67 *Dictionary of National Biography*, s.v. "Edward Pococke, Junior."

68 Twells, *The Lives of Dr Edward Pocock, the Celebrated Orientalist*, 1:334–35.

69 The first three chapters of this translation are actually by Pococke the Younger.

70 The minutiae of this ill-starred publishing history are recounted in al-Baghdādī, *Relation*, xiv–xv and Schnurrer, *Bibliotheca Arabica*, 150–53.

71 Renan may have had a point when, contemplating Silvestre de Sacy, he saw "the strange spectacle of a man, who, though he possesses one of the vastest eruditions of modern times, has never had an important critical insight" (quoted in Irwin, *For Lust of Knowing: The Orientalists and their Enemies*, 166). But we are still the beneficiaries of that erudition today.

72 E.g. it is not the Nile that supplies the drinking water of the coast dwellers (al-Baghdādī, *Relation*, 3), but rain (al-Baghdādī, *Eastern Key*, 21; cf. §1.1.4, below).

73 E.g. by turning a "trustworthy and truthful" informant (§1.4.70, below) into a person called "El Amin 'l' Sadk" (al-Baghdādī, *Eastern Key*, 171).

74 Irwin, *Night*, viii.

75 By R. H. Saunders. London: Hutchinson, 1928.

76 Al-Baghdādī, *Eastern Key*, 8.

77 Al-Baghdādī, *Eastern Key*, 8.

78 I have told the tale of ʿAbd al-Laṭīf's text and of his alleged postmortem visits to suburban London at greater length in a small study, *Ghost Writer*.

79 Manguel, *A Reader on Reading*, 151.

A Physician on the Nile

The Book of Edification and Admonition 0.1

An Eyewitness Account of the Land of Egypt and of Recent Events There

written in hope of the mercy of God, Mighty and Glorious is He,

by ʿAbd al-Laṭīf ibn Yūsuf ibn Muḥammad al-Baghdādī,

may God guide him to be His obedient servant[1]

In the name of God, the Merciful and Compassionate

Praise to God, Lord of the worlds, and may His blessings rest upon Muḥammad, the Seal of the Prophets, the Arabian prophet, and upon the virtuous members of his family. When I finished my earlier book of accounts of Egypt, comprising thirteen chapters,[2] I had the idea of extracting from it the reports of present-day events and of conspicuous monuments and other features that I myself had observed, for I saw that these passages gave the truest information and made the most striking impression. Besides, most if not all of the rest of the material in that earlier book is probably to be found in the works of previous writers, either presented as a whole or scattered throughout their pages. Realizing that all of this first-hand material appeared in two of my thirteen chapters, I excerpted them and turned them into the two parts of the present book, adding or omitting information as circumstances required. My hope is that this shorter work will prove less weighty to deliver and more finely pointed in effect when I present it to the ruling authority and leader of the age—the leader of mankind, obedience to whom is an obligation under the sacred law of Islam, God's vicegerent on His earth 0.2

and the ultimate repository of His revelation, supreme governor of the people of the world by the exercise among them of the commands and prohibitions of God the Exalted—namely, our lord and master the caliph al-Nāṣir li-dīn Allāh, Commander of the Faithful, he whose manifold status is sanctified, hallowed, and purified by prophetic heritage, is exalted and glorified by caliphal precedent, is resplendent with illumination, effulgent with benediction. My aim in offering him this book is that no news of his territories, however remote, should be concealed from the sublime corpus of his knowledge, and that nothing be hidden from him regarding the conditions of his subjects, however distant. My intention, too, is that those close to him—the entourage who serve at his threshold, the great men of his state, those who throng his beatific enclosure and who circle the sanctuary of his sacred precinct—that all these should realize how surely God the Exalted defends them by their caliph's hand, and should thus express a greater gratitude to the same Exalted God; and that He, in turn, might prolong the rule over them of the Commander of the Faithful, and bestow thereby upon them an even greater grace.[3] «And God would not chastise them while you are among them.»[4]

0.3 It is the duty of a servant to seek his master's favor by keeping him informed—even if that master already possesses prophetic and therefore ultimate knowledge.[5] God Himself, may He be glorified, has enjoined obedience by requiring His servants to address Him aloud,[6] although He knows their secrets beforehand. His purpose in concealing thoughts within their minds is so that hidden intentions will be made manifest through physical actions and so that, for each individual Muslim, all three stages of faith might thus be brought to perfection: that is, the resolution of the heart, the word of the tongue, and the deed of the hand. We beseech God to include us among those who have risen to this level of obedience to Him, by our obedience to His vicegerent on His earth, may God's blessings be upon him and upon the rightly-guided caliphs who preceded him.[7] And may the most abundant blessings of the Lord of the worlds rest upon the master of messengers, Muḥammad, blessings everlasting till the Day of Reckoning.

The Chapters of the Book

Part One, consisting of six chapters 0.4

- Chapter One: General characteristics of Egypt
- Chapter Two: Characteristic plants and trees of Egypt
- Chapter Three: Characteristic features of the animal world in Egypt
- Chapter Four: A description of the ancient Egyptian monuments examined by the author
- Chapter Five: Unusual Egyptian buildings and boats examined by the author
- Chapter Six: Unusual Egyptian foods

Part Two, consisting of three chapters

- Chapter One: The Nile and the manner of its annual rises, with an explanation of the causes of this phenomenon and the laws of nature governing it
- Chapter Two: The events of the year 597 [1200–1]
- Chapter Three: The events of the year 598 [1201–2]

Part One, consisting of six chapters

Chapter One: General characteristics of Egypt

Egypt is a land of wondrous monuments and strange stories. It consists of a valley enclosed by two ranges of hills, one to the east and one to the west, the eastern being the greater. These uplands begin at Aswan, and at Esna they come so close as to almost touch. They then diverge once more, little by little, the gap between them increasing in width the further they extend northward, until the distance from one escarpment to the other at the parallel of Fustat is as much as a day's journey. Thereafter they draw even further apart. The Nile runs between them until it reaches Lower Egypt, where it divides into branches, all of which flow out into the sea.[8] 1.1.1

The Nile is unusual in two respects. The first is its length; indeed, we know of no other river in the inhabited world that covers a greater distance. We say this because its sources are springs fed by water from Jabal al-Qamar, a mountain range situated, it has been claimed, eleven degrees beyond the Equator. Now, the latitude of Aswan, the southernmost part of Egypt, is twenty-two and a half degrees north of the Equator; the latitude of Damietta, the extreme north of Egypt, is thirty-one and a third degrees north of the Equator. The distance covered by the Nile, measured in a straight line, is thus a sixth of a degree short of forty-three degrees, which amounts to approximately nine hundred *farsakh*s. That does not include the 1.1.2

twists and turns that the river makes. If they were taken into consideration, the figure would increase greatly.[9]

1.1.3 The second unusual aspect of the Nile is that it rises at the time when all other rivers decrease, and when water levels decline in general. The rise of the Nile begins when the days are at their longest, and reaches its maximum height at the autumnal equinox; it is then that the irrigation channels are opened, inundating the agricultural lands.[10] The reason for this peculiarity is that the waters supplying its rise come from constant and heavy rains and continuous torrents, all of which feed into the Nile during this season: rain in the First and Second Climes only falls heavily at this period, from midsummer through the heat of high summer.

1.1.4 In Egypt, the land itself is also unusual in several respects. One of these is that no rain falls there, or so little that it never gets a proper soaking; this is particularly the case in Upper Egypt. More abundant rain does sometimes fall in Lower Egypt, but still not enough for agricultural requirements. Damietta, Alexandria, and their environs do, however, enjoy copious rain, and it supplies their drinking water. There are no springs in Egypt, and no rivers other than the Nile.

1.1.5 Another peculiarity of Egypt is that, although the ground is sandy and unsuited to cultivation, large quantities of a black, sticky, and extremely rich kind of mud called *iblīz* come to enrich it. This *iblīz* arrives from the land of the Blacks, mingled with the waters of the Nile when it rises; the mud settles,[11] the water soaks away, then the sediment can be plowed and planted with crops. New mud arrives every year; consequently, all the agricultural lands of Egypt can be cultivated and nothing left fallow, as is the custom in Iraq and the Levant, although the Egyptians do practice crop rotation. This annual enrichment is something the Bedouin Arabs take note of in their saying, "The more the wind blows, the better the tillage," because the wind brings the dust of foreign lands. Another of their sayings goes, "The more the wild winds blow, the better the crops will grow." It is also because of this *iblīz* that the land of Upper Egypt is so fruitful and produces such an abundance of lush crops, as it is closest to the origin of the mud, and thus receives a great quantity of it. In contrast, the soil of Lower Egypt is unproductive and lean, poor in quality and with a low mud content, for by the time the Nile water has reached it, the sediment has settled and the water has become clear. I know of nothing quite like this annual influx of mud, except what I have been told about a certain highland region in the First Clime, where it is said that, at the beginning of the time for cultivation, the winds bring in a lot of new dust; rain then falls on it and settles it, and it can be plowed and planted. Eventually, when the crops there have been harvested, other winds come and dry out the soil, so that it goes back to being as bare as it was to begin with.

Another peculiar feature of Egypt is that its seasons are quite dif- 1.1.6
ferent in character from their usual nature elsewhere. Thus, what is normally the driest part of year in other lands—I mean summer and harvest time—is the season of greatest humidity in Egypt: it is then that the Nile rises and floods, rising in summer and inundating the land at harvest time. In other lands, waters subside in this period and increase at the times of greatest humidity, namely winter and spring—which is precisely when the aridity and dryness in Egypt are at their maximum.

This mixture of heat and humidity is the reason why miasmata and 1.1.7
corruption of the air are so common in Egypt, and why the endemic diseases there are miasmatic ones that result from combinations of yellow bile and phlegm. You seldom come across purely bilious diseases among the Egyptians; instead, phlegm is the predominant humor in their diseases, even in the young and in those who have a hot humoral temperament, and yellow bile is often accompanied by raw phlegm. Diseases affect the Egyptians most often at the end of fall and the beginning of winter, but they are mostly of the sort that have a good outcome. Acute illnesses are infrequent; so too are sudden, fatal attacks caused by an excess of blood. Nevertheless, even Egyptians who are in good health are generally flabby and languid, and sallow and sickly in color; you seldom see a blooming and ruddy complexion. Egyptian children are thin, and generally have

stunted bodies and dull countenances; it is usually only from the age of twenty and upwards that their frames fill out and their features become pleasing.

1.1.8 The intelligence of the Egyptians, their sharpness of mind, and their sprightliness of limb are due to the intrinsic heat of their country, for its humidity is accidental. Because of this, the people of Upper Egypt have leaner frames and drier humoral temperaments, and are generally darker-skinned, while the inhabitants of the region from Fustat to Damietta have a greater amount of moistness in their bodies, and are generally paler.[12]

1.1.9 When the ancient Egyptians realized that the prosperity of their land depended entirely on the Nile, they made the start of the harvest time the beginning of their calendar year. This is when the rise of the Nile reaches its maximum height.[13]

1.1.10 Another distinctive feature is that the east wind is prevented from reaching part of the population by the eastern escarpment, called al-Muqaṭṭam. The escarpment acts as a barrier that deflects this salubrious wind from the land to the west; this means that the people there hardly ever enjoy a true easterly breeze, although it may occasionally blow from an angle to the east. This is the reason why the ancient Egyptians chose as their seat of royal power Memphis and the surrounding area, which are in a region lying at some distance from the eastern range, towards the western one. The Greeks, for their part, preferred Alexandria, and avoided the site of Fustat because of its proximity to al-Muqaṭṭam.[14] The "wind-break" effect of this eastern escarpment is more pronounced in its immediate lee than in areas further away. An additional effect on the inhabitants is that sunrise is delayed; thus, the air is not heated through, and remains for a time in a state of nocturnal "rawness." As a consequence of all this, you find that the parts of Egypt exposed to the east wind are in a better state than the rest of the country, where high humidity accelerates putrefaction, and where rats and mice proliferate, generated and formed from the mud.[15] In Qūṣ, for example, scorpions are particularly numerous and their stings are often fatal, and stinking, crawling bugs[16] and fleas are a chronic nuisance.

Another peculiarity of Egypt is that when the south wind blows 1.1.11
in winter, spring, or the period immediately following, it blows very cold. They call it "the Marīsī," because it passes over the region of al-Marīs in the land of the Blacks. The reason it is so cold is that it passes over pools and ponds there—the proof being that, if it blows continuously for several days, it reverts to its naturally high temperature, heating and desiccating the air.[17]

Chapter Two: Characteristic plants and trees of Egypt

1.2.1 One characteristic plant is okra, which has fruits the size of a thumb, deep green in color and something like baby cucumbers, but covered with a fuzz of tiny bristles. They are five-sided in shape, and delineated by five ribs; when cut open, five interior chambers are revealed, separated by partitions and containing round white seeds arranged in rows. These seeds are smaller than black-eyed beans, soft in consistency and sweetish in taste, but they also have an astringency to them and are highly mucilaginous. The Egyptians cook okra with meat, chopping it up small with the peel still on; it is not a bad dish. In the natural temperament of okra, heat and moisture predominate. In its cooked form no astringency is apparent; instead, there is a marked viscosity.

1.2.2 Another Egyptian plant is *mulūkhiyyah* (which physicians call "*mulūkiyyah*"). I am absolutely certain that it is none other than a cultivated version of wild mallow, just as marsh mallow is another kind of wild mallow. *Mulūkhiyyah,* however, has a higher level of wateriness and moisture than wild mallow, and is cold and moist in the first degree.[18] It is grown in market gardens, cooked with meat, and is highly mucilaginous. A little *mulūkhiyyah* is also grown in the Levant, and it is occasionally used there in cooking. Although it is bad for the stomach, it mollifies heat and has a cooling effect, and is swiftly ingested because it is so slippery. Al-Isrāʾīlī writes, "I have seen a third kind of mallow, called in Egypt '*mulūkhiyyah* of the Blacks' and known in Iraq as '*shūshandībā*.' Its potency and effect are mid-way between those of *mulūkhiyyah* and wild mallow, because it has less nutritional value than *mulūkhiyyah* but more than wild mallow."

Then there are *labakh* fruit, which come from a tree with sappy branches and verdant foliage that resembles a lote tree. The fruit are the size and color of large unripe dates, except that they are of a particularly saturated green, like the color of a whetstone. Before they are ripe, *labakh* fruit have an astringency like that of half-ripe dates, but when they are ready for eating they are pleasantly sweet to taste, and sticky. Their stones resemble plum stones or almond kernels, and are whitish to greyish in color; they are easily cracked, and split open to reveal an "almond" which is soft, white, and juicy. If the stone is left for three days, it dries out and hardens. The longer it is left, the more wizened the kernel within it becomes, while the outer skin remains as it is, but empty, or seemingly so; this skin does not contract, however, so the shrunken kernel has room to rattle about inside it. When tasted, the kernel has a noticeably bitter, sharp bite to it that lingers on the tongue. It is my hypothesis that it is one of the three varieties of *dand*. Concerning this, Aristotle and others have said that the *labakh* was a deadly poison when it grew in Persia, but became edible when it was transplanted to Egypt. Similarly, Nicolaus writes, "*Labakh* had been a deadly poison in Persia, but when it was transplanted to the Levant and to Egypt it became a luxury food." It is indeed rare and expensive, as there are only a few trees in the entire country. Their timber is a hardwood of the highest quality, variously wine-colored and black; it is costly and greatly prized. The Egyptians serve *labakh* fruits as a dessert with other fresh or candied fruits. 1.2.3

Abū Ḥanīfah al-Dīnawarī writes, "The *labakh* is a big tree, similar to the larger specimens of *athʾab*. Its leaves are like those of the walnut, and its fruit like that of the mountain fig. The fruit are bitter; 1.2.4

if you eat them, they bring on a thirst, and if you then drink water, they bloat your stomach. It is a tree of the uplands." He then quoted a man from Upper Egypt as saying that *labakh* trees are as big as plane trees, with green fruit resembling dates that are very sugary but rather unpleasant-tasting, although they are excellent for toothache. Al-Dīnawarī continued, "When the timber is sawn, it causes nosebleeds in those sawing it.[19] Nevertheless, it is sawn, and the price of a plank can reach fifty dinars. For various reasons, shipwrights use it in the construction of vessels." He then claimed that if two planks of *labakh* wood were fixed tightly together and placed in water for a year, they would fuse into a single plank. I do not know how accurate the majority of al-Dīnawarī's reports are.

1.2.5 Ibn Samajūn writes, "The *labakh* grows in Egypt. Its fruit is good for the stomach. A venomous spider is sometimes found in *labakh* trees.[20] The dried and powdered leaves staunch bleeding, and inhibit diarrhea when drunk as a potion; there is a pronounced astringency to them." He also said, "The Egyptians maintain that eating the stones of *labakh* fruit causes deafness."

1.2.6 Another characteristic tree is the *jummayz*, which is very common in Egypt; I have also seen a number of them at Ashqelon and along the neighboring coast. It is something like a mountain fig, but its fruit grows directly out of the wood of the branches, rather than from beneath the leaves. It bears seven times a year, the fruit is in season for four months, and it yields an enormous crop. A few days before the fruit is picked a man climbs the tree, taking an iron tool with which he scores the fruits, one by one; they exude a white milky juice, then the places of the incisions turn black. This operation makes the fruit sweet.[21] Indeed, some of it can be exceedingly sweet—sweeter, in fact, than the usual sort of figs; but, in the latter stages of chewing, the sweetness is invariably accompanied by a slightly woody flavor. The *jummayz* tree itself is as big as a sturdy old walnut tree. Both the fruit and the boughs, when "bled," exude that white milky juice which, if applied to a piece of cloth or some other item, will dye it red. Its timber is used to construct houses, and to make doors and other large articles of joinery. It is very durable, withstands the effects of water and sun, and seldom rots, even though it is a lightweight timber with a low resin content. The fruit is also used to make a pungent vinegar and a rough and rasping kind of alcoholic drink.

Galen writes, 1.2.7

> The temperament of *jummayz* fruit is cold and moist, midway between the temperaments of the mulberry and the fig. It is bad for the stomach. The milky juice of the tree has a strong emollient effect that helps wounds heal over and reduces swellings; it can be applied as an ointment to the stings of venomous creatures, and as a plaster to alleviate hardness of the spleen and stomach pains.[22] A linctus can be made from the fruit, for the treatment of obstinate coughs and of heavy congestions in the chest and lung. This is prepared by simmering the fruit until its potency is transferred to the water; this water, mixed with sugar, is then simmered again until it thickens and can be removed from the heat.

Al-Dīnawarī writes, 1.2.8

> The various species of fig include the *jummayz*. Its fruit is sweet and juicy, and hangs from long stalks; it can be dried. There is also another variety of *jummayz*, whose fruit is the same in form as that of the common fig, although its leaves are smaller. The fruit can be either small and yellow, or black. It grows in al-Ghawr, and is known as "the male fig." The yellow sort are sweet; the black ones cause the mouth to bleed. The fruit of this variety has no stalk, but is directly attached to the branch.

Another distinctive plant is the balsam. Nowadays, it is only 1.2.9
found in Egypt, at ʿAyn Shams, in an enclosed reserve approximately seven *faddān*s in area. The balsam bush reaches a height of around a cubit and more, and has two layers of bark, the outer one

thin and reddish, the inner thick and green. When chewed, balsam releases an oiliness and a fragrant aroma in the mouth. Its leaves are similar to those of rue.

1.2.10 Its oil is harvested at the rising of Sirius.[23] First, after the stems have been stripped of all their leaves, they are scarified with a special stone, sharpened for the purpose. This operation calls for skill, because the outer bark needs to be cut through while the inner bark must merely be split, yet not so deeply that the split reaches the underlying wood; if it does reach the wood, the bush will not produce any oil. After a bush has been scarified in this way, the balsam collector allows the gum time to seep out on to the branch, then gathers it by removing it with his finger and transferring it to a horn; when this receptacle is full, he decants the contents into glass flasks. The operation continues in this way until the gum ceases to flow and the harvesting stage ends. The greater the amount of dew in the atmosphere, the more copiously the gum will flow; conversely, in dry years when there is little dew, the crop of gum is scantier.[24] The amount produced in the year 596 [1200], which was a year of drought, was rather more than twenty *riṭl*s.[25]

1.2.11 After the harvesting stage, the flasks of gum are taken away and kept in storage until high summer, and when the heat is at its fiercest they are brought out of store and placed in the sun. From now on they are inspected daily, for the oil will be found to have risen above a layer of fluid, whose element is water, and a lower layer of sediment, whose element is earth; the oil is skimmed off, and the flasks placed in the sun once more. This exposure to the sun and the skimming off of the oil continues until no oil remains in the flasks. The extracted oil is then taken to the person in charge, who heats it; he does this in secret, without letting anyone else in on the operation.[26] He then delivers it to the ruler's treasury.[27] The amount of pure oil produced by this refining process is about a tenth of the total quantity of crude gum.[28] An expert on the subject told me that the amount of oil obtained annually is about twenty *riṭl*s.

I have seen a statement of Galen's which says that the finest balsam oil was from Palestine,[29] and the lowest grade from Egypt. Nowadays, however, we find no balsam at all in Palestine. Nicolaus writes in his *Book of Plants*, "Certain plants contain a sweet-scented aroma in some of their parts, while others have the sweet scent in all their parts. The latter include the balsam which is found in the Levant, near the Sea of Pitch. The well from which the plants are watered is called Biʾr al-Balsam, and its water is sweet." For his part, Ibn Samajūn writes, "In our time it is only found in Egypt. Its oil is extracted at the rising of Kalb al-Jabbār, which is Sirius; that is, in the month of Shubāṭ [February].[30] The amount produced is between fifty and sixty *riṭl*s, and it is sold *in situ* for twice its weight in silver." That, it seems, was the case in Ibn Samajūn's day. He also reported on al-Rāzī's authority that radish oil is used medicinally as a substitute, but that is far off the mark. 1.2.12

The oil-bearing variety of balsam does not produce a fruit, so the only way to propagate it is by taking cuttings, which are planted in the month of Shubāṭ, when they take root and grow. The fruit is produced by the wild male balsam alone, which produces no oil. It is found in Najd, in Tihāmah, in the wildernesses of the Bedouin Arabs, in the coastal regions of Yemen, and in Persia, and is known as *bashām*. 1.2.13

Provided no oil has yet been extracted, balsam bark can be made into a preserve that is a sovereign remedy for all poisons.[31] But its pharmacological properties and medical uses are a subject for which a book other than this would be more appropriate. 1.2.14

Then there is taro, which has roots the size of cucumbers, although some are smaller, the size of fingers;[32] they tend to be pinkish-red, and are peeled and sliced in the same way as turnips. The roots are dense and solid, and taste something like unripe green bananas, mildly astringent and intensely bitter, which indicates that their qualities are heat and dryness. On boiling, the bitterness dissipates completely and, along with that mild astringency, they 1.2.15

acquire a gluey viscosity; this quality was already present to a high degree, but had been masked and disguised by the bitterness. The viscosity means that they are a coarse form of nutrition, slow to be digested and heavy on the stomach. Nevertheless, because of their astringency and acridity, they serve to strengthen the stomach and bind the bowels, provided they are not consumed in large quantities. Also, because of their viscosity and stickiness, they are an effective remedy for ulceration of the intestines.[33] The peel of the roots is more efficacious in binding the bowels than the flesh, because its astringency is greater. Taro is cooked in sumac-flavored water and other such infusions. The broth takes on a viscosity that nauseates anyone who is unaccustomed to it; but if the taro is boiled, then the water poured off and the roots fried in oil until they begin to brown, they are not bad.[34]

1.2.16 In the temperament of taro, heat and moisture predominate. It is apparent from its observable state that it is a compound of two essential substances, a hot and acrid substance that dissipates when heat is applied, and an earthy and watery substance that increases with heating; it is the same with onions, garlic, and other similar vegetables. Taro in its raw state is therefore medicinal, and in its cooked state nutritional. I have seen it in Damascus, but only occasionally. I have also observed that when it dries out it becomes woody, and precisely similar to costus.

1.2.17 Turning now to its leaves, they are broad and rounded, just like the underside of a male camel's hoof in shape, but larger, with a diameter of one to two spans. Every leaf has its own stalk, as thick as a finger and two or more spans in length. Each individual stalk grows directly out of the underground root, as the plant has no central stem; neither does it bear fruit. Taro leaves are a deep green and have a delicate epidermis; they are similar to banana leaves in color, pliancy, glossiness, and lushness.

1.2.18 Dioscorides said that this plant has flowers the color of pink roses, and that when it produces a bud, the bud formed is something like shepherds' bags in miniature, as if it were a froth of water bubbles and a palm spathe.[35] In it are small "broad beans," smaller than Greek broad beans, which are located above the places where there are no beans;[36] anyone wishing to grow the plant needs only to take some of these beans, place them in lumps of mud, and throw the lumps into water, and they will sprout. Dioscorides claimed that taro can be eaten both fresh and dried, and that it is ground into flour which can be cooked and drunk like gruel; he also claimed that a pap can be made from it which strengthens the stomach and is a remedy for bilious diarrhea and ulceration of the intestines. He added that if the bitter-tasting green thing at the center of the root is dried, powdered, mixed with oil and administered as ear drops, it relieves earache.

Al-Isrāʾīlī writes, "Speaking for ourselves, we have not observed 1.2.19
that it produces flowers." He also says,

> When the root of this plant is kept in store in peoples's houses, I have noticed that, at the beginning of its growing season, rootlets will sprout from the "beans" which are attached to it, and the plant will produce new growth without any flower or fruit appearing. The bean itself, however, is similar to rose flowers in color, for when it germinates and begins to grow, the emerging growth is of a fine white hue tinged with a delicate pink.

Al-Isrāʾīlī also writes, "We have not found that it dries out sufficiently to be ground and made into gruel. Instead, we observed that it retains its moisture all year long, like the bulbs of narcissus, saffron, and other such plants," adding, "Neither have we seen this green part at its center mentioned by Dioscorides; rather, we have found that, at all times of the year, the root merely resembles green bananas."

On the contrary, it is Dioscorides's statement that is correct. 1.2.20
Taro dries out quite sufficiently to be ground, and can therefore be made into gruel, as we have seen with our own eyes. And when it does dry out, the roots are no different in appearance from those

of dried ginger, except that they are bigger; when you taste them, there is a sharpness and a bite to them, as with ginger. I would say, therefore, as a hypothesis constructed on the basis of evidence observed and heard, that taro is an Egyptian variety of ginger; but that the ground in Egypt has imparted additional moisture to it and, as a result, its heat and sharpness have decreased. Similarly, East African and Indian varieties of ginger are stronger and sharper than Yemeni ginger; moreover, the Yemenis use ginger in cooking just as the Egyptians cook with taro, although not in very large quantities.[37] I have questioned a number of merchants and other knowledgeable people about where ginger is grown in Yemen and what it looks like, and they all assured me that it resembles taro, except that taro roots are bigger, and its leaves are bigger than those of Yemeni ginger. I myself have observed how, when it dries, taro is no different from ginger in outward appearance, and shares its sharpness and mild bite. Another informant told me that the ginger and onion plants resemble each other, and that taro is found in those ginger-growing regions, but seems to be a garden plant.

1.2.21 ʿAlī ibn Riḍwān writes, "Of all foods, taro is the one that converts most quickly into black bile." Other Egyptian physicians have said that taro increases potency in copulation. Both claims need examining, but that would not be appropriate to this book.

1.2.22 Another plant of Egypt is the banana. (It is also widespread in Yemen and India, and I have seen bananas in al-Ghawr, too, and in Damascus, where they are brought in for sale.)[38] The plant forms from suckers that appear at the base of the tree,[39] just as offshoots appear from a date palm. The fruit-bearing tree is called the "mother"; when its crop of fruit has been harvested, it too is cut down, and the biggest of its "daughter" suckers takes its place. The banana tree grows to the height of a man or twice that, and resembles a slender date palm.

1.2.23 People have claimed that the banana tree is in origin a hybrid, and that it was produced from taro and date stones by embedding a date stone in the middle of a taro root and then planting it. The claim, although hard to believe, is based on demonstrable evidence, so the senses incline one to accept it. You will find that the banana tree has leaves just like the leaves of a date palm, except that you have to picture the individual segments of the banana leaf forming a seamless whole, as if it were a green silken mantle outspread, or a green banner lush with fragrance and freshness.[40] It is thus as if the banana had acquired its moisture from the taro, and its outward form from the date palm. Moreover, you should be aware that the only reason the leaves of the date palm segment into leaflets is the dryness that predominates in the palm's temperament; conversely, it is the banana's high moisture level that causes the segments of its leaves to remain connected, and not to split apart. On the basis of this evidence, therefore, the taro should be equivalent to the constituent matter of the banana, and the date palm to its outward form. Furthermore, if you were to examine carefully the woody parts and leaves of a banana tree that had dried up, you would find they had the same sort of splintery and fibrous grain that you see in the trunk and leaves of a date palm—with the difference that those of the banana are combined with sufficient moisture to fuse them together, and to fill the interstices between them. The same applies to the taro, as anyone eating it fried will discern.[41]

Turning now to the fruit, you will observe that bananas grow in 1.2.24
bunches like the bunches on date palms; a tree may bear upwards of five hundred individual bananas. At the lower extremity of the bunch there is a banana also called the "mother," which contains no flesh and is inedible. Cut open, you find it is composed of layers like an onion, with the layers arranged concentrically and the inner layer of each adjacent pair half the length of the outer.[42] Below each layer, at its base, there form white flowers the size of pistachios, or like orange-tree blossoms, eleven in number and arranged in two rows; the number seldom varies, and if it does, it will only be one more or less. Each layer is equivalent to the integument of a palm spadix, while the flowers are equivalent to the spadix itself. Over time these layers split open, spontaneously and by degrees, layer by

layer from the outer inward, to reveal the above-mentioned flowers, which are white and the equivalent of immature dates; they are juicy and sweet. The petals of the flowers then fall off and miniature bananas bud up out of them. When these tiny bananas begin to grow a little bigger, another layer of the "mother" splits open in the same manner, and so on until the bunch is complete.

1.2.25 You will find that the peel of the banana fruit is similar to that of a fresh ripe date, but much thicker, on account of the characteristics the banana tree has acquired from the substance of the taro. Its flesh is sweet, but with a blandness to it, so that it tastes like ripe dates with bread; the sweetness derives from dates, and the blandness from taro. In shape, it has the form of a date but is the size of a large cucumber; in color, it tends to be yellowish-white, the yellowness deriving from dates and the whiteness from taro. When the fruit is first cut from the tree, however, it is a particularly intense green and cannot be eaten, but after being stored for some days it turns yellow and becomes edible. You will find that it consists of a single morsel of flesh, with no stone in it and nothing to be discarded other than the peel alone; in fact, you might imagine it to be a lump of *khabīṣ* pudding—it is soft and easy to chew, and slips down easily. If, however, you examine it carefully in a good light, you will find in the center of the fruit numerous seeds, smaller than mustard seeds and nearly black or light brown in color; they are something like fig seeds, but extremely tender. It is as if these seeds are the vestige of date stones which, owing to the extra moisture present in the banana, have softened, fragmented, and mingled with the flesh, so that they slip down with it when it is eaten. The fruit has a rather pleasing, fragrant odor, with a touch of sweet yeastiness to it. And when bananas cause someone who has eaten them to bring up wind, as they can do in the early stages of digestion, the belches are pleasant in odor.

1.2.26 The banana's temperament is hot and moist; its moistness exceeds its heat, as if it were hot in the first degree and moist in the second. It increases potency in copulation, has a diuretic effect, and produces wind in the stomach. Given all this, its nature is thus not far from that of ripe dates, except for the high degree of moistness which the banana has acquired from the taro. If this is indeed the result of artificial hybridization, then empirical experience has confirmed the truth of the report; conversely, if the hybridization is due to nature, then the banana is only one of a whole series of marvelous and beautifully contrived hybrids, both animal and vegetable, which the natural world contains.

Al-Dīnawarī writes, 1.2.27

> The original habitat of the banana is Oman.[43] The banana tree grows like the papyrus reed, having a thick root beneath the surface and long, broad leaves about three cubits by two; the leaves do not grow to a point, as do those of date palms, but are squarish in shape. The banana tree grows to over and above the height of a man, and continually puts out suckers around itself, which diminish in size the younger they are. As soon as the mother tree has "borne her litter"—that is, when its fruit has reached full size—the tree is cut through at the base and felled, and the bunch is removed. The largest of its suckers now grows and becomes the next mother, while the rest remain as suckers to this new tree, and so on, *ad infinitum*. This explains the exchange that took place, according to al-Aṣmaʿī, between Ashʿab and his son: when the father said, "Boy, why can't you be like me?" the son retorted, "I'm like a banana tree. It's no use until its parent dies."[44] From the tree's initial growth out of the sucker to the time it can bear fruit is two months; the period from the fruit's first emergence until it reaches full size is a further forty days.[45] The fruit is available in its native lands all year round, and a single bunch contains between thirty and five hundred bananas.

I once saw, in the stock of one of the India merchants, some finely 1.2.28
woven rush mats of superb quality. They were patterned and double-sided, and of the most beautiful colors, dyed in brilliant, pure

hues like those used for silk. Each mat was about two and a half cubits in breadth, and yet the entire width was made from a single rush with no central join.[46] When I began to say how surprised I was at the length of the rushes, which in Egypt are called *samār*, the merchant told me that the mats were made not of rushes, but of Indian banana leaves. He explained that the ribs of the leaves are first split and dried, then dyed and woven into these mats. A single one sells in al-Maʿbar for two dinars, but there are others that sell for only two dirhams. He showed me both sorts.[47]

1.2.29 Many kinds of citrus fruits are found in Egypt which I have never seen in Iraq. They include citrons so large that it would be all but impossible to find anything of similar size in Baghdad, and sweet citrons which do not contain any acidic pulp.[48] There are hybrid lemons, too, that come in different varieties, some of which can be about as big as a melon. Among these hybrids is the "seal-stamped lemon," which is intensely orange in color—indeed, of a deeper shade than an actual orange—of a noticeably rounded shape, flattened at the top and bottom, and indented at each end as if by the impression of a seal.[49] There is also the "balsam lemon," which is about the size of a thumb and like an elongated egg in shape, although some specimens are perfectly conical, rising from a base and culminating in a point. As for their color, scent, flesh, and pulp, these differ in no respect from citrons.

1.2.30 One sometimes comes across a citron with another citron inside it, covered by its own yellow skin. A trustworthy person informed me that he had found inside a single citron seven miniature citrons, each encased in its own fully formed skin. What I myself have seen is a citron with a second, but incompletely formed, citron inside it; I have also seen a few of this kind in al-Ghawr. These intrusive citrons only occur inside the sort that contain acidic pulp.

1.2.31 In addition, these different types of citrus fruit are cross-bred, so that a great many varieties are produced.

1.2.32 Another Egyptian fruit is a variety of apple, found in Alexandria in a single orchard called Bustān al-Qiṭʿah. These apples are very small in size and deep red in color. Their scent is indescribably fragrant and more pungent than musk, and they are a great rarity.

The kind of lucerne known in Egypt as *qurṭ* is what is called in Iraq *raṭbah*, in the Levant *fiṣṣah*, and in Persian *aspist*. 1.2.33

Egyptian date palms are numerous, but one finds that their fruit, compared with that of Iraqi palms, tastes as if most of the sweetness had been "stewed" out of it, leaving the fruit lacking in potency. The dry dates that people in Iraq call *qasb*, people in Egypt call *tamr*; conversely, the sticky lumps of dates known in Iraq as *tamr* they call *ʿajwah*. Only occasionally, indeed very rarely, will you find dates in Egypt that approach those of Iraq in quality. They are from a limited number of palms, and are regarded as delicacies to be given as gifts. 1.2.34

The green gram called *māsh*, which is the same as *majj*, is not grown at all in Egypt.[50] It is only available imported from the Levant, in the apothecaries' shops, where it is sold by the ounce for invalids. Sorghum and millet are not known in Egypt—that is, unless they are known in the furthest part of Upper Egypt, which may be the case with millet in particular. 1.2.35

A crop in which Egypt specializes is opium, which is harvested in Upper Egypt from the black poppy. The harvesters often adulterate it, sometimes with human excrement, but a sure sign of the pure product is that it will melt in the sun; it will also catch light when placed in a lamp, without giving off any dark smoke, and when extinguished will give off a pungent aroma. In addition, adulterated opium will rapidly become infested with maggots. Aristotle proscribes the use of opium as an ingredient of eye and ear remedies, because it causes blindness and deafness. 1.2.36

Another Egyptian specialty is *aqāqiyā*, which is the juice of the leaves and fruit of the *qaraẓ* tree. The liquid is extracted by pounding and pressing, and placed in wide, shallow vessels in the full light of the sun until it thickens; it is then formed into round cakes. This is the pure, top-grade product. In the case of the ordinary sort that is imported to foreign lands, the *qaraẓ* is crushed and kneaded with a solution of gum arabic. The mixture is then formed into round cakes 1.2.37

which are stamped with a mark and dried. The tree is actually the *sanṭ*, also known as the "Egyptian thorn"; *qaraẓ* is in fact the term for the leaves of this tree, which are additionally used for tanning hides. The juice from these leaves, from which *aqāqiyā* is produced, is called "*qaraẓ* concentrate." Egyptian women drink both the pure *aqāqiyā* juice and cordials made from it, as a cure for diarrhea.[51]

1.2.38 *Sanṭ* are very large trees with numerous sharp, hard thorns, which are white in color. The trees bear fruit called "*qaraẓ* carobs," which are round and flat, rather like lupine seeds in shape, except that they grow in rows, in pods like black-eyed bean pods. Inside these fruits are tiny seeds. If the *aqāqiyā* is made from *qaraẓ* before it is fully ripe, it will be more astringent and more effective in binding the constitution. However, if it is made from thoroughly ripe ingredients, it will be inadequate for binding the bowels. The sign of ripeness is when the *qaraẓ* pods are a deep, shiny black in color.

1.2.39 Al-Dīnawarī writes,

> *Qaraẓ* are large trees, like walnut trees. Their timber is as hard as iron, and as it ages it turns as black as ebony. Its leaves resemble those of the apple tree, and it has a pod like the bean pods of black-eyed beans, containing seeds which are used as weights in scales; its leaves and fruit are used for tanning. It grows both on the lowland plains and in the mountains. The pod of the *qaraẓ* is smaller than the fruit-pod of the *ṭalḥ*. When camels graze on it, their mouths and their softer hair turn red; even their droppings go red, so that you would think they were lumps of safflower pigment. The camels get fat on it. The variety of *qaraẓ* that grows in Egypt is the kind called *sanṭ*. It catches fire readily when lit, and produces little ash. It bears balls of yellow flowers, but they do not have a pungent scent like the flower balls of acacias in Iraq.

1.2.40 Another Egyptian crop is the *faqqūṣ*, which is a small serpent melon. It never grows to a large size: the longest ones do not exceed the distance between the tips of a man's thumb and index finger when stretched apart, and most of them are the length of a finger. They are sweeter and more tender than the serpent melon, and yet there is no doubt that they are a variety of the latter; it is as if they are those miniature serpent melons called *ḍaghābīs*. The gherkin known as *qathad* is, however, a common cucumber.[52]

In Egypt there is a melon called the ʿAbdalī or ʿAbdallāwī, which is said to be named for ʿAbd Allāh ibn Ṭāhir, al-Maʾmūn's governor of Egypt. The market gardeners, however, call it the Damīrī melon, a name derived from Damīrah, a village in Egypt. These melons have twisted necks and thin peel; they taste insipid, and only occasionally sweet. A very few specimens can reach thirty *riṭls* and more in weight, but the majority weigh between one and ten *riṭls*. The Egyptians consider their flavor superior to that of the hybrid melon they term "Khurasani" and "Chinese," and maintain they are good for the health; they eat them with sugar. Their flavor is closest to that of the variety called in Iraq *shilinq*, but they have a better flavor and are more tender than the latter. They look like the gourds of Iraq, except that their color is a particularly beautiful yellow, and they feel rough and slightly prickly to the touch. Ibn Wahb writes, "The melons called *ṭibbīkh* are the rounded, rough-skinned, ribbed ones without necks. Those called *khirbiz* are small *biṭṭīkh* melons with long necks, smooth skins, and rounded bodies." Yaḥyā reports, however, that "Al-Akhfash said, '*Ṭibbīkh* is the same as *biṭṭīkh*, but the Bedouin Arabs swap the letters around and metathesize them.'" 1.2.41

These ʿAbdalī melons, when they are still small and and immature, are like gourds in color and shape, but are like serpent melons in taste, and they have rounded bellies, and also have necks. They are sold as the equivalent of *faqqūṣ*, but are called *ʿajjūr*. A man who grows them informed me that it is the usual practice to go through the plot every day, and that the grower will harvest any melons he thinks worth cutting while still young and green, and will sell them as *ʿajjūr*; those that he decides to leave until they grow to maturity and turn yellow are what become ʿAbdalī melons. 1.2.42

1.2.43 You will seldom find Egyptian melons that are perfectly sweet (equally, one does not find any that go wormy or rotten); the majority are insipid and watery. In Egypt, all types of melon are sold by weight, with the exception of the green watermelon. This green watermelon is called the *dullāʿ* in the West, the *zabash* melon in the Levant, and in Iraq the "Raqqī" melon, as well as being called "Palestinian" and "Indian." As for the sort of gourd that the common people invariably call "pumpkin," in Egypt it is elongated in shape and of the appearance of a serpent melon, reaching as much as two cubits in length and a span in breadth.

1.2.44 The green broad beans that the Egyptians call *fūl* are continuously in season for about six months; this is also the case with roses. Jasmine is in season all year round, for the jasmine shrub is always in flower. There is a white variety and a yellow one, but the white is both more common and more fragrant, and from it is produced the *zanbaq* oil which is a specialty of Damietta. Similarly, lemons are produced year-round; it is only that they are less or more abundant, according to the season. Violets are highly fragrant in Egypt, but the Egyptians are not proficient at producing oil or conserve from them.[53]

1.2.45 Quinces in Egypt are of very poor quality, small, tart, and expensive, though apples, even the low-quality ones, are not bad. Egyptian pomegranates, however, are of the very highest grade, although they are never perfectly sweet. Cherries are not to be found in Egypt, but rather in the Levant, Asia Minor, and elsewhere. In Egypt there is only a small, sour kind of plum that they call "cherries." In Damascus, they call this same kind of fruit "bears' peaches," because in the Levant plums are called "peaches," peaches "nectarines," and pears "plums."[54]

1.2.46 Another common species in Egypt is the golden shower tree, which is a big tree that resembles the Levantine carob tree. Its flowers are large, intensely yellow, and radiantly beautiful, and when the fruits form they hang down like green batons. In Egypt there are also almond trees. Lote trees are plentiful there; their fruit is the jujube, and it is very sweet. Indigo is also plentiful in Egypt, but it is inferior to the Indian sort.

Chapter Three: Characteristic features of the animal world in Egypt

One distinctive feature is the incubation of chicks using cattle dung.[55] In Egypt, you will rarely see chicks incubated by the mother hen; indeed, for many Egyptians, it is unheard of. Instead, the incubation of chicks is viewed in Egypt purely as an industry, and as a means of earning a livelihood by doing business and making profits. In every Egyptian town you will find several sites at which the operation is carried out, called "chick factories." The factory consists of a large yard in which are constructed between ten and twenty chambers, described below. Each chamber holds 2,000 eggs, and is called a "bedding chamber." 1.3.1

To describe one in detail, a quadrangular chamber is constructed, eight spans in length by six in breadth and four in height. A doorway is placed in one of the shorter sides, having a width of two spans and an arched top of the same height.[56] Above this doorway is situated a round aperture, one span in diameter. The structure is then roofed with four wooden beams on which is placed an underlay of reeds (that is, of woven reeds) and, on top of that, a layer of *sās*, which is the refuse of flax and its dried stalks; on top of this comes the coating of clay. All this is then covered with a layer of bricks, and the whole chamber is plastered with clay—outside and in, top and bottom—so that no vapors can escape from it. You must also make 1.3.2

an opening in the center of the roof measuring one span square. The roof imitates the hen's breast.

1.3.3 You must then construct two troughs from clay into which *sās* has been thoroughly mixed, each trough six spans in length by one and a half in breadth; the clay should be as thick as a knuckle, and the walls approximately four finger-breadths in height. The base of the trough must be a single slab; you form it by spreading the clay out on an even surface. This trough is called the *ṭājan*. When the two *ṭājan*s are dry, you mount them on the two edges of the roof, one at the end where the doorway is and the other opposite, at the other edge. You must position them precisely, and fix them in place very carefully with clay; the *ṭājan*s must sit on the roof beams in such a way as to be in contact with them.[57] These two *ṭājan*s play the part of the hen's two wings.

1.3.4 Next, the chamber is carpeted with a basketful of straw, evenly spread, on top of which are laid fiber or reed mats,[58] that is, papyrus matting, of the same extent as the floor. The eggs are then arranged on this in neat rows, touching each other but not piled one on top of the other, so that the heat will be evenly distributed through them; a chamber having the dimensions proposed has a capacity of 2,000 eggs. This latter procedure is called the "bedding down."

1.3.5 The incubation process: First, you seal the doorway by hanging over it a pad of felt, of the precise shape of the opening. You then seal the round aperture with *sās*, and the opening in the roof too, also with *sās*, further covered with dung; the object is to leave no outlet for the escape of vapors. You then load the two *ṭājan*s with two basketfuls, which is three *waybah*s, of dried cattle dung, set fire to it all over using a lighted wick, and wait for it to burn down to ashes. At the same time, you must examine the eggs hour by hour, by placing them on your eye to test the heat. This procedure is called "tasting." If you find that the heat of the eggs produces a burning sensation in your eye, then you must give them three turns—that is, turning the eggs upside down, one by one, and repeating all that three times.[59] This imitates the way the hen turns her eggs with her beak and examines them with her eye.[60] This stage is called "the first hearing."[61]

When all the dung has turned to ash, you remove it and leave the *ṭājans* without fire until midday—that is, if the "bedding down" took place at daybreak. If the "bedding down" began from the first part of the night, however, you must keep watch until the eggs get warm, so that you can give the fire its "hearing," as in the foregoing operation; similarly, you then leave the two *ṭājans* without fire until daybreak. 1.3.6

Next, you place three *qadaḥs* of dung in the *ṭājan* over the doorway of the chamber, and two and a half *qadaḥs* in the *ṭājan* over its far wall, spreading the dung out with a small but stout spatula of iron. Set fire to the dung in each *ṭājan* in two places. (Whenever you come out of the chamber after examining the eggs in it, be sure to let down the covering of the doorway: on no account forget to do this, to avoid letting the vapors out and the air in, and thus ruining your work.) In the early evening, when the dung has turned to ashes again and the warmth has penetrated down to the eggs in the bottom of the chamber, replace the ashes in the *ṭājans* with new dung, as at first. At all times, you must feel the eggs and "taste" them with your eye. If you find their heat to be above a moderate level, such that it burns the eye, then, instead of the three measures of dung for the *ṭājan* over the doorway, put in two and a quarter, and for the *ṭājan* over the far wall only two. 1.3.7

For a period of ten days, you must never cease continually replacing the ash with new dung and kindling fire in it, to ensure that the supply of warmth is never interrupted. Ten days is the amount of time it takes for the visible bodies of the chicks to form, by the will and power of God; it is also half of the embryonic stage of the animal's life. At this point, you must go into the chamber with a lamp and pick up the eggs one by one, placing them upright between yourself and the lamp. An egg that appears black inside contains a chick. In contrast, one that looks like yellow fluid in glass, with no dark patches in it, is "glimmery" and contains no embryonic seeds; 1.3.8

this kind is called a "widow," and you must remove it, as it is of no use. You must then rearrange the eggs evenly in the chamber, having gone through them and weeded out the "glimmery" ones. This procedure is called "glimming."[62]

1.3.9 Beginning from the morning after "glimming," you must decrease the initial quantity of dung, reducing the amount in each trough by a handful at daybreak and by the same amount at close of day; thus, by the end of the fourteenth day, no dung at all will remain to be put in. At this point, the embryo is assuming its complete form, becoming downy and filling out;[63] you then deprive the eggs of all fire. If, despite this, you find them so overheated as to burn the eye, you must unblock the aperture in the side with the door. Leave it open for two days, then "taste" the eggs again with your eye: if you still find them overly hot, then unblock half of the opening in the roof. At the same time, you must turn the eggs, and also move those at the far end of the chamber out towards the area by the door, while moving those by the door to the back. This is so that the cooler ones that were by the door can get warm, and the warm ones by the back wall can cool off by "taking the air": they will thus all be on course to a balanced state, for it is through these alternate periods of warming up and cooling down that the temperament of the eggs achieves its balance. This procedure is the stage actually called incubation, and is the same as that followed by the birds themselves.

1.3.10 You go on repeating the process of swapping the eggs around, twice in the daytime and once at night, for a full nineteen days from the "bedding down." The living creatures will now, by the power of God the Exalted, be emitting sounds inside the eggs. On the twentieth day, some of them will throw off, "throwing off" being the term for breaking through the shells and hatching. By the end of twenty-two days, all of them will have hatched.

1.3.11 For the incubation process to be successful, the most favorable times are Amshīr, Barmahāt, and Barmūdah, which fall in Shubāṭ, Ādhār, and Nīsān [February, March, and April].[64] This is because during this period eggs contain plenty of liquid and big embryonic seeds, and have sound temperaments; the season is itself temperate, and suitable for generation and formation; the eggs, too, ought to be fresh, as they are at this time. Also, eggs are abundant in these months.

Another distinctive animal is the donkey. In Egypt, donkeys are extremely mettlesome. They are ridden saddled, and can hold their own when racing against horses and the most prized mules; on occasion, they even outpace them. At the same time, they are very numerous. There are donkeys so tall that, when they are ridden saddled, they are mistaken for mules. The leaders of the Jews and the Christians ride them, and they can fetch as much as twenty and even forty dinars.[65] 1.3.12

Their cattle are big-bodied, fine-looking beasts. They include a variety, the finest and most valuable of all, called Khaysī cattle. These have horns like archers' bows, and produce copious amounts of milk. 1.3.13

Their horses are champion thoroughbreds, and some fetch 1,000 to 4,000 dinars. As well as breeding male donkeys with female horses, they also breed male horses with female donkeys, producing a mule whose mother is a she-ass. However, such mules will not be big-bodied like those whose mothers are horse mares, because it is the mother that provides the substance.[66] 1.3.14

Another Egyptian animal is the crocodile. Crocodiles are numerous in the Nile, and especially in the far reaches of Upper Egypt and in the Cataracts; there, in the water and among the rocks of the Cataracts, they teem like worms. There are both large and small ones, and they reach a maximum length of more than twenty cubits.[67] On the surface of their bodies, next to their bellies, they have a swelling like an egg that contains moist and bloody matter; it resembles a musk pod, both in appearance and fragrance.[68] A trustworthy informant told me that, on rare occasions, the substance inside this swelling can be of as high a quality as musk itself, no less. Crocodiles lay eggs similar to hens' eggs. 1.3.15

I have seen in a book attributed to Aristotle the following passage: "*The crocodile*: Its liver stimulates copulation, and its kidneys 1.3.16

and their suet are even more efficacious to that end. Iron has no effect on its hide. Between the vertebrae of its neck and the base of its tail, its spine is a single bone, so if it is turned on to its back, it is unable to right itself."[69] The author also says,

> It lays elongated eggs like geese do, and buries them in the sand. When they are hatched, crocodiles are like agama lizards as regards the size and constitution of their bodies. Then they grow big, until they reach ten cubits and more. They lay sixty eggs, because their constitution is patterned on the number sixty, with sixty teeth and sixty blood vessels;[70] during coitus, they ejaculate sixty times; and they can live for sixty years.

1.3.17 Another animal encountered in Egypt is the dolphin. It is found in the Nile, and in particular in the vicinity of Tinnīs and Damietta.

1.3.18 Yet another Egyptian animal is the skink, which is common in Upper Egypt and Aswan. It develops from the offspring of the crocodile on dry land,[71] and is a species of varanus. In fact, it is a varanus, but with a short tail. The varanus, the crocodile, the agama, the skink, and the "fishlet of Sidon" all have one and the same shape. They only differ in how small or large they are, the crocodile being the largest of them and the fishlet of Sidon the smallest. The latter is about the size of a finger, and it can be used to the same ends as the skink, namely to heat various parts of the body and act as an aphrodisiac. It is as if the crocodile is an aquatic varanus, and the varanus a terrestrial crocodile. All these species lay eggs.

1.3.19 The skink is found on the banks of the Nile. When in the river, it lives on small fish; by land, it lives on *ʿaẓāʾ* lizards and similar creatures, and it swallows its food down in one gulp. Male skinks have testes resembling those of cockerels, to which they are similar both in size and in the way they are placed within the body. The females lay more than twenty eggs, burying them in the sand, and the embryos are brought to a complete state of development by the heat of the sun. On the basis of this information, therefore, the skink is actually a separate genus.[72]

Dioscorides said that the skink is found in the environs of al-Qulzum, and in certain places in India and Abyssinia, and that it is distinct from the varanus in its habitat: the varanus is a denizen of the uplands, whereas the skink is amphibious because it goes into the water of the Nile. Furthermore, Dioscorides said, the back of the varanus is rough and hard, while that of the skink is soft and smooth. Also, the varanus is dusty yellow in color, while the skink has yellow and black variegations. 1.3.20

It is the male skinks alone, not the females, that are esteemed as an aphrodisiac. They are trapped in the spring, because that is the season when their desire to mate is aroused. When one is caught, it is slaughtered on the spot and its limbs cut off, but its tail is not cut off too far down.[73] Its belly is then slit open and its innards removed, except for the fat of its belly and its kidneys. It is then stuffed with salt, sewn up, and hung in the shade until it dries out; when it is dry, it is taken down. 1.3.21

From one to three *mithqāls* of its kidneys, the flesh of its back, its fat and its belly are administered in honey water, reduced grape juice, or the yolk of a soft-boiled egg, either on its own or with rocket seeds and "cockerel's testes," both the latter ingredients being dried then powdered.[74] The salt it was stuffed with can also have the desired effect, if it is mixed with other aphrodisiacs. The flesh, too, may be compounded with other medicines, but it is more efficacious when used as a simple.[75] 1.3.22

Another characteristic animal is the "river horse."[76] It is found in Lower Egypt, and particularly in the branch of the river at Damietta. It is a creature vast in form, mighty to behold, and highly aggressive. It goes after boats, sinks them, and kills any of the passengers it can get hold of. It is actually more like a buffalo than a horse, even though it lacks horns and emits a sort of grating sound that does in fact resemble the neighing of a horse or, rather, of a 1.3.23

mule. It has a massive head, gaping jaws, sharp fangs, a broad chest, a great pot belly, and short legs. It attacks savagely and suddenly, charging with great force, and is terrifying in appearance and menacing in its destructiveness.

1.3.24 I was informed by a man who had hunted them several times and had cut open those he had killed, enabling him to see their interior and exterior parts, that they are large pigs: these interior and exterior parts, he said, are in no way different from those of pigs in appearance, or only in their inherently enormous size.[77] I have seen in Anatolius's book on animals a passage that corroborates this claim. To quote, "The 'water pig' is found in the river of Egypt. It is the size of an elephant. Its head resembles the head of a mule, and it has hoofs like a camel's." He also writes, "If a woman drinks the fat from its back, melted and stirred into gruel, it will cause her to put on weight to an exceptional degree."

1.3.25 In the river at Damietta, one such animal had become so addicted to sinking boats that anyone traveling through the locality did so in peril of their lives. Elsewhere, another became addicted to killing buffaloes, cattle, and humans, and to ruining crops and livestock. The local people tried every stratagem to kill these two creatures: they set sturdy traps, deployed men armed with all sorts of weapons, and took various other measures, but to no avail. Eventually, an appeal was sent to a group of the Marīs, a race from the land of the Blacks: they claimed to be experts in hunting hippopotami, and said there were many in their home country. Armed with short spears, they made straight for the creatures, killed both of them in the shortest time and with the least effort, and brought them to Cairo.

1.3.26 I saw them with my own eyes. Their skin was black, hairless, and very thick. The animal's length from head to tail is ten medium paces; its body is about three times broader than a buffalo's, and so too are its neck and head. In the front part of its mouth it has twelve fangs, six above and six below, the outermost ones measuring half a cubit and more, and those between them a little less. Behind these fangs are four rows of other teeth, running the length of the mouth in straight lines, ten in each row, and looking like hens' eggs lined up; two of the rows are in the upper jaw and two, opposite them, in the lower. Opened to its greatest extent, the mouth would be wide enough to take in a big sheep. The tail is half a cubit and more in length, broad at the base, but with a tip like a finger in size that is just skin and bone;[78] it is similar to the tail of a varanus. The legs are short, about a cubit and a third long; they end in something like a camel's hoof, except that the edges are split into four sections. These legs are exceedingly stocky, and the body as a whole is so enormous that it seems like the hull of a capsized boat.

Altogether, it is longer and bulkier than an elephant, except that 1.3.27
its legs are much shorter than those of an elephant, although they are as stocky, or more so.[79]

Another Egyptian creature is the fish known as the "jolter," 1.3.28
because anyone who takes hold of it when it is alive is shocked by a jolting sensation that makes him unable to maintain his composure. The jolt is accompanied by such shivering, severe numbness, tingling in the limbs, and heaviness that the person affected can neither control himself nor keep a grip on any object at all. The numbness spreads upwards to the upper arm and shoulder, then to the entire side of the body, even when one only gives the fish the lightest and most fleeting touch. A man who caught them told me that, when a jolter had been netted, the fisherman would be overcome by this sensation even if there was a gap of a span or more between him and the fish, without him even having to place his hand on it. When the fish dies, however, this peculiar property disappears. It is one of the kinds of fish that have no scales, and its flesh has few bones but much oil. Its skin is thick—as thick as a finger—and easy to peel off, and is inedible. Both small and large ones are found, weighing between one *riṭl* and twenty *riṭls*. A person who often swam in areas that this fish frequents mentioned that, if it brushes against the body of a swimmer, whatever place it touches will, for a while, be so numb that he will nearly fall over if he tries to stand. There are many of these fish in Lower Egypt and in the region of Alexandria.

1.3.29 The Egyptians have many other sorts of fish, because their land is the meeting place of fish from both the Nile and the salt sea. Indeed, there are so many kinds, and such a variety of shapes and colors, that words are not enough to describe them. For example, there is the sort called by the Egyptians the "water snake." It is a fish just like a serpent, between one and three cubits in length.[80] Then there is the *sarb*, which is a fish caught in the waters of Alexandria. It gives anyone who eats it terrifying nightmares, particularly when the person is from outside the region or not used to eating it. The funny anecdotes about these hallucinations are well known.

1.3.30 Another sea creature is the "shield," also called a "turtle." This is an enormous tortoise weighing around four *qinṭār*s, but differing from a tortoise in that its "bowl"—I mean the shell on its back[81]—is like a shield, with flanges that project about a span beyond its body. I saw one in Alexandria whose flesh was being cut up and sold like beef. The flesh of a "shield" exhibits a variety of colors, ranging from green through red and yellow to black and other shades.[82] Out of its belly come around four hundred eggs, which are just like hens' eggs except that they have soft shells. I made an omelette from some of these eggs, and when they congealed they took on various colors—green, red, and yellow—similar to the colors of the flesh.

1.3.31 Yet another sea creature is the clam called *dillīnus*, which has a shell that is oval in shape and somewhat larger than a fingernail. When opened, one finds inside it a moist, mucous, white substance with a black spot, nauseating to look at. It has a salty taste that they claim is appetizing, and is sold by the measure.[83]

Chapter Four: A description of the ancient Egyptian monuments examined by the author

To turn now to the ancient monuments in Egypt, these are such as I have never seen nor even heard tell of in other lands. I will restrict my account to the most remarkable ones I have personally examined. 1.4.1

First among them are the pyramids, already so extensively discussed, described, and surveyed by so many. They are very numerous; all are situated on the Giza side of the Nile, and extend in the direction of Memphis, spread out along a distance of about two days' journey, with a large number at Abusir. Some are big, others small; some are of clay and mud brick, but most are of stone; some are stepped, but most of them taper smoothly.[84] 1.4.2

There used to be a great number of pyramids at Giza; most, however, were small, and were demolished in the time of Saladin by Qarāqūsh, one of the emirs, a eunuch of Greek origins and lofty ambitions who was in charge of public works in Egypt. It was he who built the city wall of stone that surrounds Fustat, Cairo, and the area between them, and which also encompasses the Citadel on al-Muqaṭṭam. It was he, too, who built the Citadel itself and excavated its two well shafts, still extant today. These shafts, also, are among the wonders of Egypt: one descends to the water in them via a staircase of about three hundred steps. 1.4.3

1.4.4 In addition, Qarāqūsh took the stone from those small pyramids, and used it to construct the arches to be seen today at Giza. These arches, too, are marvellous structures, to be numbered among the works of giants; there are over forty of them. At the time of writing, however, namely the year 597 [1200–1], a person devoid of foresight was placed in charge of them. He had them blocked up, hoping to provide a reservoir of water with which to irrigate Giza; but the flow of water was too great for them, and three of the arches were so shaken that they cracked.[85] And after all that, the area he had hoped to irrigate never got its irrigation. Of the pyramids that were demolished, the inner cores and infill still remain; they are of rubble and other stones too small to have been suitable for the arches, and were therefore left in place.

1.4.5 Turning now to the pyramids that everyone talks about, points at, and characterizes in terms of their sheer size, there are three, laid out in a straight line at Giza, across the Nile from Fustat. The distances between them are short, and their angles are all orientated alike, with one angle of each pyramid facing east. Two of them are particularly enormous, and are of one and the same size.[86] It is with these two that the poets have been infatuated, likening them to a pair of breasts swelling from the bosom of the Egyptian motherland.[87] They stand very close together and are built of white stone. The third pyramid is shorter than the first two by about a quarter,[88] but it is built of speckled red granite of extreme hardness: iron tools take a long time to make any mark at all on it. At first, this pyramid seems small in comparison with those other two; then, when you move closer to it until it alone fills your field of vision, the spectacle is so awe-inspiring that your sight will falter as you try to take it all in.

1.4.6 The construction of the pyramids was carried out according to a methodology remarkable in respect both to design and to precision of execution. This is what has enabled the pyramids to endure time's passing eras; or rather, it has meant that time itself has had to endure the Era of the Pyramids.[89] When you meditate in depth upon them, you discover that noble intellects gave the pyramids their all, that pure minds exhausted their every effort for their sake, and that enlightened souls outpoured their loftiest capabilities on their design. Architectonic expertise then brought them forth into the realm of reality, to stand as exemplars that are the pinnacle of the possible. Because of this, they all but speak aloud of their builders, telling us what sort of folk they were, giving voice to their scientific attainments and their intellects, relating the stories of their lives and times.

All this is apparent in the way the pyramids are constructed, 1.4.7
namely in a tapering form that rises from a square base and culminates at a point. It is a property of this tapering form that its center of gravity lies at its midpoint, meaning that it is self-supporting, bearing down upon its own mass and having its weight distributed throughout its parts; the form has no salient point in the direction of which it might subside. A further notable feature of the layout is the way in which its four-square form has been orientated so that its angles face the directions from which the four cardinal winds blow. Thus, the force of the wind is broken when it strikes the angle, which is not the case when it meets a flat surface.

Let us return to our account of the two great pyramids. Those 1.4.8
who have surveyed them state that each has a base four hundred cubits in length and the same in breadth, and that their vertical height is also four hundred cubits, all these dimensions being measured by the "black cubit."[90] The tapering form, they add, is truncated at its uppermost part, where there is a flat top with an area ten cubits by ten.

Speaking of my own observations on the two pyramids' dimen- 1.4.9
sions, an archer who was with us shot an arrow up the middle of the face of one of them, in line with its highest point, and the arrow fell short of the halfway mark.[91] We were then informed that, in the village next to the two monuments, there were people who were accustomed to climbing the pyramid with no effort, so we sent for one of their men and gave him a small inducement. He began to go up it as one of us might climb the staircase at home—in fact, even

more swiftly. Moreover, he climbed wearing his sandals and outer robes, which were long and trailing.[92] I had told him that, when he reached the flat top, he should measure it with his turban; when he came down, we used the turban to find the length in cubits of the distance he had measured, and it came to eleven cubits, measured by the "cubit of the hand."

1.4.10 I have seen a certain expert in mensuration stating that the pyramid's vertical height is approximately 317 cubits and that, of the four triangular planes which form its surrounding faces, each side measures 460 cubits in length. My opinion, however, is that this measurement is at fault, and that if he had made the vertical height four hundred cubits, the figure would have been correct. If circumstances permitted, I would undertake to measure it myself.[93]

1.4.11 In one of the two great pyramids there is an opening that allows people to gain entry; it leads them into narrow corridors, labyrinthine passageways, well shafts, pitfalls, and other such features as appear in the accounts of those who venture inside and explore the innermost parts. Many people, obsessed by the pyramid and filled with fanciful ideas about it, are inspired to penetrate its depths; but they always end up at some place beyond which they cannot go. The route usually followed—the beaten track—is a slippery ramp that leads to the upper part of the pyramid, where there is a square chamber containing a stone sarcophagus. This entrance is not the doorway with which the pyramid was provided when originally constructed; it was merely a hole tunnelled into the side that, by chance, met with success.[94] It has been said that al-Maʾmūn was the one who opened it up.

1.4.12 Most of the people we were with went inside, and ascended to the chamber in the upper part. When they came back down, they spoke of the grandiose sights they had seen. They spoke also of how the pyramid was so full of bats and their droppings that the way was all but blocked, and how these bats grow to the size of pigeons. Inside, there are apertures and shafts leading upwards, which seem to have been incorporated to admit the breeze and to allow light in.

I ventured inside with a group of people on another occasion, and got about two-thirds of the way in; but I suffered a fit of vertigo, fell into a swoon, and only made it back out at my last gasp.

These pyramids are built of massive stones. The length of the stone blocks varies from ten to twenty cubits, their height from two to three cubits, and their width is about the same again. The wonder of all wonders, however, is the way in which one stone is laid on another with such precision that it would be impossible to improve on it—so exactly, in fact, that you will find no space wide enough to insert a needle between them, nor even a gap of a hair's-breadth. Between the stones there is a paper-thin layer of clay mortar; I do not know what kind of clay it is or indeed, if not clay, what it is. In addition, there are inscriptions on the stones written in the ancient characters that no one understands: in the entire land of Egypt, I have never found a single person who so much as claimed to have heard of anyone who knew how to read them. These inscriptions are so numerous that, even if the ones on the two great pyramids alone were copied down on paper, they would amount to about 10,000 leaves.[95] 1.4.13

I have read in certain ancient books of the Sabians that one of these two pyramids is the tomb of Agathodaimon, and the other the tomb of Hermes. The Sabians maintain that these two were great prophets, and that Agathodaimon was the earlier and greater. People used to go on pilgrimage to these pyramids, they say, drawn to them from all corners of the Earth. Concerning such accounts, taken from earlier authorities, we have written extensively in our longer book on Egypt, to which anyone wanting fuller information should refer; the present book is limited to what I have personally observed. 1.4.14

When al-Malik al-ʿAzīz ʿUthmān, the son of Saladin, succeeded his father as sole ruler, some of his more foolish friends inveigled him into the idea of demolishing these three pyramids. He began with the small, red one—and it proved to be the proverbial third stone under the cooking pot.[96] He sent the Ḥalabiyyah, miners, and 1.4.15

stonemasons out to the Pyramid, together with a crowd of the great men of state and the emirs of the kingdom, charging and commanding them to demolish and destroy it. They set up camp by the pyramids, recruited laborers and artificers for the work, and provided them with funds.

1.4.16 For about eight months, they camped out there with their cavalry and foot soldiers.[97] Each day, after expending so much effort that they exhausted themselves, they would dislodge one or two stones: one crew would be stationed above, levering the stone out using wedges and crowbars, another below, tugging at it with cables and ropes. Whenever a block fell, it would do so with a mighty crash, audible from far away and so powerful that it would make the hills tremble and the earth quake. The block would bury itself in the sand, so they would have to exhaust themselves all over again in order to dig it out. They would then drive wedges into it, having first chipped out a place for them, and leave them overnight; as a result, the block would split into pieces, each of which had to be hauled away on a wagon to be discarded at the tail end of the plateau, a short distance away.

1.4.17 In the end, after camping there so long, using up all their funds, and overstraining themselves so repeatedly that their resolve was in tatters and their stamina spent, they gave up and withdrew in abject defeat, without achieving a single ambition or attaining a single goal. Instead, the only goal they attained was that of disfiguring the pyramid and exposing their own impotence and incompetence. These events took place in the year 593 [1196–97].

1.4.18 And despite everything, even though someone seeing the quantity of stone removed might imagine that the pyramid had been utterly extirpated, yet if he then looked at the pyramid itself, he would think that none of it had been demolished, and that only some of the outer facing had been stripped from one side.[98] When I saw for myself the toils they underwent to extract each and every stone, I interviewed the foreman of the stonemasons and asked, "If you were paid 1,000 dinars to replace just one stone in its original position, with the original degree of precision, could you do that?" And he swore by God the Exalted that they would be unable to do so, even if they were paid many times that sum.

On the part of the east bank of the Nile opposite the three great pyramids are numerous grottos of enormous size, containing cavernous chambers. They interconnect, and some have three levels; they are known as "the City."[99] A horseman might well enter them holding his lance upright, ride through them for a whole day, and still never get to the end of them—so many are they, and so spacious and far-reaching. To judge by their appearance, it seems they are the quarries that supplied the stone for the pyramids. The quarries for the red granite, however, are said to be in the regions of al-Qulzum and Aswan.[100] 1.4.19

Over by the three great pyramids themselves are the remains of other gigantic buildings and of many other grottos, worked with superb precision. You will seldom find any part of these monuments that is not inscribed with those unknown characters.[101] 1.4.20

Also by the three pyramids, at a distance from them of rather more than a bowshot, the likeness of a most enormous head and neck protrudes from the ground. The people call it "Old Father Dread,"[102] and assert that its body is buried in the ground; judging by analogy, the body, to be in proportion to the head, would need to measure upwards of seventy cubits.[103] There is a ruddiness to its face, and it is colored with red pigment that shines brilliantly as if still fresh. The face is handsomely, indeed admirably portrayed, with a touch of elegance and beauty about the features, as if a smile were playing across them. 1.4.21

A learned man once asked me what was the most marvelous sight I had seen, and I replied, "The harmonious proportions of Old Father Dread's face." I said this because its features, such as the nose, the eye, and the ear, are in proportion to each other, just as nature itself produces forms that are in proportion. A child's nose, for example, will be in suitable proportion to the child, and the child will look comely with that nose. If the same nose belonged 1.4.22

to a grown man, he would be disfigured by it; by the same token, if the young boy had the man's nose, the boy's appearance would be disfigured. The same applies to all other features: every feature must be of a certain size and shape in comparison and relation to the particular figure to which it belongs; if harmonious proportion is lacking, then the figure will be unsightly. The wonder is how the sculptor of Old Father Dread was able to follow the rules of harmonious proportion in the figure's features, given that they are so enormous, and that nothing in the works of nature resembles the sculpture, let alone corresponds to it.[104]

1.4.23 There is another group of monuments at ʿAyn Shams. This is a small city whose wall may still be seen encircling it, albeit in a ruinous state. To all appearances, the place was once a center of worship: in it are a number of awe-inspiring idols of massive form, sculpted from stone, a single one of which may be about thirty cubits in length, with all its members proportionately enormous.[105] Some of these idols once stood on plinths, while others were seated in various curious postures, all portrayed with precision and skill. The city gate is also still extant today. On most of this stonework are engraved representations of humans and other living beings, and many inscriptions in the unknown characters; you seldom see a stone that is blank, without either an inscription or some other engraving or image on it.

1.4.24 Also in this city are the two celebrated obelisks called "Pharaoh's Obelisks."[106] To describe them in detail, each obelisk has a square plinth, ten cubits in length by the same in width and about the same in height, placed on foundations set firmly in the ground. On this plinth a column was then erected, square in section and tapering, over one hundred cubits in height, having an initial dimension of perhaps five cubits across at its base and culminating in a point. The top of the obelisk is sheathed with a copper cap like a funnel, covering about three cubits of its upper part. Owing to the effects of rain and the long passage of time, this cap has acquired a patina of verdigris and turned green; some of the green color has run down the face of the obelisk. The obelisk is entirely covered with inscriptions in those unknown characters.

I saw that one of the two obelisks had fallen and cracked in half, on account of its enormous weight, and the copper had been removed from its top. Around it are countless other obelisks, a half or a third of the enormous one in size. You seldom find one of these small obelisks formed from a single piece of stone; they are instead made up of superimposed blocks. Most of them have collapsed, with only their plinths remaining upright. I also saw two obelisks in Alexandria, on the seafront in the middle of the built-up area, bigger than these small ones but smaller than the two enormous ones.[107] 1.4.25

Concerning the great temples of Upper Egypt, innumerable accounts already exist of their huge size, precise workmanship, and skillfully executed forms; of the marvelous figures, engravings, representations, and calligraphy which they contain; of the precision with which they were built; and of the massiveness of their architectural features and masonry. The fame of these temples means that another lengthy description would be superfluous.[108] 1.4.26

In Alexandria I saw the Pillar of Columns. This is a red, speckled pillar carved from that exceedingly hard granite, so enormous in girth and soaring so tall that a height of seventy cubits and a diameter of five cubits may not be far off. Beneath it sits an enormous base, appropriate to the scale of the shaft, and on its summit is a correspondingly enormous capital: the perfect symmetry with which this is positioned atop the shaft must have called for a masterful understanding of how to raise heavy masses, as well as expertise in applied engineering.[109] A certain reliable person told me that he had measured the Pillar's circumference, and that it came to seventy-five full spans. 1.4.27

I then saw on the seashore next to the city wall more than four hundred pillars, all broken into two or three pieces, of the same type of stone as the Pillar of Columns, but a third or a quarter of its size. All the Alexandrians agreed that these used to stand around the Pillar of Columns, but that one of the governors of Alexandria, 1.4.28

by the name of Qarājā, who had governed on behalf of Saladin, had seen fit to pull down these columns, break them up, and heave them down to the seashore. They were to act as a breakwater to protect the city wall from the force of the waves, or would prevent the enemy's ships mooring hard by the wall—or so he claimed, for it was really an act of wanton and puerile vandalism, and the deed of someone who cannot distinguish between what is useful and what is harmful.[110]

1.4.29 I did, however, also see around the Pillar of Columns a number of surviving examples of these lesser pillars, some of them intact and others broken. It appears from the look of them that they were once roofed over, with the lesser pillars supporting part of the roof, and the Pillar of Columns surmounted by a dome for which it was itself the support. It is my opinion that this was the colonnade in which Aristotle and the later adherents of his school taught, and that it was the academy Alexander built when he built his city.[111] I believe, moreover, that here in this academy was situated the library which ʿAmr ibn al-ʿĀṣ burned, with the sanction of ʿUmar (may God be pleased with him).[112]

1.4.30 Turning to the Lighthouse, its appearance is so well-known that it needs no detailed description here. Authorities known for their thoroughness have stated that its height is 250 cubits.

1.4.31 I have also read a report written in the hand of a certain research scholar, saying that he had measured the Pillar of Columns together with its base and capital, and that it was sixty-two and a sixth cubits tall,[113] and that it stood on a hillock twenty-three and a half cubits in height, giving a total of eighty-five and two thirds cubits; the height of the base was twelve cubits, and that of the capital seven and a half cubits.

1.4.32 He also measured the Lighthouse and found it to be 233 cubits in height, being composed of three sections: the first section is square and 121 cubits in height, the second section is octagonal and eighty-one and a half cubits in height, and the third section is circular and thirty-one and a half cubits in height.[114] And on top of it all is a mosque which is around ten cubits high.

Then there are the monuments at "Ancient Miṣr." This city is situated on the Giza bank of the Nile, a little upstream from Fustat. It is the same place as Memphis, which was the residence of the pharaohs and the royal seat of the rulers of Egypt. It is this city that is referred to in the words of God the Exalted about Moses, peace upon him, «And he entered the city at a time of inattention on its people's part,» and also in the words of God the Exalted, «So he [Moses] went out of it, fearful and wary of danger.»[115] This is because the residence of Moses, peace upon him, was in a village on the Giza side, near to this city, called Damūh, where today there is a monastery belonging to the Jews. 1.4.33

Today, the ruins of Memphis cover an area half a day's journey in length by about the same in breadth. It was a flourishing city in the time of Abraham, Joseph, and Moses, peace upon them all, and before that for a period known only to God the Exalted.[116] After their era, it prospered until the time of Nebuchadnezzar: he it was who laid waste to the land of Egypt, and it remained in ruins for forty years. The reason he wrought this destruction was that the king of Egypt had taken the Jews under his protection when they sought refuge in his country, and had not allowed Nebuchadnezzar to gain power over them. As a result, Nebuchadnezzar marched on him and annihilated his realm. Later came Alexander, who took control of Egypt, built Alexandria, and made it his capital there. The city retained this status until the coming of Islam, when it was conquered by ʿAmr ibn al-ʿĀṣ; he moved the capital to Fustat. Last of all, al-Muʿizz came from the Maghrib, built Cairo and made it, in turn, the seat of power, as it still is today. All this we recount and explain in full detail in the longer book. 1.4.34

To return to the description of Memphis, also known as Ancient Miṣr, it is a city of broad extent and high antiquity, ruled over by nation after nation and rooted up by people after people. These invaders have erased its monuments and effaced its relics, carried away its stones and its fittings, destroyed its buildings, and disfigured its paintings and sculptures—all in addition to the decay 1.4.35

brought about by four thousand years and more.[117] And yet, in spite of these vicissitudes, you still find in Memphis wonders to elude the understanding of the most meditative mind, and to tie the most eloquent tongue that tries to describe them. The deeper you contemplate them, the more marvelous they seem; the closer you look at them, the more they move you. Whatever significance you draw from them, they hint to you at meanings yet more curious; whatever knowledge you elicit from them, they show you that, beyond, lies knowledge that is greater still.

1.4.36 One of these wonders is a chamber called the Green Chamber. It is formed from a single block of stone, nine cubits in height by eight in length by seven in breadth, with a room hewn out of its center. Its walls, roof, and floor are all two cubits thick; the remaining volume is taken up by the internal space of the room. Both the exterior and interior are entirely covered with engravings, images, and inscriptions in the ancient characters. On the exterior there is a depiction of the sun, facing the direction from which it rises, and there are also representations of many of the stars and heavenly spheres, as well as images of people and other living beings, shown in different postures and guises—variously standing or walking, with their feet spread apart or side by side, with clothes girt up in order to perform tasks, and carrying various implements and gesturing with them. The obvious implication is that these depictions were intended as an allegory for higher matters, nobler activities, and more elevated forms of being, and to be pointers to occult mysteries; one may infer, too, that they were not executed as an idle pastime, and that so much effort would not have been expended on producing them for merely decorative and esthetic ends.

1.4.37 In former times, this chamber stood fast upon large and sturdy granite supports; but ignoramuses and imbeciles dug beneath them in their lust to find buried treasure. As a result, the chamber was displaced, its symmetry upset, and its center of gravity disturbed, so that its own unequally distributed weight caused it to fracture, albeit with hairline cracks. This chamber stood inside what was an enormous temple, built of hard-textured, massive stones to the most perfectly symmetrical design and with the most exacting skill.

In Memphis there are also capitals atop great pillars. Throughout the ruins of the city, the debris of masonry stretches in every direction in a continuous layer. In places, there are the remains of walls, built of those abovementioned massive stones, that are level with the ground; in other places, only foundations remain; elsewhere, ruins stand above ground. I saw a towering arched doorway, each of whose jambs was formed from one single stone; its arched head was also made of one stone, but it had fallen down in front of the doorway. 1.4.38

Even though this stonework was laid with such exact symmetry and precision, you will also find indentations about a span long by two finger-breadths in height, carved out between each pair of blocks, which show traces of copper oxide and discoloration by verdigris. I realized that this was due to the use of clamps in the stonework of the buildings, to stabilize it and act as trusses tying the masonry together: the clamps would be positioned across the joint between the two blocks, then molten lead poured on to them.[118] Despicable good-for nothings have, however, gone about looking for these clamps and have pried out so many that only God the Exalted knows what they have taken, and they have smashed much of the stonework in order to get at them. I swear by God that they have spared no effort in extracting them—and that, in doing so, they have displayed the heights of avarice and the depths of rascality. 1.4.39

To speak next of idols, it is impossible to give a true picture of their sheer numbers and huge dimensions, and hard even to give an estimate. The perfection of their figures, the precision of their forms, and the manner in which they imitate nature are all in truth cause enough for admiration. To give an example, we measured one idol and found that its height, not including the plinth, was over thirty cubits; from right to left it extended about ten cubits, and the distance from back to front was in proportion to that. It was carved from a single block of red granite, and embellished with a red pigment to which the passing of time seemed only to have added extra 1.4.40

freshness.[119] The greatest wonder of all, however, was how the rules of nature and of true proportion had been strictly observed in its execution, in spite of its huge size.

1.4.41 As you are aware, every single part of the body, whether compound or simple,[120] has its own particular size; it has also its own particular proportion to all the other parts, dependent on the said size. It is from this proportionality that beauty of form and comeliness of figure derive; if there is any defect in the proportions, it will result in a degree of unsightliness according to the magnitude of the defect. In these idols, the rules of natural proportion have been implemented with astonishing accuracy, not least with respect both to the sizes of the individual parts, and to their proportions one to another.

1.4.42 If you look closely at such an idol, you will see with what eloquent proportion the trunk commences, at the division of chest from neck at the clavicle; then how the chest begins to rise at the upper ribs, towards the pectoral muscles; these rise in turn above the surrounding area, and are rendered distinct from the remainder of the chest by the use of admirable proportion; they ascend further, to their apex at the nipple, which is depicted in proper proportion to the whole vast figure. It then slopes down to the flat plane in the middle of the breast, to the depression above the sternum, and to the metasternum;[121] also to the corrugations and undulations of the lower ribs, all depicted just as in the actual living being. The downward slope continues to the cartilaginous tips of the ribs, to the soft parts of the belly, and to where the sinews curve and the abdominal muscles, right and left, make the belly taut and raised. It further follows the descending plane from below the navel down towards the flanks; the navel itself is then fully realized, together with the tautness of the muscles surrounding it. There is a further slope down to the region between navel and pubis, to the groin and the inguinal ligaments;[122] finally, the trunk merges into the hip bones.

1.4.43 You will find similarly admirable skill in the way the shoulder is divided from the neck and connected with the upper arm, and in the latter's connection with the forearm; also, in the twist of the vein of the forearm, and in the depiction of the trapezium and the pisiform bone of the wrist,[123] the tip of the bone at the elbow, the two grooves at the articulation of forearm and upper arm,[124] and the muscle of the forearm. The softness of flesh, too, the tension of sinew, and so many other features are depicted that it would take too long to enumerate them.

Sometimes the hand of an idol is shown gripping a pillar one span 1.4.44
in diameter that might be intended to represent a written scroll, and in these cases the depiction even includes the creases and wrinkles that occur in the skin of the palm, next to the little finger, when a person clenches his hand.[125] Regarding the idols' faces, their beauty and harmony of proportion are the utmost accomplishment man could achieve, and the most perfect embellishment stone could receive; the only thing lacking in them is the portrayal of actual flesh and blood. The way the ear is shown, too, with its rim and its intricate convolutions, is the ultimate in visual mimicry.

I saw the statues of two lions, facing each other and separated 1.4.45
by only a short distance. The figures were absolutely enormous, yet the rules of nature and the proportions of living beings had been adhered to in their design, even though their bodies were so very much larger than those of the actual animal. They had broken into pieces, and earth had been piled on top of them.[126] We also found an intact section of the city wall of Memphis, built of small stones and of fired brick. These bricks are large, heavy, and elongated in form; they are half the size of the Kasrawī bricks in Iraq, just as the Egyptian baked bricks of today are also half the size of bricks in Iraq today.

A person of discrimination, on seeing these monuments, would 1.4.46
forgive the common people their beliefs about their ancient predecessors; that is, that they lived to a great age, and that their bodies were of a huge size; or that they possessed a magic wand which, when they struck a stone with it, would set the stone bowling along in front of them. Such beliefs arise in intellects that are insufficiently

equipped with what is necessary for producing such monuments: a knowledge of engineering,[127] the ability to focus one's energies, an abundance of tenacity, perseverance in one's labors, competence in the use of tools, devotion to work; also, a knowledge of the anatomy of living beings, and particularly that of humans—the size of individual members, their proportions one to another, how they are assembled and positioned, the extent of the locations they occupy relative to each other.

1.4.47 To give an example, in contrast to other living beings, the lower "half" of a human is in fact greater than the upper "half"—I mean the trunk—by a known amount.[128] A person of medium frame is eight spans tall, measured by his own span; the length of his hand and forearm to the inner angle of his elbow—I mean the place where his blood is let[129]—is two of his own spans; his upper arm measures a span and a quarter. It is the same with all his bones, small and great, including those of his fingers and toes, his vertebrae, metacarpals and metatarsals: they all keep to the rules of size and of relative proportion.

1.4.48 The same rules apply to all parts of his anatomy, internal and external: to the manner in which the crown of his head slopes down from its vertex, for example, and in which the crown protrudes from the area below it; to the width of the front and sides of his forehead, and the degree to which his temples are indented; they determine how prominent his cheekbones are, and how flat his cheeks; they dictate how sharp his nose will be and how pliant its cartilage, how wide his nostrils will flare and how broad will be the flesh that separates them; they govern the fineness of his lips, the roundedness of his chin, the sharpness of his jawline—and many other details, besides, for which our vocabulary is not extensive enough, and which can only be understood through observation, dissection, and minute examination.

1.4.49 Aristotle included a section in the eleventh chapter of his *Book of Animals*[130] which shows that, while the people of his time had proficient and indeed expert knowledge of the members of living beings and of their proportions, the sum of their understanding, great though it was, was an inconsiderable trifle when measured against the actual state of things created by nature. He demonstrated how a person's knowledge of the subject only seems great when measured on the scale of his own feeble powers, and when compared with the even feebler abilities of others of his own human kind. It is as if an ant carrying a barleycorn should be cause for wonder, whereas an elephant carrying a load weighing many *qinṭārs* were to inspire no wonderment at all.[131]

Here is my version of Aristotle's exact words: 1.4.50

> It is surprising that we should consider a knowledge of the rules of figurative art and of the sculpting and casting of idols to be so desirable, and that we should strive to grasp the philosophy underlying this knowledge—and yet that we should *not* think it desirable to learn about things whose perfection is due to nature, and especially when we are capable of learning their efficient causes. Given this gap in our knowledge, we ought not to shrink from inquiring into the natural characteristics of humble creatures that are considered "ignoble." Such inquiries ought not to be wearisome to us, as they would be to small children. For in everything in the world of nature, there is something to be marveled at: we ought therefore to strive to understand the natural characteristics of every single species of living creature, and to be aware that in all creatures there is something of these characteristics that is noble. The reason for this innate virtue is this: that nothing formed by nature is ever devoid of *some* purpose or other; nor do natural forms turn up by chance, or result from luck. No; everything that exists by virtue of nature can only exist *for* something—I mean, to contribute to a state of perfection. And as such, it has gained its rightful place, its due rank, and its proper merit.

May God be blessed, for He is the best of creators.

1.4.51 When it comes to the internal parts and cavities of living beings, and all the marvels therein whose descriptions are included in the anatomical writings of Galen and others, and in Galen's *On the Use of Parts*,[132] the very least of the least of them would baffle an artist trying to depict them; his powers would fall far short, his endeavors find no support, and he would realize the truth of the words of God the Exalted, «And humans were created weak.»[133]

1.4.52 Furthermore, I would say that to admire the works of human hands is no different from admiring the works of nature. This is because man-made artefacts are, in a certain regard, also natural, inasmuch as they result from capabilities that are endowed by nature. For example, if an engineer moves an enormously heavy object, he will be worthy of admiration; but, by the same token, if he were to make a figure of wood, say, and that figure were itself to move some heavy object, then the engineer would be even more deserving of admiration. «And God has created not only you, but also what you make.»[134]

1.4.53 Blessed is He Whose sovereignty pervades both the invisible and the visible universes,[135] «and also your own selves. Do you not see?»;[136] the light of Whose majesty shines unbedimmed by any veil; Who «knows the import of each surreptitious glance, and what is hidden in men's breasts.»;[137] by Whose power the manifest forms of all existent things derive their being, and by Whose will they are in motion or at rest; in the execution of Whose commands, fulfilled in themselves, these beings delight, rejoicing in their own proximity to the presence of His sanctity; Whose unity is affirmed in their plurality, and Whose eternity is avowed by their mutability. «And there is not a thing but it proclaims His glory.»[138]

1.4.54 To return to our earlier subject of discussion, we should remark that, although idols are so numerous in Egypt, the passage of time has fretted all but a very few of them to fragments, and frayed them into scraps.[139] That said, I have myself seen a large idol from the top of whose forehead someone had hewn out a millstone two cubits in diameter; yet the idol's appearance did not seem to have been particularly impaired or appreciably changed for the worse.[140] I have also seen an idol that had another idol at its feet, attached to it, and of such relatively small size that, on the scale of the larger one, it was like a newborn child—even though it was, in absolute terms, the size of the biggest living man.[141] There was something especially attractive about its features—the sort of beauty that draws the onlooker's eye, and at which one never tires of gazing.

In ancient times, the making of idols for worship was prevalent throughout the world, and common to all nations. For this reason, God the Exalted said concerning Abraham, peace upon him, «In truth, Abraham was a nation, obedient to God, a *ḥanīf*, and not one of the polytheists.»[142] That is, in his time, he alone was a monotheist, and was thus "a nation" in himself, for he set himself apart from the polytheists, and adopted a unique point of view that contradicted their beliefs.[143] In contrast, the Children of Israel saw the Copts worshipping these Egyptian idols with great adulation, honor, and devotion; because of their long sojourn among the Copts, they not only became accustomed to these practices, but also began to find them attractive. This is why, when they later also saw one of the communities in the Levant paying their devotions «to their idols, they said, "Moses, make us a god just as they have gods!" And he said, "In truth, you are a people who are ignorant."»[144] 1.4.55

Later, in the time of the Christians, the overwhelming majority of them, both Copts and Sabians, became nostalgic for their roots and gravitated towards the ancient practices of their forefathers—namely, by making figurative images for their churches and larger places of worship. In this they excelled themselves in scope and diversity; often, too, they would try to outdo each other in ignorance and folly, and would go so far as to portray what they claimed to be their God, surrounded by angels. This was all due to the survival of elements from the practices of their earliest ancestors—even though those same ancestors had, in fact, regarded the Deity as far too great to submit to being apprehended, by either the 1.4.56

intellect or the senses, let alone by figurative portrayal. The Christians' belief in the divinity of a human being only aided and abetted them in producing such portrayals.[145] We have supported our statements on this subject with further proofs, in our treatises refuting their beliefs.[146]

1.4.57 Later rulers never ceased to take an interest in the survival of the ancient monuments. They prevented people from tampering with them or damaging them, even if they themselves felt hostility towards the monuments' masters.[147] This policy had several benefits. One was that the monuments would survive as a historical record that drew attention to past eras. Then, they would stand as testimony in support of divinely revealed scripture: the Glorious Qur'an mentions such monuments, and also mentions their builders; by seeing them, therefore, one has empirical proof of the account, and confirmation of written tradition.[148] They also remind one of the fate of past peoples and recall the end that befell them. Not least, they give some indication of the circumstances of those peoples of old, of how they lived, of the wealth of their knowledge and the clarity of their thinking, and of much else besides. All these are matters to stimulate a soul's appetite for learning, and to provide choice food for thought.

1.4.58 In the present day, however, people have been left to their own devices, at liberty to roam day and night.[149] They have been given free rein to go wherever their fancy takes them, running after their own whims and ambitions. Each and every one of them acts by his own rules, and on the impulse of his own nature, according to the temptations of his ego and the enticements of his passions. Confronted by great monuments, such people are awestruck at first sight—but then go on to view their implications in the worst light. Their fancies have steered them relentlessly towards their darlings, their hearts' dearest desires: the dinar and the dirham. They are thus like the wine drinker of whom it was said,[150]

> Everything he saw, he thought to be a cup;
> Everything he saw, the boy who tops it up.

These people see every sign that catches their eye as a marker flagging loot, and every crack that cleaves a hillside as leading to treasure. Moreover, they view every great idol as a guardian of riches buried beneath its feet, standing as a deadly warning to all. They have taken to using every device to destroy them, and they spare no efforts in demolishing them; they disfigure the idols, not only because they hope to get money out of them, but also because they fear that the idols can cause their own destruction.[151] They chip holes in rocks, too, never doubting that they are locked coffers filled with treasure, and they creep through clefts in the hills like cat burglars who have found devious ways into houses and stolen a march on their rivals. Some of these clefts can only be entered on all fours, some only by crawling on one's belly, others by dragging oneself flat on the ground, and yet others contain such tight spots that only a lean and skinny person can squeeze through. Most are in fact natural clefts in the hillsides. 1.4.59

Any treasure seeker with his own money ends up losing it in his quest. Those who are hard up to begin with, however, will target some well-off person and build up his hopes, till his desire for gain seems all but fulfilled. This they do with solemnly sworn oaths; they also make claims about information of which they are the exclusive possessors, and about portents they pretend to have witnessed. Eventually, the backer will end up insane, insolvent, and in dire straits. 1.4.60

Nevertheless, the hopes of such people are constantly reinforced, and they never cease to persist in their quest. Part of the reason is that some treasure seekers do indeed find spacious, well-built underground crypts containing vast and innumerable throngs of the ancient dead. The bodies are swathed in linen wrappings, at times up to about a thousand cubits of cloth on a single corpse. First, each member—for example, the hands, the feet, the fingers, and the toes—is individually wrapped in fine bandages, then the entire body is wound about until it ends up like an enormous bundle. The wrappings are taken by the Bedouin Arabs, by the country folk,[152] and by other people who go looking for these crypts. Any of the cloth that 1.4.61

is still soundly woven they make into garments, or else they sell it to the paper makers who turn it into packaging for druggists.

1.4.62 Some of the dead are interred in coffins of *jummayz* wood, hewn thick, others in stone sarcophagi of marble or granite; yet others are found in large jars full of honey. A reliable person informed me that once, when some people were on the trail of treasure near the pyramids, they came across a sealed storage jar. On breaking open the seal, they were surprised to find the jar full of honey. They had begun tasting it, when one of the company found some hair sticking to his finger. He pulled at it—and out popped a small boy. All the parts of the child were still in one piece, the flesh of his body was soft to the touch, and he was wearing some pieces of jewelry and other ornaments.

1.4.63 The foreheads, eyes, and noses of these dead ancients are sometimes covered with an outer skin, as it were, of gold foil; this is sometimes also placed over a female corpse's genitalia. At times, a gold integument of this sort covers the entire body, like a sheath. Also, the corpse may be accompanied by some pieces of gold, and by various ornaments and items of jewelry, or even by the tools with which the dead person plied his trade in life. A reliable informant told me that he had found with one corpse a barber's kit, consisting of a whetstone and a razor, with another, a cupper's instruments, and with a third, a weaver's equipment. Judging by appearances, it thus seems that it was the ancient Egyptians' practice to bury a man with the tools of his trade and with his worldly wealth.

1.4.64 I have heard that there are certain Abyssinian communities who also follow this practice, and that they regard it as inauspicious to touch a dead man's possessions, or to make any use of them. A relative of ours moved to Abyssinia and made money there, including 200 *ūqiyyah*s of gold.[153] When he died, the local people compelled an Egyptian who had been in his company to take the money—and so he did, with all due acknowledgement to them.

1.4.65 It seems—though God knows best—that it was also part of the practice of the ancient Egyptians to place a quantity of gold bullion with the dead person. One of the judges in Abusir, which is situated next to the ancient burial grounds, informed me that they had dug up the bodies from three graves, and had found each one to be covered with an integument of gold so thin that it barely held together. In the mouth of each corpse they had found an ingot of gold; when the judge put the three ingots together, they weighed nine *mithqāl*s in total. There are so many stories about such finds that this book could not contain them all.[154]

Let us turn to the substance they call *mūmiyā*, which is found in the body cavities and brain pans of ancient corpses. It is exceedingly plentiful: the country folk bring it into the city, where it is sold for a trifling sum. I myself have bought three heads full of it for half an Egyptian dirham; the man who sold them to me showed me a sack filled with the stuff, in which there was a thorax and abdomen packed with *mūmiyā*. I noticed that it had infiltrated the bones, and that they had become saturated with it; indeed, the *mūmiyā* had permeated them so thoroughly that they seemed to have become part of it. I also saw a mummified cranium that had the marks of the cloth wrappings and the pattern of their weave impressed on it, just as they will be imprinted on wax if you use it to seal a cloth wrapper. 1.4.66

This *mūmiyā* is black, like mineral pitch.[155] I observed that, when exposed to the high temperatures of summer, it became runny, and stuck to anything it touched; when placed on lighted charcoal, it boiled and emitted smoke, and I smelled the odor of mineral pitch or asphalt coming off it. Indeed, it seems likely that it is a mixture of asphalt and myrrh.[156] 1.4.67

As for *mūmiyā* proper, it is a substance that comes down from the mountain peaks with the waters that run off them, then coagulates like tar; it gives off an odor of asphalt mixed with mineral pitch. Galen writes, "*Mūmiyā* wells up from springs, as do tar and naphtha."[157] Other authorities have said that it is itself a type of tar, and that it is called "the menstruation of the mountains." Whatever the case, the substance that is found in the cavities of corpses in Egypt is not far different in its properties from the natural characteristics of 1.4.68

true *mūmiyā*, and near enough to be used as a medicinal substitute when true *mūmiyā* is unavailable.

1.4.69 Of all the interments to be found in their ancient burial grounds, some of the most surprising are those of various types of animals—birds, beasts, and insects. Each is swathed in any number of cloth wrappings, cosseted and coddled in its coverings. A reliable person told me that some people had discovered a subterranean chamber, solidly built, and on opening it had found inside it a mass of linen wrappings that had become threadbare with age. These they managed to remove, innumerable though they were—and found them to contain a perfectly preserved calf, which had been swaddled with the utmost skill. Another informant told me that they had come across a falcon: after an exhausting time unwinding its wrappings, they also found it intact, with not a feather missing. I have also been told similar stories about a tom-cat, a sparrow, a beetle, and other creatures, but recounting them would involve too much long-winded and extraneous detail.[158]

1.4.70 A trustworthy and truthful informant also told me how some treasure hunters had come to him when he was in Qūṣ, and explained that a sink hole had suddenly opened up beneath their feet, leading them to suspect that there was something buried in it. My informant went out with them to the spot, accompanied by a group of armed men, and they began digging. They eventually found a large jar, its top firmly sealed with gypsum plaster. They eventually opened it, with some difficulty, and discovered some objects like fingers, wrapped in strips of cloth. When they unwound the wrappings, they found them to contain sprats—that is to say, small fish—which had as good as turned to dust, and would fly away at a puff of breath. Nevertheless, the men carried the jar to the town of Qūṣ and placed it before the governor. About a hundred men gathered around it, and set about unwrapping the rest of its contents. At last, they got to the bottom of it—and it was all wrapped sprats, and nothing but.

1.4.71 Some time later, I myself saw in the ancient burial grounds at Abusir more marvels than this book could possibly contain. For example, I found there subterranean grottos, constructed with great skill, each of which held countless mummies.[159] One grotto would be filled with the mummies of dogs, another with those of cattle, yet another with those of cats, all of them wrapped in strips of linen. I noticed, too, a certain amount of human bones that had become so splintered with age that they resembled the white fibers of a date palm.[160] However, most of the remains I saw were hard and still very much in one piece; indeed, they looked better preserved than the remains of the people who perished in the year 597 [1200–1] (I shall describe those recent corpses in the last part of the present book). This was particularly true of the ancient bodies that had been steeped in asphalt or in tree pitch. You find that these latter corpses resemble iron in color, hardness, and density.

I saw God knows how many skulls of cattle, and also of sheep and goats, and was able to distinguish between the heads of goats and of sheep, as well as between those of cows and bulls. I found that the flesh of the cattle had adhered to its wrappings and become one piece with them, red to black in color; the bone, where it protruded, was a pure and brilliant white. Some bones, however, were red, and some black; human bones displayed the same variety of color. Undoubtedly, the mummy cloths were first soaked in aloes and tree pitch and, when saturated, were used as wrappings. This is why they impregnated and preserved the flesh; any of the wrappings that happened to be in contact with bone impregnated it also, turning it red or black. 1.4.72

In several places, I also found entire hillocks composed of the remains of dogs, containing in all perhaps 100,000 individual dogs or more.[161] These are the spoil heaps from what the treasure hunters rummage up: a whole mass of people make their living from these graves, carrying away whatever bits of wood, rags, and so on that they chance upon. Regarding other animals, I looked through all the possible sites, but in none did I find a single horse, camel, or donkey. The absence of these species kept puzzling me, so I questioned the shaykhs of Abusir about it. They told me straight away 1.4.73

that they themselves had already pondered the question and had investigated it themselves, but had also found no trace of those animals.[162]

1.4.74 Most of the ancient coffins are of *jummayz* wood. Some examples are still strong and solid, but others have turned to the consistency of ashes. One curious piece of information the judges of Abusir shared with me was their discovery of a stone sarcophagus which they unsealed, only to find that it enclosed a further sarcophagus. This too they unsealed, and discovered a coffin inside. On opening it, they found it contained an "albino lizard"—that is, a gecko—very carefully cocooned in cloth wrappings.[163]

1.4.75 Around Abusir we came across many pyramids, including one that was in ruins but whose core had survived. We took its measurement from the original line of its foundations, and found it not far short of the two great pyramids of Giza.[164] Regarding all these features of the burial grounds at Abusir that we have described, comparable and, at times, precisely similar features are to be found at ʿAyn Shams, in the great temples of Upper Egypt, and elsewhere.

1.4.76 On the subject of pyramids, you should note that I have found no reference to them in the Torah or other scriptures.[165] I have not come across any mention of them in Aristotle, either, but only a statement in the course of a passage of his on politics: "just as building was part of the tradition of the Egyptians." Alexander of Aphrodisias wrote a short history in which he spoke of the Jews, the Magians, and the Sabians, and also went to some extent into accounts of the Copts. Galen, however, I have noted making an actual reference to pyramids at one point, and deriving their name, *haram*, from the *haram*, or "decrepitude," of old age.[166] He also said, speaking of Egypt in his *Commentary on the "Airs and Lands" of Hippocrates*,[167] "Whoever wishes to learn the craft of astrology should head for Egypt, for its people have applied themselves to it with unstinting devotion." That, anyway, is the drift of his statement. In addition, Galen said in his *Anatomical Procedures*,[168] "Whoever wishes to see for himself how bones are articulated, and to examine their individual forms, should set out for Alexandria and look at the ancient dead."

You must also be aware that the Copts in Egypt are the counterparts of the Nabataeans in Iraq, that Memphis is the counterpart of Babylon, and that the Romans and the Caesars in Egypt are the counterparts of the Persians and the Kisrās in Iraq;[169] also that Alexandria is the counterpart of al-Madāʾin, and Fustat that of Baghdad. Today, all these peoples and places come under the aegis of Islam, and are embraced by the mission of the Abbasid caliphate.[170] 1.4.77

Chapter Five: Unusual Egyptian buildings and boats examined by the author

1.5.1 Turning now to their latter-day buildings, these are not only distinguished in their architecture, but are also very cleverly planned—so much so that it is rare for the Egyptians to leave any spot vacant, and not utilize it to some end. Their residences are spacious; they live for the most part in the upper storeys, with the windows of their dwellings facing north, open to the pleasant breezes. Also, you seldom find a dwelling that does not have a wind tower.[171] Their wind towers are big and wide, and thus subject to the full force of the breeze. They build them to the very highest standards: the construction of a single one can cost from one hundred to five hundred dinars. If they are wind towers for small dwellings, however, one might cost a single dinar.

1.5.2 Their markets and streets are broad, and their buildings lofty. They build in cut stone and fired red brick—that is, baked brick—and their bricks are half the size of Iraqi bricks. They construct the drainage channels of their lavatories so solidly that, even when the rest of the house falls into ruin, the channel remains standing.[172] They dig the shafts of their privies down to flowing water,[173] so a long period of time can pass without them needing to be emptied out.

1.5.3 When they want to build a residential compound,[174] a palace complex for a ruler, or a bazaar,[175] an architect is called in and commissioned to carry out the work. He heads off to the site, which will be a hummock of dust or some such spot, and divides it up in his mind's eye, planning the layout for it according to the recommendations he has received. He then concentrates on the subdivisions of the site in turn: on each one, he starts to build and takes the work through to completion, so that the part in question can be utilized independently and inhabited immediately. This done, he turns his attention to another subdivision. And so he continues in the same manner until, when all the parts are finished, the whole complex will have been completed without any hitches or amendments.

In the construction of dams, which they call *zarbiyyahs*, they dis- 1.5.4
play admirable expertise.[176] To describe the work in detail: first, a shaft for a foundation pile is dug down to a level where moisture and water seepage begin to appear. At this point, a frame made of *jummayz* or some other such wood is placed on the damp floor, after the ground has been levelled. The rim of the frame is about two thirds of a cubit wide, and the circular opening within it is about two cubits in diameter; it is like the frames placed at the bottom of wells. Next, fired bricks, mortared with lime, are laid on top of the rim, and built up to a height of about two fathoms; the result is something like a cylindrical oven. At this stage, the "divers" arrive, go down the shaft, and dig deeper. Whenever water wells out, they scoop it up, together with the mud and sand. They also dig beneath the frame: as the soil under it loosens, and as its own weight increases with the brick courses laid upon it, it goes down into the ground; as it sinks ever deeper, the divers go down and dig beneath it. Simultaneously, the bricklayer builds on top of it, adding to the height of the brick lining. With the builder continually adding courses and the diver digging under it, the frame sinks under its own weight until eventually it comes to rest on firm ground and thus reaches its maximum depth, which they know by experience.

At this point, they move on to repeat the process, at a spot in 1.5.5
line with the first shaft and about four cubits beyond it. And so they continue, following the same procedure along the entire designated

length of the foundations. Finally, they build the foundations of the dam in the normal manner, having first packed the shafts with rubble: these shafts are thus transformed into underpinnings that will anchor the construction firmly, and piles to support and stabilize it.

1.5.6 Speaking next of the public bathhouses in Egypt, in no other land have I seen any that are more skillfully planned, more perfectly thought out, or finer either in appearance or to experience.[177] To begin with, the plunge pools in them are each big enough to hold between two and four *rāwiyah*s, or even more. Two gushing spouts, one hot and one cold, supply the pool; the water from them first pours into a cistern, very small and set high up, in which the two streams mix before flowing down into the big pool. Of this pool, about a quarter of its height projects above floor level; the remainder is sunk into the ground, so that the bather goes down into it to immerse himself. Further into the bathhouse, there are private compartments with their own doors, and there are also private compartments off the changing area: all these are for the more exclusive class of bathers, so that they can avoid mixing with the common crowd and giving anyone a glimpse of their private parts.

1.5.7 The changing area and its associated private compartments are beautifully laid out and elegantly built. In the center is a pool faced in marble, surmounted by columns supporting a cupola, and the entire space has ceilings embellished with colored patterns, walls striped below and whitewashed above,[178] and floors paved with different types of marble in a variegated design of contrasting colors; the marble work in the interior parts of the bathhouse is always finer than that in the outer areas. In addition to all this, the bathhouse is well lit, with lofty vaulted ceilings and glass roundels of various colors and brilliant hues.[179] The overall effect is such that, once one has entered the place, one is loath to leave it: even if some member of the ruling elite were to spare no expense in building a palace for receiving guests in state, and were to see his plan through to perfection, it would not be finer than one of these bathhouses.[180]

The heating system of Egyptian bathhouses, too, is remarkably clever. The fire chamber is built with a domed top, open to the fire so that the flames can reach up to it. Placed around ledges inside this dome is a series of four cauldrons made of tin,[181] similar to the cauldrons used by makers of *harīsah*, but bigger; these cauldrons are also connected to channels consisting of pipes, positioned near their brims. First of all, water enters via the main channel bringing it from the well; it goes into a large tank and, from there, into the first cauldron. At this point it is at its normal, unheated temperature. It then flows into the second cauldron, where it heats up a little, then into the third, where it gets hotter still; finally it goes into the fourth cauldron, where it attains its maximum heat. From here it flows into the channels supplying the actual bathhouse. Constantly running hot water is thus provided at the lowest possible cost, with the least possible effort, and in the shortest possible time. In this heating process, the Egyptians have imitated what nature does in the bellies of living creatures, and the way nutriments are "cooked" in them. The nutriments pass through the guts and other alimentary organs common to all living creatures; at each stage, they undergo a particular phase of digestion and attain a particular degree of concoction,[182] until they reach the last gut, by which time they are completely digested. 1.5.8

Note that the cauldrons need to be renewed regularly, because the fire gradually depletes them. Moreover, the first cauldron, the vessel containing the unheated water, always suffers a visibly greater degree of depletion than the cauldron containing the hottest water. The phenomenon is due to a physical cause, but this is not the place to go into it.[183] Note, also, that they line the floor of the furnace—that is, the base on which the fire is laid—with about fifty *irdabb*s of rock salt, as they also do with the floors of commercial ovens. This is because it is a physical property of salt that it retains heat. 1.5.9

Turning now to Egyptian boats, they come in many types and shapes, but the most remarkable sort that I myself have seen is a vessel they call an *ʿushayrī*. Its general form is that of the *shabbārah* 1.5.10

of the Tigris, except that it is much broader and longer, and has more elegant proportions and shapelier lines. It is decked with stout planks of excellent joinery, and from this decking project ledges, rather like balconies, about two cubits wide. On the deck itself a wooden superstructure is built: this is rounded off with a cupola, and is provided with portholes and skylights, furnished with shutters, that open on to the river on all sides. Within this cabin a separate closet is then erected, together with a lavatory. Finally, the cabin is embellished with patterns in various colors, including gilding and the finest quality paintwork.

1.5.11 This type of vessel is built for princes of the sultan's family and members of the ruling classes, and designed so that its high-ranking owner can sit in state on his cushion, surrounded by the closest members of his circle, while his pages and military slaves stand to attention, girt with waist sashes and swords, on the projecting balconies. The passengers' food and other requirements, meanwhile, are down in the vessel's hold. The boatmen are below deck, too, or in other parts of the vessel, rowing. They know nothing of their passengers' affairs and, similarly, the passengers will not be bothered by the crew; each group is totally separate and involved in its own business. If the high-ranking owner wishes to be alone, away from his companions, he goes into the small interior cabin; if he wishes to answer the call of nature, he goes into the lavatory.

1.5.12 Boatmen in Egypt row facing backwards, which means that their rowing action makes them look like rope makers doing their backward walk.[184] In their manner of propelling boats, they thus also resemble someone walking in reverse and dragging a weight placed in front of him. The boatmen of Iraq, however, are the equivalent of someone propelling a weight forwards by shoving it along before him. Iraqi boats, therefore, head the way the boatman is facing, while Egyptian boats move in the opposite direction to the one the boatman is facing. As to which of the two techniques is easier, and how to prove it, the question belongs in the realm of physical science and, in particular, kinetics.

Chapter Six: Unusual Egyptian foods

One Egyptian specialty is *naydah*. It is comparable to the sweet called *khabīṣ*, ranges from red to black in color and is sweet-tasting, but not overly so.[185] It is made from wheat that has been allowed to germinate and is then simmered until the starch and nutritional potency have been transferred to the water. The water is then strained off and simmered again until it begins to thicken. At this point, wheat flour is sprinkled into it, and the mixture sets and is taken off the heat. It is sold at the same price as bread, and is known as *naydat al-bawsh*. The water, after straining, may also be simmered on its own until it sets without the addition of flour. In this case, it is called "set *naydah*," and is more expensive and higher in quality. 1.6.1

The Egyptians also specialize in extracting oil from the seeds of radish, turnip, and lettuce, which they use as fuel for their lamps and to make soap. Their soap is soft-textured and red, yellow, or green in color—hence the name of the sweet known as "soap cakes," from its resemblance to this soap. 1.6.2

Regarding main dishes in Egypt, the vinegar-flavored and plain ones are the same as, or close to, their familiar equivalents in other lands.[186] Their "sweet" main dishes, however, are unusual, in that they prepare chicken with various ingredients of sweets. The method of cooking involves boiling the chicken, then sousing it 1.6.3

in rose water[187] and adding ground hazelnuts, pistachios, poppy seeds, purslane seeds, or rose petals. The mixture is simmered until it thickens, spices are added, and it is removed from the fire. These dishes are called "pistachio chicken,""hazelnut chicken,""poppy chicken,""rose chicken," and "Nubian Lady" in the case of the one thickened with purslane seeds, because of its dark color. In all these recipes, they display a degree of inventiveness that deserves a longer description than this.[188]

1.6.4 Similarly, their sweets made from cane sugar are of so many kinds that to examine them all would take us away from the main point and, indeed, would require a separate monograph. One might, however, single out for mention those that are beneficial in the treatment of illnesses, for invalids on diets, and for convalescents who feel a craving for sweet things. Such sweets include *khabīṣ* made with gourd[189] and with carrots, rose sweets made with roses, and ginger sweets made with ginger; also, those such as aloeswood pastilles, lemon pastilles, pastilles infused with musk, and other similar sweets.

1.6.5 In place of almonds, the Egyptians often use pistachios in their main dishes and sweets. (Pistachios are one of the foods that unblock obstructions of the liver.) They use them to make a kind of hash called "pistachio *harīsah*," which is particularly delicious, and also fattening. The ingredients are: flesh of boiled chickens, shredded, one part; rose water, two parts; pistachios, peeled and pounded, an eighth or a ninth of the sum of the other ingredients. The method of cooking is as follows: the shredded chicken is coated with sesame oil then placed in the pan so as to get a scent of the fire;[190] the rose water is then poured on, and the mixture stirred until it thickens; the pistachios are added and stirred in so that the ingredients blend; finally, it is removed from the fire.

1.6.6 Another of the unusual dishes they make is "platter pie." The recipe is as follows: take thirty Baghdadi *riṭl*s of best white flour, and knead it with five and a half *riṭl*s of sesame oil (knead it as you would the dough for *khushkanān* bread). Divide the dough in two, and use half of it to line a copper platter made specially for this pie:

it is roughly four spans in diameter and provided with stout handles. Next, on this dough base arrange three whole roast lambs, stuffed with a mixture of ground meat fried in sesame oil, pounded pistachios, and aromatic hot spices such as pepper, ginger, cinnamon, mastic, coriander seed, cumin, cardamom, nutmeg, and other similar spices.[191] Sprinkle the whole with musk-infused rose water. Then, on top of the lambs and in the gaps between them, place twenty full-sized chickens, twenty young chickens, and fifty squabs,[192] some of them roasted and stuffed with eggs, others stuffed with meat, and the rest stewed in the juice of sour grapes, lemons, or similar. Next, embellish the pile with triangular and flask-shaped pastries,[193] some filled with meat and others with cane sugar and sweets. If at this stage you wish to add another lamb, carved into slices, and some fried cheese, it is not a bad idea.

When all these ingredients have been neatly piled up in the shape of a dome, sprinkle them with rose water in which musk and aloeswood have been infused. Now cover the ensemble with the other portion of dough, spread out into a round. Seal the edges of the two rounds of dough together, as one does with *khushkanān*, so that absolutely no breath of air can escape. The platter should then be transferred to the top of the cylindrical oven, and left there until the dough casing becomes firm and begins to cook through. At this point, the attached handles should be used to lower the platter, very gradually, down into the oven. One then needs to wait patiently to give it time for the pastry to become fully cooked. When it has browned nicely, remove it, wipe the surface with a sponge, then sprinkle with rose- and musk water and serve. 1.6.7

This is a culinary creation fit to accompany royalty and lovers of luxury to their distant hunting grounds and remote picnic spots. It is an entire feast of many courses all in one; it is easy to transport and hard to spoil; it is splendid in appearance and a pleasure to experience; and it retains its heat for a long time. 1.6.8

As for the common people of Egypt, few of them have even the slightest experience of such luxurious fare. Instead, their diet 1.6.9

consists mostly of the salt fish called *ṣīr* and *ṣiḥnāh*, clams, cheese, *naydah*, and similar foods. They drink a kind of beer called *mizr*, which is an intoxicating beverage made from wheat. There are certain sorts of people who eat the mice that are generated in desert areas and fields when the Nile's inundation ebbs away; they call them "field quails." Moreover, in Upper Egypt there is a tribe of people who eat snakes, and also donkeys and other beasts of burden that have died.[194] In Lower Egypt, an intoxicating drink is sometimes made from the green melon; in Damietta, a lot of fresh fish is eaten, and is served with all the ingredients that accompany meat, such as rice, sumac, meatballs, and so on.

1.6.10 Here ends Part One. Praise to God, Lord of the worlds, and may He bless the foremost of His emissaries, Muḥammad, and the pious and virtuous members of his family.

Part Two, consisting of three chapters

Chapter One: The Nile and the Manner of Its Annual Rises, with an Explanation of the Causes of This Phenomenon and the Laws of Nature Governing It

In the name of God, the Merciful and Compassionate

Egypt's River Nile, you will recall, rises at the time when the waters of the Earth's other rivers fall, namely when the sun is in Cancer, Leo, and Virgo.[195] During this season, it inundates the land, covering it for some days. When the water recedes, the land is plowed and sown; the nights then become very humid with dew, and this dew nourishes the crops until they are ready to be harvested. 2.1.1

The maximum rise required for the needs of normal irrigation is eighteen cubits. If the Nile rises more than this, it will also irrigate areas of higher ground: this is a bonus, as it were, amounting to a free gift. The maximum rise—and this is by way of an exceptional occurrence—is a few finger-breadths above twenty cubits. When such a rise occurs, there are places where the water sits for long periods, turning these tracts into lakes; thus, they miss out on being cultivated. However, while this part of the land that is customarily planted is left without crops, another part of it that is usually left "sun-dried," as they say, but which has now been watered, can now be planted in compensation. 2.1.2

Let us therefore call the figure of eighteen cubits "the maximum of necessity," and the figure of twenty "the maximum of superfluity." 2.1.3

Each of these maxima has a corresponding minimum starting point. The starting point of necessity is sixteen cubits, and is called "the Sultan's Water," because when it is reached, the land tax becomes payable.[196] With that rise of sixteen cubits, about half the normally cultivable lands are watered, and will yield a sufficient quantity of grain to provide for the people of the country for the whole year ahead, and amply, too. The remainder of the lands normally cultivated will be watered to satiety by any additional rise, that is, over and above sixteen cubits and up to eighteen cubits; an eighteen-cubit rise will yield sufficient produce to supply the people of the country with food for two years or more.[197] A rise of less than sixteen cubits, however, will not water enough land, so will not provide food stocks to last the coming year; the shortage of food will be proportional to the shortfall below sixteen cubits.

2.1.4 At such times of shortfall, it is said in Egypt that the land "has become sun-dried," that is, *sharraqat*. The word derives from the standard Arabic expressions "the sun has risen," meaning that it has come up and into view, and "I sun-dried the meat," meaning that I put it in the sun to dry out. From the latter sense comes the expression the "Days of *Tashrīq*," that is, sun-drying, because the meat of the sacrificial animals is sun-dried during these days: that is, it is spread out in the sun.[198] Also from the same root comes *shariqa*, "he gagged on the water, or on the drink," meaning that he choked on it, because when someone chokes and his throat closes, the water re-appears and emerges into view, rather than going down. In a comparable sense, in years when the Nile has not risen as expected and the earth is open to view, neither hidden by the water nor concealed by the flood, it is said that the land has "become sun-dried" and has not been covered, and that the Nile has given it nothing.[199]

2.1.5 Another plausible interpretation is that the verb *sharraqa* means "to become wind-dried" and comes from the term, "a *sharqiyyah*, or easterly, wind." This is because winds from the east and from the direction of Mecca—that is, the south[200]—are, according to the Egyptians, not only the indicator of a coming shortfall in water, but also the actual cause of it. In contrast, winds from the west and from the direction of the Mediterranean Sea—that is, the north—are, to their thinking, the indicator and cause of the Nile's rise. On this basis, then, when they use the verb *sharraqa* of the land, they mean that the east wind has blown so much that it has dried up the water and exposed the ground to view. As a consequence, such ground is itself called *sharqiyyah*, "easterly," from the name of the wind, and given the plural form *sharāqī*—the same plural pattern as that of *kursī–karāsī*, "chair–chairs," and *bukhtī–bakhātī*, "Bukhtī camel–Bukhtī camels."[201]

As regards the derivation of *al-Nīl*, "the Nile," it is a verbal noun from the verb *nāla-yanālu-naylan*, "to give generously," or from *nāla-yanūlu-nawlan*, "to give."[202] One says, for example, *nawwaltuhu tanwīlan*, "I gifted him a gifting," and *nultuhu nawlan*, "I gave him a giving," if one has presented anything to anyone. *Al-nīl*, however, is the noun for "the actual thing which is given": it is the same as *al-raʿy* being used for the infinitive noun, "the act of grazing," while *al-riʿy* is used for the thing which is grazed, "the grazing lands."[203] This is admittedly not part of our main theme; but the topic popped up, so we have given our opinion about it. 2.1.6

To resume: any rise of less than the sixteen cubits will be inadequate, because sixteen is also the starting point of "insufficiency," the antithesis of "superfluity." In our longer book, we have already listed the years of superfluity and insufficiency from the start of the Hijrah era up to this current year;[204] in this book, however, we will keep to our brief and only relate what we have personally witnessed. 2.1.7

In the event, the Nile's rise in the year 596 [1200] amounted to twelve cubits and twenty-one finger-breadths. Such a low figure is very rare; indeed, throughout the entire period from the Hijrah until now, the information we have shows that the Nile only ever failed to rise above this point once, in the year 356 [967], when the rise ceased at four finger-breadths below this amount.[205] Counting instances when the rise has ceased at thirteen cubits and various amounts of finger-breadths, these have occurred about six times 2.1.8

over that same long period; rises of fourteen cubits and some finger-breadths have occurred about twenty times; those of fifteen-plus cubits have been frequent.

2.1.9 In what follows, we will give an account of the phenomena that accompanied the Nile's rise in the year in question, that is, 596 [1200]. We will then follow this up with information we have obtained about the causes of these phenomena and the laws of nature governing them. We should explain first that, in the normal course of things, the rise begins in Abīb [July], grows in magnitude in Misrā [August], and reaches its height in Tūt [September] or Bābah [October], after which the level goes down.[206]

2.1.10 In this year, 596 [1200], at the start of Abīb [the end of June], the Nile went through the initial motions of its rise. About two months earlier, a green color like that of beet leaves had begun to appear in its waters. This green color then grew more noticeable, and a strong and disagreeable odor became discernible, together with an algal putrescence:[207] the water resembled the juice of beet leaves when left some days and allowed to rot.

2.1.11 I placed a sample of it in a vessel with a narrow opening at the top, and a cloudy green layer formed on the water's surface. This I gently removed and left to dry out, whereupon I discovered beyond doubt that it did contain algae. The water, meanwhile, after the removal of the cloudy layer, was colorless, with no green tint left in it; however, its taste and odor remained as they had been. You could also see that it contained specks of vegetable matter, dispersed throughout it like dust motes, which refused to sink. People on dietary regimes began to avoid drinking it, and would only drink well water.

2.1.12 I heated and boiled some, as physicians recommend one to do with tainted water, imagining that it would thus become potable; but its taste and odor only became more disagreeably foul. The cause, I discovered, was that the heating process affected the vegetable particles dispersed in the water, by rarefying their essential substance; as a result, they became mixed with the water even more thoroughly than before, making the tainted odor and taste more noticeable. My boiled sample was therefore comparable to water in which the leaves of beet, radish, or some similar plant have been cooked, when the fire causes the water and the subtle vegetable matter to combine.[208] The kind of water which becomes potable on heating—and this is what the physicians speak about—is water tainted by an admixture of particles of the earthy element. Earthy particles are separated from the water on the application of heat, because water when heated becomes rarefied, thus permitting the particles to sink down.

To resume: the green discoloration persisted for the latter days of Rajab [early to mid May], and through Shaʿban [May–June] and Ramadan [June–July], finally fading away in Shawwal [July–August]; together with the greenness, the sort of worms and other organisms found in stagnant water were also present. The amount of pollution would have been higher in Upper Egypt, because it is nearer to the origin and source of the Nile. 2.1.13

On 11 Tūt [8 September], the river stopped rising at twelve cubits and twenty-one finger-breadths, then began to fall. In Shawwal [July–August], an envoy had arrived from the king of Abyssinia, bearing a letter that contained news of the Abyssinian archbishop's death and a request for a replacement.[209] The letter also mentioned that the rainfall in their land had been meager this year, and that as a result the Nile had risen only a little. 2.1.14

In our other book, we gave a full account of the state of the Nile in this year and in previous years. In doing this, we hoped to reveal any relationships that might exist between these annual data, and any symptoms displayed by them: such information might help identify which of the phenomena displayed by the Nile are ones that recur, both in years when it rises sufficiently and in years of deficient rises. We would then be able to make the knowledge thus gained available in advance, in order to be on the alert and able to give warning of foreseeable events. 2.1.15

Regarding such forecasts, the Copts of Upper Egypt claim that they can predict the amount of the Nile's increase in any year, by 2.1.16

means of a type of mud of known weight. They expose it to the influence of the stars[210] on a particular night, then, on weighing it in the morning, find that it has become heavier; basing their judgement on the increase in weight, they pronounce upon the Nile's coming increase.[211] Another group of people make similar forecasts based on the quantity of the date crop, and yet others on how much honey the bees have produced.[212]

2.1.17 Note that the term "the bottom" means the floor of the pool in the Nilometer, a gauge which registers the Nile's maximum level in both deficient and sufficient rises; also, that when the maximum level it attains is particularly low, the Nile is said to be "burned out." Now, I have observed, regarding the state of the bottom, that if the quantity of water in it is already less than normal, then the rise in that particular year will usually also be less than normal; this is the general rule.[213] If, in addition, the green discoloration appears at the start of the rise, and a little before it, this reinforces one's suspicion that the flow will be weak; if the green color then persists for many days, and the initial rise is indeed weak, that suspicion of a low total rise will be greatly reinforced; and if the greenness lasts through Abīb [July], then one can be sure that the increase in level will be deficient.

2.1.18 The causes of these phenomena are obvious. First, the low level of water in the bottom of the Nilometer acts as an indicator of a deficient rise for the following reasons. The rainfall that causes the rise must be abundant enough, in the first place, to restore the water in the bottom to its usual level; on top of that, it must supply additional water for the usual increase. It is not every year that the rains provide a great enough quantity: such an abundance is not always available. To give an example, if the water in the bottom were, say, one cubit deep, then the rise would have to amount to fifteen cubits so as to reach the level of the Sultan's Water. If, however, the water in the bottom were already six cubits deep, it would need a rise of only ten cubits, which is more easily achieved than the first amount.

2.1.19 Then again, while the water for the primary flow of the Nile is supplied by springs, the water supplying the rise comes from rains.

But any shortfall in the springs is in itself an indication that the year is already "burned out," the atmosphere dry, and the humidity low: these conditions lead, in turn, to low rainfall.

Furthermore, the increase to the water already in the bottom is generally thirteen cubits at most. If the bottom is only a cubit or two deep to begin with, and this usual maximum rise of thirteen cubits is added, it will not reach the level of the Sultan's Water. I have, however, seen an increase of fifteen cubits; this occurred in the year of plenty that came after the drought. 2.1.20

Second, the green color acts as an indicator of a low rise because the Nile's passing floodwater leaves behind ponds and pools; some of these soak into the ground, but others grow algae, stagnate, and stink. If the subsequent rains are scanty, when the rainwater passes through this stagnant water, it mixes with it and washes it into the main stream of the Nile. Light rainfall is not abundant enough to predominate over the pondwater and purify it; instead, the pond water predominates over any rainwater that has had contact with it and alters it, making it putrid. Little by little, quantities of the stagnant water flow out of the ponds, and make their way successively downstream to us in Egypt. The lighter and scantier the rain, the longer the flow of green discoloration will persist. If, on the other hand, the rain is heavy, it will scour out those stagnant waters, overcoming them and sending them rushing swiftly downstream, charged with a load of mud that is swept along by the force of the downpour. In this case, the green color disappears, leaving no trace. 2.1.21

The green color is also due to the fact that the rivers which emerge from Jabal al-Qamar all eventually empty into a great basin that covers an extensive area; it is from this basin that the Nile flows out.[214] Now, it is certain that the water of this basin stands there permanently and thus grows algae, particularly at its margins and in its shallows. When the early summer rain falls, therefore, and the ensuing torrents flow into the basin, they stir up matter from its bed and disturb the layers that had lain motionless. In addition, material from the margins is swept into the middle of the basin and drawn 2.1.22

towards the place where the water does flow, and the current carries this material away with it.

2.1.23 Third, the presence of green discoloration in Abīb [July] is an indicator of a deficient rise because Abīb is the likeliest month for the rise to start, and for the floodwater to overcome that mishmash of detritus. If the water retains its green taint now, at the beginning of the rise, it is a sure sign of deficiency to come. Those waterborne particles of plant matter, noted earlier, are nothing but the debris of vegetation generated in and around the river, such as papyrus, reeds, rushes, algae, and the like; these plants decompose in the water and break down into ever-smaller particles, which are carried along with the flow. An additional factor causing their dispersal operates when the water in the abovementioned basin is at a low level. If there is too little water, the current will reach down to the bed of the basin, and the slime and sediment there will be drawn up. If, however, the basin is full, then the current will flow in its clear upper layer. This is something else to bear in mind. It is also evident from all this that the water of the Tigris, the Euphrates, and other comparable rivers is superior to that of the Nile, and particularly at times when they are low. That is because the former rivers come all the way from their sources as they are, in their pristine form. The Nile, in contrast, flows via a marsh where the water stands permanently and is putrid.

2.1.24 For all these reasons, the green color will only appear in a year in which the Nile is "burned out"; the more severely "burned out" the Nile is, the more noticeable the greenness will be. In a year in which the Nile is not "burned out" but is full, you will not see the green color: this is because the high level of the river is due to its headwaters also being high, and thus flowing well above the layers where slime has settled.

2.1.25 In short, then, if all or most of these indicators appear together in a particular year, it may be strongly suspected that the Nile's rise that year will be a low one. To understand that fact is one benefit to be gained from this detailed account of mine. But there are other benefits, too. One is that future readers, if they add the information in this account to their own observations, will be in a position to discover in the combined data some other relationship between, or indicator of, the annual amounts of the rise, both high and low.

There is also another benefit, for those who practice astrology.[215] 2.1.26
If they were to look into the periodicity of lower and higher rises, and were then to examine the various positions of the stars and the astral conjunctions occurring at the times in question, as well as the ascendant stars for Egypt, the land of the Blacks, and for those entrusted with their government—if they were to do all this, and were then to work out the resulting temperaments, the recurrent features would enable them to set up an experimental model relating to the amount of high and low rises.[216] And yet, up to the present, I have seen no interest shown in these matters by the astrologers of Egypt; indeed, I have found no pronouncement of theirs that a soul might trust—nothing but digging over the same ground without building on a sound basis.[217] It is by the method just described that the majority of astrological lore has been deduced: people have witnessed earthly events happening in conjunction with certain astronomical dispositions and celestial motions; on closer observation, they have found that such conjunctions recur; and they have attributed the earthly events to those particular heavenly patterns and dispositions. Consequently, when, in plotting the future motions of the celestial bodies, they happen upon a forthcoming disposition and pattern like one they have previously observed, they decree that the same accompanying event will take place as before.

It is related on the authority of the ancient Coptic empiricists 2.1.27
that, if the water level twelve days into Misrā [i.e. on 5 August] has reached twelve finger-breadths above twelve cubits, it will be a year of sufficient water. If it has not yet reached this level, then the water will be deficient. This is proven by experience.

I have also seen a statement on forecasting by one of the com- 2.1.28
mentators on Ptolemy's *Karpos*, in the course of his explanation of the book's final aphorism. The aphorism begins with the assertion

that "Shooting stars are an indication that the water vapors will dry up. If the shooting stars appear in one quarter, they are a sign that winds will blow from that quarter. But if they are present in all quarters, they are a sign that the water will be insufficient, the air disturbed, and armies at odds." The commentator in question said of this,

> I remember well how, in the year 290 [903], meteors showered over Egypt, filling the whole of the sky. The people were terrified, and yet the meteors went on falling ever more numerously. Then, after only a little more of the year had passed, the population was afflicted by drought: the Egyptian Nile reached only thirteen cubits, and the resulting public disturbances led to the end of Ṭūlūnid rule in the land.[218] In the year 300 [912–13], also, meteors showered from all quarters of the sky. Once more, the Nile failed to rise sufficiently, and there were riots and disturbances in the kingdom.[219]

2.1.29 Upon my life, these phenomena are potent indicators indeed; but they are general to all climes, and not peculiar to Egypt alone. That said, this very same set of events has also taken place in this present year: stars scattering all over at the start of the year, water levels falling at the end of it, and the ruler of Egypt being replaced during it by his uncle, al-Malik al-ʿĀdil, following a war between the two of them.[220]

Chapter Two: The events of the year 597 [1200–1]

And then came the year 'seven—that monstrous year, that predatory date, "seven," the severer of lives.[221] People had already abandoned hope of the Nile rising. Prices went up, and the land was stricken with drought. The populace sensed the coming calamity, and fear of famine made them riotous. The villagers and country folk took refuge in the main towns. Many emigrated to the Levant, the Maghrib, the Hijaz, and Yemen: "they dispersed through the lands like the people of Sabā" and were torn apart «and scattered in every direction».[222] A vast throng of these creatures also made their way into Cairo and Old Fustat; but their hunger only grew more severe, and they began to die off. Then, when the sun entered Aries,[223] the air became pestilential, and diseases and deadly contagions struck. 2.2.1

The paupers became so famished that they ate carrion, however rotten, as well as dogs, and the droppings and dung of animals.[224] 2.2.2
Then they went beyond that—so far beyond as to eat human children. Often, they would be discovered in possession of young children, roasted or stewed; the chief of police would give orders for the perpetrator and anyone else who had eaten the victim to be executed by burning. I myself saw a basket containing a roasted child, which had been brought to the prefect's residence along with a man and a woman people claimed were the child's parents; the prefect

ordered them to be burned.[225] During Ramadan [June–July 1201], the discovery was made in Old Fustat of a man whose flesh had been stripped off his bones and eaten, leaving the victim in the form of a "lattice"—just as chefs do with sheep.[226] Nothing like this was ever available for Galen to examine, and he tried every trick to get hold of such a skeleton—as, indeed, has every avid student of anatomy.[227]

2.2.3 At first, when the paupers fell into the habit of eating human flesh, people would exchange all the news and gossip about their doings, simultaneously shocked by the whole business and excited by so bizarre a development.[228] But the paupers' flesh-lust intensified, and they became increasingly addicted to cannibalism: they made it a way of life, a source of enjoyment, and a means of sustenance, and became ever more inventive in its practice. Moreover, the habit spread beyond them, until it could be encountered in every corner of Egypt. At this point, people ceased to be excited or appalled by it; to tell or listen to stories about it was now deemed to be in the worst taste. Indeed, I once saw a woman, her head smashed in, being dragged through the market by a gang of hooligans: she had been caught with a roasted child on which she had been feeding. And yet the market traders were going about their business oblivious of her, and I did not see a single one of them show any surprise at the spectacle, or express any disapproval of it. At this, my amazement at these people increased. And yet their indifference was due to nothing but the effect upon their sense perception of the frequent repetition of such scenes, which had entered the category of the familiar, and as such were not worthy of provoking amazement.

2.2.4 Two days earlier, I had seen a young lad, about the age of adolescence, who had been roasted. Two young men had been arrested in possession of him; they confessed to killing, roasting, and partially eating him.

2.2.5 It also happened, one evening just after the sunset prayer, that a maidservant was playing with an infant child whom she was babysitting for a certain well-to-do family. One moment he was by her side, the next—while the maid-servant was momentarily distracted—a vagrant woman seized her chance and the child, ripped open his belly, and began to devour him raw. Several other women told me of being similarly pounced upon by people attempting to snatch their children, and of their struggles to keep them safe. For example, I saw one woman with a plump and, I thought, particularly attractive infant. When I advised her to take good care of him, she told me that, while she had been walking by al-Khalīj, a big, rough man had pounced on her and tried to wrest the child from her grasp. She had thrown herself to the ground on top of the child, and had lain there until a horseman got to her and drove the ruffian off. She assured me that the assailant had been utterly set on devouring any part of the child he caught sight of, and that the child had been ill for some time after, as a result of the violence with which she and the predator had fought over him.

You would come across pauper children, toddlers and older ones, bereft of guardian or other protector, dispersed throughout the country regions and the alleys of the city quarters like scattered swarms of locusts. Paupers, men and women, would hunt these little ones and eat them, but would seldom get caught, and only when they did not take proper precautions. Most cases that did come to light involved women: I believe the reason for this was merely that women are not as wily as men, and are less adept at slipping away and hiding. 2.2.6

In the case of Old Fustat, and in the course of only a few days, thirty women were executed by burning, each one of whom had confessed to eating a number of children. I saw a woman who had been brought before the prefect with a young roasted child slung around her neck. She was given more than two hundred strokes of the lash to make her confess, but she gave no answer to the accusation—nor could she have done, for you could see that she had become utterly devoid of human nature. She was dragged away, but died there and then. Whenever people who had eaten human flesh were burned, they would be found the next morning to have themselves been eaten, being ready-roasted and needing no further cooking. 2.2.7

2.2.8 In time, cannibalism became so widespread among the paupers that most of them were wiped out. It was then that a number of people from the affluent and moderately well-to-do classes got into the habit, some out of necessity, others for the sake of the novel culinary experience.[229] A man told us of a friend of his who had become mired in this affliction. This friend invited him to his house for a meal, as had been their regular custom before the famine. On entering the house, he found his friend in the company of a group of men wearing paupers' rags; in front of them was a stew rich in meat, but no bread to go with it.[230] The scene aroused his suspicions, and he asked to visit the lavatory. Next to it, he came across a storeroom packed with human bones and freshly butchered meat. Terrified, he fled.

2.2.9 It also emerged that some of these abominable folk were using various forms of ensnarement to trap people, and employing different scams to lure them to their lairs. Three of the physicians who were frequently in my company had experiences of this. In the case of one, his father went out and never came home. Another was given two dirhams by a woman on the pretext of accompanying her to treat a sick member of her household. When she led him deep into a warren of narrow alleys, however, he began to have his doubts: he hung back from her, accusing her of evil designs, and at this she abandoned her two dirhams and slipped away.

2.2.10 The third physician was induced by a man to go with him to (as he claimed) "a sick person in al-Shāriʿ." On the way, the man began handing out scraps of bread in charity[231] and saying, "Today a reward will be gained, and a manifold recompense be earned. «For the like of this let the doers perform their deeds.»"[232] He went on doing this so many times that the physician grew suspicious of him; even so, his mind was put at ease—by the lure of good fat fees.[233] Eventually, however, when the man led him into a big, tumbledown house, his sense of foreboding increased, and he paused on the stairs. The man went up ahead of him, and knocked on a door. Out came a crony of his, saying, "You've taken your time. Have you caught us a bit of game that's worth the wait?" When he heard this, the physician turned to jelly. Luckily for him, there happened to be a window nearby, and he threw himself out of it and landed in a stable—only to find the owner of the stable coming over to him and saying, "What's the matter with you, then?" Fearing the worst from the keeper of the stable too, the physician did not let on. But the man said, "Don't tell me: it's that lot in this house here, luring people to the slaughter."

In Iṭfīḥ, a number of large storage jars were found in a druggist's shop, full of human flesh preserved in brine. When they questioned him about his motives for laying in such a stock, and so much of it, the druggist replied, "I was afraid that, if this drought went on much longer, people would get even skinnier."[234] 2.2.11

Back in the capital, a gang of paupers had made their lair on Roda Island, where they hid away in mud huts in which they trapped people. The authorities learned of them and sought to have them killed, but they escaped. A large number of human bones were found in their huts: a trustworthy person informed me that the cache discovered there comprised four hundred skulls. 2.2.12

Another story that gained wide circulation, and was heard out of the prefect's own mouth, concerned a woman who had appeared before him, unveiled and in a state of shock.[235] She said she was a midwife, and that some people had called for her and, during her visit, had given her a plate of *sikbāj* stew, beautifully cooked and flavored with all the appropriate spices. When she realized, however, that it was particularly rich in meat, and that this meat was different from normal meat, the discovery turned her stomach. She managed to get a word in private with a little girl of the family, and asked her about the meat. "Oh," said the girl, "Mrs So-and-so, the fat lady, came to visit us, and Daddy cut her throat. There she is, hanging up in bits." The midwife went over to the storeroom, and found pile upon pile of flesh. When she had finished telling her story to the prefect, he sent a squad with her to raid the house and arrest its inhabitants, but the owner got away. Later, the man made a secret deal and paid a bribe of three hundred dinars to escape execution. 2.2.13

2.2.14 Another extraordinary occurrence of this sort involved one of the army wives, a woman of property who led a comfortable life. She was pregnant; her husband was away on service. Next to her lived some vagrants. One day, she caught the smell of stew coming from their direction and, as pregnant women are wont to do, asked them for some. Finding it delicious, she asked for more; they told her that there was none left, so she asked for the recipe—whereupon they confided to her that the meat was human flesh. At this, she cajoled them into catching children for her, for which she rewarded them generously. This happened many times; she became addicted, and fell under the sway of her bestial nature. At this point, her maidservants, in dread of her, informed on their mistress. As a result, her house was raided, and such quantities of flesh and bones were discovered as to corroborate the accusation. The woman was imprisoned and kept in irons, though she was granted a stay of execution, both out of respect to her husband and to preserve the child in her womb.

2.2.15 If we were to set out to recount in detail everything we caught sight of and heard tell, we would surely be suspected of exaggeration, or would babble on too long. And yet all the scenes we personally witnessed and describe above result from experiences that we neither sought out, nor went looking for in likely places; we came across them purely by accident. Indeed, I often fled from such sights, so gruesome were they to behold. On the other hand, anyone going to look for evidence of cannibalism in the prefect's residence would find all manner of horrors turning up at all hours of the night and the day. For example, two, three, or more victims might be found in a single pot. One day, a pot was discovered that contained ten hands, cooked just like sheeps' trotters; another time, a large pot was found containing the head of an adult and certain extremities of the body, stewed with wheat. There were many more variations on this type of discovery, too numerous to list.

2.2.16 Near the Mosque of Ibn Ṭūlūn, there lurked a gang who would snatch people. Into their snares fell an elderly and portly bookseller, one who supplied us with books. He got away, but had been a hair's breadth from death.[236] Similarly, one of the gatekeepers of the Mosque of ʿAmr ibn al-ʿĀṣ[237] fell into the snares of another gang at al-Qarāfah, but some townspeople caught up with him, and he slipped the noose and took to his heels. That said, the number of people who parted from their families, never to return, was enormous.

Someone in whom I trust told me that he had passed by a ruined building and seen there a woman with a dead man in front of her. The corpse had swollen and blown up, but she was eating bits of its thighs. When he reproached her, she claimed that the dead man was her husband. It often happened that the person eating would pretend that the person being eaten was a child, a spouse, or some other relative. For example, one old woman who was seen eating a young child excused herself by saying, "It's only my daughter's son, so he's not from outside my family. It's better for *me* to eat him than for someone else to do so." There were very many similar incidents—so many, in fact, that you could find no one in Egypt who had not seen something of this kind, not even among those who led the most cloistered lives,[238] or women secluded in purdah. 2.2.17

Another phenomenon that also became widespread was the grubbing up of graves so that the corpses could be eaten and their flesh sold. This further scourge that we describe was present throughout Egypt.[239] In every single settlement, whether in Aswan, Qūṣ, Faiyum, al-Maḥallah, Alexandria, Damietta, or any other province, newly interred people were gobbled up immediately. One of my friends, a trustworthy merchant, told me on his return from a trip to Alexandria of numerous such scenes he had beheld there with his own eyes. Most extraordinary of all, he described to me how he had found himself eye to eye with the heads of five small children, stewed in a single pot with high-grade spices. 2.2.18

But enough of these accounts of cannibalism—even if I believe, though I have gone on at length, that I still have not told all that should be told. 2.2.19

2.2.20 Turning to cases of murder and violent assault in the provinces, these incidents were frequent and, indeed, ubiquitous in «every mountain pass,»[240] especially on the routes to Faiyum and Alexandria. On the Faiyum route there were boatmen who would offer passengers a low fare but, when they had taken them halfway, would cut the travelers' throats and divide up the plunder. When the governor captured a group of these boatmen and subjected them to exemplary punishment, one of them, tortured by being beaten, confessed that his personal share, not counting those of his accomplices, had amounted to six thousand dinars.

2.2.21 The total death toll of paupers from emaciation and starvation is a matter known only to God, glorified and exalted is He. All we can do is mention some facts and figures by way of a representative sample, from which a person of sound judgement might infer how shocking an affair it was. What we personally observed in Old Fustat, Cairo, and the adjoining areas was that anyone going on foot, wherever he happened to walk, would at all times find himself treading or gazing on some person who was either dead or in the throes of death, or on a large mass of people in this condition. In the particular case of Cairo, the daily number of corpses brought to the public place of ablution was between one hundred and five hundred.[241] The dead of Old Fustat, meanwhile, were numberless: they were just thrown together, and not given a decent burial. In the end, the survivors were too weak even to dispose of them in this way, and the corpses were simply left where they were, in the markets, or between the houses and shops, or inside them. You would see one of the dead from the neighborhood, chopped up—and there, beside the butchered corpse, barbecue men, bread sellers, and others in the catering trade.

2.2.22 In the rural fringes of the capital and in the villages, the inhabitants sometimes perished altogether, or all but a very few whom God willed to survive; others abandoned their homes. This may not have been the case with the principal towns and larger settlements, such as Qūṣ, al-Ushmūnayn, al-Maḥallah, and similar places; even so, in these, too, only a token number remained.[242] Indeed, a traveler could well pass through a town and find not a living, breathing soul in it:[243] he would find its houses left wide open, and their inhabitants ranged opposite one another, dead, some in a state of decay, others still fresh. A house might still contain all its furnishings, as there would be no one to make off with them.

More than one person described such scenes to me, and each account bore out what the others stated. One said, "We went into one city and found not a single living creature, either on the ground or in the air. So we went into the houses, and came upon their inhabitants just as God, mighty and glorious is He, says in the Qur'an, «We made of them a harvest of the dead.»[244] In every dwelling you would find the occupants dead—the man of the house, his wife, his children." He continued, "Then we moved on to another town, where we had been told that there had been four hundred weaving workshops, and found it in the same state of devastation as the first: there would be the weaver in the pit of his loom,[245] dead, with his family dead around him. Such scenes brought the words of God the Exalted in the Qur'an to mind, «There was but one single cry, and—lo!—there they were, dead.»"[246] He also said, "Then we moved on to yet another town, and found it like the previous one: not a soul there to welcome us, and crammed with the bodies of its inhabitants. We needed to spend some time in the place, to deal with the cultivation there. So we hired some people to remove the corpses from around our accommodation and take them to the Nile, at the rate of one dirham for every ten corpses. But," he said, "the land had been transformed into a land of wolves and hyenas, feasting on the flesh of its people."[247] 2.2.23

One of the curious scenes I myself witnessed occurred when I was looking out over the Nile one day with a group of companions and, in the course of an hour or so, about ten corpses floated past us, looking like inflated waterskins. We were not intentionally trying to spot them, and we could not even take in the whole width of the river in our field of vision. Then, the following morning, we went on 2.2.24

a trip by boat and, in both al-Khalīj and all the other waterways,[248] we saw the remains of the dead just as Imruʾ l-Qays described them in his simile, like "plucked-up roots of squills."[249] I was also given an account originating from a fisherman in the port of Tinnīs that told how, over the course of part of a day, four hundred water-borne corpses had floated past him as the Nile swept them out to the sea.

2.2.25 Concerning the road to the Levant, accounts came thick and fast, telling how it had become a field sown with human beings—or, rather, a reaping ground, and one that turned into a banquet of human flesh for bird and beast—and how it was the victims' own dogs, which had accompanied them from their abandoned homes, that were feeding off their masters. The first to perish on this road were the people of al-Ḥawf, when they set out for the Levant in search of new pastures. They ended up scattered along the entire way, great though the distance is, like a swarm of locusts killed off by the cold; their dead still lie there in an unbroken line, to this day. The search for new lands took the survivors to Mosul, Baghdad, and Khurasan, as well as to Anatolia, the Maghrib, and Yemen: they were torn asunder «and scattered in every direction» through the lands.[250] Often, a woman would lose hold of her children in the crush; they would be left, wailing with hunger, until they died.

2.2.26 Another phenomenon was the sale into slavery of freeborn people: this became common practice—indeed, common law—among those who had no fear of God.[251] It got to the stage where a pretty young girl would be sold for a few dirhams. I myself was offered a pair of adolescent girls for a single dinar; another time, I saw a couple of girls, one of them a virgin, with someone crying out over them, "Eleven dirhams!" Once, a woman asked me to buy her daughter, a pretty girl and still immature, for five dirhams. When I got her to understand that this was unlawful in Islam, she said, "Then take her as a gift." Often, women and good-looking young boys would throw themselves at people's feet, wanting to be bought or sold by them. This was deemed lawful by a great many people, and those sold into captivity were dispersed to Iraq, deepest Khurasan, and elsewhere.

More astonishing than anything else we have related, however, is the fact that people, despite all these portents following one upon another, remained unrepentantly devoted to the idols of their lusts, wallowing in the sea of their errors, as if they themselves were exempt from the rule of divine law.[252] For example, not only did they take to selling freeborn people as an article of commerce and source of gain, but they also used those enslaved women as prostitutes: some men claimed to have deflowered fifty virgins, others seventy, and all for scraps of bread.[253] 2.2.27

That the land and its villages became a waste, and the dwellings and shops were deserted, was one of the inevitable consequences of this whole catalogue of events that we have recounted. Suffice it to say that you could pass by a village which, before, had contained around ten thousand souls, but would now seem like an abandoned livestock pen; perhaps there would be a handful of people left in it, but perhaps not even that. 2.2.28

Old Fustat was largely deserted. As for the houses of al-Khalīj, and those in Zuqāq al-Birkah, Ḥalab, al-Maqs, and the adjoining quarters, not a single one remained occupied at all—when, before, each local neighborhood in these quarters had been so thronged with people that it was virtually a city in itself. Even in the case of the residential compounds, individual residences, and shops in the most desirable part of the very heart of Cairo, most were empty and dilapidated. In one residential compound, situated in the most densely built-up part of Cairo and consisting of more than fifty dwellings, all the units were empty, except for four rooms which were used as accommodation for people guarding the place. Also, the people still left in the city no longer had any fuel for their cylindrical ovens, public bakery ovens, or houses, except for timber from roofs, doors, and folds.[254] 2.2.29

Something that occasions particular wonder is how, this year, quite a number of people whom prosperity had previously always 2.2.30

eluded, struck lucky in their worldly affairs. They included those who grew rich from the wheat trade, and those who grew rich from property that passed to them by inheritance; there were those, too, whose financial position improved for no known reason. Blessed be He by Whose hand all gifts are withheld or bestowed, and to Whose every creature comes the share of His provision it is owed.

2.2.31 Turning to news of the Nile in this year, it was so severely "burned out" in Barmūdah [April] that the Nilometer was left high and dry on a bare mudbank, while the water receded from it towards the Giza side: a great, long island appeared in the middle of the river, together with sections of previously submerged buildings. The water began to smell and to taste tainted; it then deteriorated further, until eventually the cause was revealed to be an algal green discoloration which, like that which had appeared in Abīb [July] of the previous year, became ever more noticeable and intense with the passing days. This green color continued to increase until the last part of Shaʿban [early June]; thereafter it gradually diminished, and finally disappeared. Only some dispersed vegetable particles lingered in the water, and it tasted and smelled sweet again.

2.2.32 Then, in Ramadan [June–July], the river started to rise and its flow to gain strength; this continued until the sixteenth of the month. On that day, Ibn Abī l-Raddād measured the water level in the bottom of the Nilometer pool. It stood at two cubits, and began rising still higher, but only feebly—more feebly even than in the previous year. This slight increase continued until 8 Dhu l-Qaʿdah, i.e. 17 Misrā [10 August], when it rose another finger-breadth—then stopped rising for three days. At this, people realized that disaster was inevitable, and resigned themselves to destruction; but then the river underwent a series of substantial rises, of which the largest was one cubit. These lasted until 3 Dhu l-Hijjah, i.e., 6 Tūt [4 September], when the level reached fifteen cubits and sixteen finger-breadths—only for it to fall on that very same day, sinking in sudden defeat. The water had touched some of the farmlands—but a token touch at most, like some dream-visit from the river's ghost.

Only the areas of least elevation benefited from this abortive rise. Low-lying regions such as al-Gharbiyyah, therefore, were irrigated—except that the villages were utterly devoid of both farmhand and plowman; as God the Exalted says in the Qur'an, «And they became such that nothing could be seen but their empty dwellings.»[255] It was only those landholders with substantial means who could afford to bring the displaced farmworkers together and gather up the surviving individuals, since plowmen and their oxen were by now in such short supply that a single bull would be sold for seventy dinars, although a scrawny one fetched less.[256] 2.2.33

Across much of the land, however, the water ebbed away, without supplying the due amount of irrigation for the due time; this was because there was no one to hold it back and keep it dammed in.[257] Such land was thus left uncultivated, even though a sufficient quantity of water had reached it. Also, much of the land that did get enough water was left unplanted for the further reason that the local people were unable to provide the "strengthenings" necessary to set about its cultivation.[258] And on top of all this, in cases where a crop could be sown, much of it ended up eaten by grubs, while much of what escaped the grubs subsequently withered and perished. 2.2.34

As a result, the price of wheat rose this year as high as five dinars for the *irdabb*, while that of *fūl* and barley reached four dinars.[259] In Qūṣ and Alexandria, meanwhile, wheat reached six dinars. From God alone, may He be glorified, is relief to be hoped for: He is the provider of all good things, through His grace and generosity. 2.2.35

Chapter Three: The events of the year 598 [1201–2]

2.3.1 At the beginning of the year, conditions in the markets remained in the same state, outlined above, that they had been in during the previous year; or, rather, prices went on rising higher still. This situation continued until about halfway through the year. It was then that the mortality rate began to decline among the paupers—because there were so few of them left, not because the causative factor had been removed. Cannibalism declined, too, and reports of it eventually petered out altogether. Also, there were fewer cases of food being snatched from the markets, because the vagrants previously responsible had died off, and had all but disappeared from the city.

2.3.2 Prices then fell, until an *irdabb* of wheat was down to three dinars; this was on account of the dearth of mouths to be fed, rather than any abundance of food to feed them. The city's burden of population had grown lighter: it was now a reduced version of itself, and everything in it had been reduced in proportion. Even so, people had become so inured to high prices and continual crisis that they had begun to seem like a natural temperament.[260]

2.3.3 I was told that, in Old Fustat, there had been nine hundred workshops where rush mats were woven; now only fifteen remained. From this you may deduce figures for all the other tradespeople ordinarily found in the city, such as vendors, bakers, druggists, cobblers, tailors, and other categories: of each class of traders, there remained about the same fraction as that of the surviving mat weavers, or fewer still.

Chickens would have disappeared altogether, if a number had not been imported from the Levant. I was told that a certain Egyptian man had been on the brink of destitution, but then had the heaven-sent idea of buying from the Levant sixty dinars' worth of chickens. He sold them in Cairo to the poultry breeders for about eight hundred dinars.[261] When, consequently, eggs reappeared in the market, they fetched a dirham an egg. Thereafter, a dirham would buy two, then three, and eventually four eggs; the price stayed at that last level. Young chickens fetched as much as one hundred dirhams for a single bird; later, the price remained for some time at a dinar and upwards each.[262] 2.3.4

Bakeries had no fuel for their ovens, other than the timbers of houses. A bakery owner would buy a house at a bargain price, use the wood from its folds and the timbers of the house itself as fuel for a few days, then go on to buy another house. Sometimes, too, certain bakery proprietors would be prompted by a lack of scruple to slip out at night and snoop about the houses, gathering firewood, without coming across anyone to scare them off. It also often happened that the owner of a property would end up alone in an otherwise uninhabited house, for which he could find no buyer: he would remove its timbers, doors, and other fixtures, and sell them, and would then abandon the house in this dilapidated state. People did the same with rental properties.[263] 2.3.5

In al-Hilāliyyah, most of al-Shāriʿ, the houses of al-Khalīj, Ḥārat al-Sāsah, al-Maqs, and the adjoining districts, not a living soul remained. All you would see was the townspeople's houses, «fallen in upon their own roof beams,»[264] and many of their occupants dead inside the ruins. That said, Cairo—when compared with Old Fustat—was still in an excellent state of repair, and its population positively numerous. 2.3.6

2.3.7 The rural fringes of the capital and the rest of the country, however, were an utter wasteland: a traveler might journey in any direction for days and not come across a living creature—only the remains of dead ones. The exceptions were the biggest towns like Qūṣ, Ikhmīm, al-Maḥallah, Damietta, and Alexandria, where some life survived. Other than these and places of similar size, towns that had comprised thousands would be deserted, or almost so.

2.3.8 Of properties that had commanded considerable rents, the majority now lay empty. Their owners' only concern was to safeguard them, by sealing their doors and securing the places where intruders might climb in, or by paying a live-in guard. The exception, perhaps, was property in the city center, of which some was still tenanted at very low rents.[265] I myself know one residential compound in the most built-up spot in the city, which had previously been let for 150 dinars a month, where the rent went down this year to about twenty dinars. I know another compound, too, in a similar spot, for which the monthly rent had been sixteen dinars but went down to a little over one dinar. And in all the other cases which we have not mentioned, the fall in rents was comparable; of that you can be sure.

2.3.9 Regarding the number of the dead, entries in the statistical records for those who were provided with shrouds, had names entered in the Dīwān, and were received in the place of ablution, over the period of twenty-two months beginning with Shawwal 596 [mid July 1200] and ending with Rajab 598 [late April 1202], amount to a few individuals short of 111,000 souls.[266] Huge though this figure is, it is insignificant when compared with the number of people who perished in their houses, or on the outskirts of the city, expiring, for example, at the base of enclosure walls. The combined total, in turn, is insignificant compared with that of the dead who perished in Old Fustat and its environs; the total so far is itself insignificant in comparison with the number of people eaten in the two cities;[267] and the sum total of all those figures is exceedingly insignificant when compared with the numbers of those who perished or were eaten in the rest of the country districts, in the provinces, and on the roads, particularly the Levant route. Of the persons arriving from one or other of the provinces whom I questioned about the roads, all without exception related that they were fields planted with dismembered corpses and bones. The same was true of the roads I myself traveled.

The next crisis to come about was that Faiyum, al-Gharbiyyah, Damietta, and Alexandria were struck by a massive outbreak of fatal pestilence, which was extremely contagious—and especially so just at the busiest time for agricultural work. Thus, it might happen that a number of farm laborers would die working in succession at one and the same plow. We were also told, "the people who did the sowing were a different lot from those who did the plowing, and the reapers were a different lot again.[268] We undertook some agricultural work on behalf of one of the high-ranking officers,[269] and workers were dispatched to do the actual labor of cultivation; but then came the news that all of them had died. Replacements were sent, but most of them died, too. This happened several times, in different parts of the country." 2.3.10

We heard from reliable informants, concerning the pestilence in Alexandria, that the imam led funeral prayers one Friday over a total of seven hundred biers.[270] They also told us that the property left by one deceased person had passed, during the course of one month, to fourteen heirs.[271] Our informants said, too, that a large section of the city's population, numbering more than twenty thousand, had moved to Barqah and its dependent provinces, resettling there and developing the land. Barqah had been a considerable domain, but it had fallen into decay in the time of al-Yāzūrī, and because of his mishandling of it: he was such an oppressive minister that the people of the place left their land, and many of them moved to Alexandria. So it was as if this recent event was a settling of the score in nature.[272] 2.3.11

An extraordinary incident occurred, meanwhile, involving an elder of the Jewish physicians of Old Fustat, one of the medical men who were frequently in my company (though not one of those 2.3.12

mentioned earlier).[273] A regular patient of his, a man of elegant appearance known for his retiring nature, devoutness, and material prosperity, sent a message requesting the physician to attend him. No sooner was he inside the house, however, than the patient locked the door, sprang on the physician and, putting a noose around his neck, grabbed his testicles and began making mincemeat of them. In the event, as neither of them knew anything about fighting, the resulting struggle dragged on, while the physician's yells rose higher and higher. Eventually, people heard the din, got into the house, and rescued the venerable doctor, who was *hors de combat* but still with a faint breath of life in him. With his testicles pounded to a pulp and his two front teeth broken, he was carried unconscious to his house. The perpetrator, meanwhile, was brought before the prefect. "Whatever induced you to do this?" the prefect asked him. "Hunger," the man replied. The prefect had him beaten and banished.

2.3.13 Another event, which took place before daybreak on Monday 26 Shaʿban, or 25 Bashans [21 May], was the occurrence of a huge earthquake.[274] People were panic-stricken: they sprang awake from their beds, alarmed and crying out aloud in supplication to God, may He ever be glorified. The quake lasted a long time; its motion was like the shaking of a sieve, or the beating of a bird's wing, and it ended with three particularly powerful shocks that rocked buildings, slammed doors, and made roof beams and other timbers creak. Buildings that were already weak, or were particularly tall, were cracked beyond repair. The earthquake then recurred, halfway through the day on the same Monday, although most people did not feel it, as it was not so noticeable and of short duration. That night had been so very cold that, in contrast to normal nights, one needed a blanket; the following day, however, the cold gave way to very high temperatures, accompanied by an excessively hot and pestilential wind that left one short of breath and choking. It is rare for an earthquake of this magnitude to happen in Egypt.

2.3.14 Reports then began to come in, one after the other, of how the earthquake had occurred in far regions and distant lands at precisely the same hour as in Egypt. What I was able to verify was that, in a single hour, it had set in motion a whole swath of the Earth extending from Qūṣ to Damietta and Alexandria, and on through the entire coastland of the Levant and the length and breadth of the Levant itself. Many towns were so utterly wiped out that no trace of them remained, and a great multitude of people perished, from countless communities. Meanwhile, I know of no town in the Levant more secure from dangers than Jerusalem, and indeed the only damage the earthquake caused there was inconsiderable. The damage the earthquake wrought in the lands of the Franks, however, was much greater than that in the lands of Islam.

We also heard that the quake reached as far as Akhlāṭ and the 2.3.15
adjoining territories, and to the island of Cyprus. We heard, too, that the waves of the sea piled up and raged, and that its pleasant vistas turned ugly. In places, the sea parted, and the wave crests rose up like great mountains;[275] ships ended up aground, and the sea cast many fish upon its shores.

Letters then began to arrive from the Levant, and in particular 2.3.16
from Damascus and Ḥamāh, containing reports of the earthquake. Of those that reached me, I quote two here, verbatim.

A copy of the letter which arrived from Ḥamāh: 2.3.17

> Before daybreak on Monday 26 Shaʿban [20 May], an earth- 2.3.18
> quake occurred that all but set the ground off tripping and the mountains rearing and dipping. Every single person had the same thought—that it was the earthquake of the Last Hour.[276] On this occasion, it came in two shockwaves: the first wave lasted for the space of an hour or more;[277] the second was shorter but more violent, and some castles suffered from its effects. The first of these was the castle of Ḥamāh, though it is a structure of the highest quality; then Bārīn, for all its elegance and solidity; Baalbek, too, despite its strength and its stability. So far, no news worth

mentioning has arrived concerning further lands and more distant castles.

2.3.19 Next, on Tuesday 27 Shaʿban [21 May], at the time of the midday prayer, there occurred another quake. It made itself known equally to those asleep and those awake, and left those sitting and those standing all ashake. It then struck again, this same day, at the time of the afternoon prayer.

2.3.20 Reports arrived from Damascus, telling how the earthquake had damaged the eastern minaret of the Umayyad Mosque, as well as most of al-Kallāsah and all of the Hospital. In addition, a number of houses had collapsed on top of their inhabitants, killing them.

2.3.21 *A copy of the letter which arrived from Damascus:*

2.3.22 Your obedient servant informs you that an earthquake occurred in the early hours of Monday 26 Shaʿban [20 May], at the time when dawn was beginning to break. The tremor went on for a period which, according to one of our companions, was the time it took him to recite the Chapter of the Cave.[278] One of the shaykhs in Damascus commented that he had never before experienced an earthquake like it. The damage it caused in the city included the collapse of sixteen pinnacles from the cresting of the Mosque, and of one of the Mosque's minarets; the other minaret was cracked, as was the lead dome (that is, the dome of the Eagle).[279] Also, the ground caved in at al-Kallāsah, and two men died there; another man died over by Bāb Jayrūn. The Mosque was cracked in many places, and a number of houses in the city collapsed.

2.3.23 Concerning the Muslim towns,[280] it was reported that part of Bāniyās had collapsed; also that Ṣafad had collapsed too, and that, other than the children of its lord,[281] the only ones left there were the dead. Tibnīn was in a similar state, while at Nābulus not a wall was left standing, except in the quarter of the Samaritans. It is reported, however, that

Jerusalem is intact—God be praised. Of Bayt Jinn, nothing—not even the foundations of walls—was left that had not caved in. Similarly, most of the towns of Ḥawrān suffered subsidence. Indeed, there is no known locality in the region of any town there, of which it might be said, "This is the village of Such-and-Such."[282] It is also said that most of Acre collapsed, and a third of Tyre, and that ʿIrqah and also Ṣāfīthā were swallowed up.

Finally, reports tell of Jabal Lubnān, which is a place people enter by passing between two mountains, and where green rhubarb is gathered.[283] It is said that the two mountains closed together, trapping the people who happened to be between them, and that the number of victims amounted to nearly two hundred men. 2.3.24

People have given numerous such accounts of the earthquake. For four days after that first tremor, it kept recurring, day and night. We pray to God for His benevolence and providence: He is «sufficient for us» «and a most excellent protector.»[284] 2.3.25

There are yet other wonders of Egypt that we personally witnessed. In one case, the opportunity arose on account of a group who came regularly to me to study medicine. They had progressed as far as *The Book of Anatomy*,[285] but I was finding it hard to explain it to them, and they to understand it, because words alone are no match for seeing for oneself. We were then told that there was a hillock in al-Maqs on which there were many human remains. So we went out to the place and saw what was, in fact, a hillock *of* remains, extending for some considerable distance. The quantity of earth in it was almost less than the quantity of the dead who, to estimate those visible to an observer, numbered upwards of twenty thousand; they lay in strata, according to how recent or ancient they were. 2.3.26

We were thus able to see, at first hand, such a variety of forms of bones, of their joints and the manner of their connection, and of their relative proportions and positions, that we acquired 2.3.27

knowledge that we could never gain from books—either because they say nothing about the bones concerned, or because the books' wording is not sufficiently clear to guide one to that knowledge, or because what we witnessed was actually at variance with what was said in the books.

2.3.28 One's own senses are a more effective guide than reports heard from others—even from Galen. His powers of discrimination and his attention to detail may have been of the highest rank, both in his practice of anatomy and in his written accounts, and yet the senses provide a truer picture than he can ever give. After putting them to use, one may then ponder a way to justify what Galen says, if that is possible.

2.3.29 Consider, for example, the lower jawbone. Everyone has agreed that it consists of two bones, with a rigid joint at the apex of the chin. (Now, when we say "everyone," in this case we really mean Galen, and no other: it was he who, all by himself, took the science of anatomy in hand, making it his vocation and the constant focus of his vision; he wrote a number of works on the subject, most of which are available to us, although some remain that have not been put into Arabic.) And yet this part of the skeleton, according to what we have personally observed of its form, is in fact a single bone with no joint or suture at all. We examined it God knows how many times, inspecting numerous individual examples—over two thousand skulls—by various methods of examination, and we never found it to be anything but a single bone, in all aspects.

2.3.30 We then enlisted the help of a group of colleagues who, on different occasions, both while we were present and in our absence, also examined specimens. They could add nothing to what we had already observed and reported about the jawbone, and this was also the case in other matters than these. If, with the aid of destiny, we were ever able to do so, we would compose a treatise on this subject, in which we would report on our personal observations as compared with the information we have from Galen's works.[286]

Subsequently, I also examined this same bone in the ancient burial grounds of Abusir (mentioned above), and again found it to be as I have reported, with no joint or suture. Moreover, it is a feature of inconspicuous sutures and rigid joints that, given a long enough period of time, they will become visible and begin to open up. The lower jawbone, however, whatever its state of antiquity, is only ever found to consist of one piece. 2.3.31

Looking briefly at the sacrum together with the coccyx, Galen has said that it is composed of six bones. To me, however, it appeared at first sight to be a single bone, and on examining it from every aspect, I found it indeed to be one bone. But I then examined a specimen belonging to another corpse, and found it to be made up of six bones, as Galen had stated. Likewise, I found the part in question to conform with his statement in the case of all other corpses, with the exception of just two, in which I again found it to be one bone.[287] In all the examples with six bones, the joints were rigid. I am not as certain of this, however, as I am of the lower jaw being a single bone. 2.3.32

Later, we went into Old Fustat, and saw streets and great marketplaces that had formerly been choked by throngs of people: all were now empty, with not a living creature in them, save the occasional wayfarer flitting by. Passing through these places, one felt utterly alone—even though there were few spots without a corpse and some scattered bones. The same scenes continued until we emerged into a place called Uskurjat Firʿawn. Here, we saw every single bit of ground chock-full of bodies and dismembered remains. The dead had taken over the hillocks hereabouts so completely that they covered every spot, and almost exceeded in quantity the dust of those hummocks. And when we looked down into Uskurjat Firʿawn itself, an enormous depression in the ground, we saw the skulls—white, black, dark brown, stacked on top of each other in layers. So numerous were they, and piled so high, that they had completely hidden all the other bones and might have been heads without bodies. To an 2.3.33

onlooker, they resembled a newly cut crop of watermelons, heaped together at the harvest. I saw them again, some days later, when the sun had scorched the flesh off them and they had turned white; this time, they seemed to me like ostrich eggs piled up.

2.3.34 When I saw how empty of people were those neighborhoods and marketplaces, and how crowded those wastes and hillocks, an image came to mind—that it was a band of travelers who had departed, vacating one place to occupy another.[288] Yet, to tell the truth, one might head in any direction one chose and, along the way, come upon devastation as great we have described, and several times greater, too.

2.3.35 In Dhu l-Hijjah [August–September], in Old Fustat, a woman was found to have cut a young boy's throat, meaning to eat him. She was arrested, and executed by drowning. However, during the time since the phenomenon of cannibalism had petered out, and since reports and sightings of it had ceased, no case other than that of this woman came to light.

2.3.36 During the period I have chronicled, several freakish happenings occurred. These included the birth, in the year 597 [1200–1], of a baby with two heads. Another baby was born with hair that was white. I saw it, and observed that it was not like the white hair of old age, but instead had a touch of reddishness to it.[289] In this year, too, a female mule gave birth to a stillborn foal; it remained for many days in the prefect's residence.[290] Then, in the year 598 [1201–2], came the discovery of a baby lamb that produced milk: it came out of its nipple in a trickle like a fine thread. The lamb was put on display in the prefect's residence several times, and at its last appearance it was four months old.[291]

2.3.37 Regarding information about the Nile this year, we will present only a summary account. At first, the river "burned out" in Ṭūbah [January]; then, gradually, the "burning out" became so much worse that the waterway turned into a series of shallows, fordable by people and pack animals. Later, in Jumada al-Thani, which coincided with Barmahāt [March], the green discoloration first appeared in the water. In Rajab [April], the greenness became so much more marked that it was immediately obvious in the color, taste, and odor of samples; thereafter, however, the discoloration diminished, eventually disappearing altogether.

2.3.38 The Nile reached its most "burnt out" state in Ramadan [June]; by then, it had receded about eight hundred cubits from the Nilometer. Ibn Abī l-Raddād carried out his inspection when the water had sunk to its lowest level, which was on the Tuesday five days before the end of Baʾūnah and four before the end of Ramadan in the year 598 [20 June 1202]: the water in the bottom of the Nilometer pool stood at one and a half cubits, whereas in the previous year it had measured two cubits. In the previous year, too, the river had begun to rise from this same date onwards; this year, however, the rise was late, and did not begin until 25 Abīb [19 July]. Over the intervening period, the level had increased so little—no more than four finger-breadths—that minds dwelt on the coming doom, and all the folk were wrapped in gloom. They even began to suppose that some accident had befallen the Nile's headwaters, at its outflow.

2.3.39 And then, at last, the river began to rise, so that by the end of Abīb [24 July] the level stood at three cubits—at which point it ceased rising for two days. Now, people grew even more despondent: for the rise to stop at this stage was such a departure from the norm. But then the river surged with enormous force, one rise following hard upon another, mountains of water all churning together in spate. In the space of ten days, the level increased eight cubits, three cubits of which came in one uninterrupted rise. On 4 Tūt, which was 12 Dhu l-Hijjah [2 September], it reached its maximum—one finger-breadth short of sixteen cubits. It remained at that level for two days, then began to fall slowly, gently ebbing away.

2.3.40 That being as much detail as I intended to provide about the event of this year's rise, let it be the conclusion of this second part, and the close of the book. *Praise to God, Lord of the worlds, and may He bless the foremost of His emissaries, Muḥammad, the gentile prophet,*[292] *and the pious and virtuous members of his family.*

2.3.41 Written in the hand of its author
and in hope of the mercy of God the Exalted
by ʿAbd al-Laṭīf ibn Yūsuf ibn Muḥammad al-Baghdādī
in Ramadan of the year 600 [May 1204] in Cairo.

Notes

1 The words "may God guide him," *waffaqahu llāh*, probably allude to ʿAbd al-Laṭīf's scholarly courtesy title, Muwaffaq al-Dīn, "God-guided in Religion."

2 No copies of this longer work are known to have survived.

3 In the second half of this sentence there is an echo of the Qur'an: «If you give thanks, I [i.e. God] will give you more» (Q Ibrāhīm 14:7).

4 Q Anfāl 8:33.

5 "Prophetic . . . knowledge" probably refers to the special innate wisdom supposedly enjoyed by the caliph, by virtue of his office and his ancestry. (There was a belief that members of the family of Muḥammad, from whose uncle the Abbasid caliphs descended, were heirs to a body of esoteric lore.)

6 Cf., in the Qur'an, «Invoke me that I may respond to you» (Q Ghāfir 40:60). The point is that even the omniscient God insists on being kept informed. It seems that intention alone, unless professed, is not enough.

7 Although parts of the foregoing passage are elliptical in the Arabic, the gist is this: ʿAbd al-Laṭīf hopes (and prays) that by "delivering" (*inhāʾ*, cf. §0.2) this book to God's vicegerent, the caliph, and by "keeping him informed" (also *inhāʾ*, i.e. delivering information), he will gain the favor of God Himself. The book, in other words, is an act of faith.

8 The Arabic says "the *salt* sea," to differentiate it from the Nile, which is itself often called a *baḥr*, "a sea."

9 The Nile is about 4,130 miles long, including its "twists and turns." ʿAbd al-Laṭīf either made a mistake in adding degrees (11° + 31⅓° should = 42⅓°) or, more likely, meant to give the latitude of the Mountains of the Moon as eleven *and a half* degrees south (a figure attested elsewhere; cf. al-Baghdādī, *Relation*, 705). In fact, the sources of the Nile are only about 3° south of the Equator. ʿAbd al-Laṭīf's straight-line estimate of nine hundred *farsakh*s, or ca. 3,230 miles, is thus considerably more than the actual figure of ca. 2,420 miles.

10 It was in the Cairo region that the Nile would reach its maximum at about the autumnal equinox; further south and north, the maximum occurred respectively earlier and later. Since the completion of the Aswan High Dam in 1971, the Egyptian river's immemorial rhythm has ceased.

11 In the MS, the words *fa-yarsubu*, "forms a sediment," appear as an afterthought or correction, written above the word "settles."

12 I.e., while all of Egypt is "intrinsically" hot, the amount of "accidental" moisture is greater in Lower Egypt, and this affects the inhabitants' appearance.

13 The ancient Egyptian calendar year began with the first month of the season called Akhet, "Flood."

14 "The Greeks" translates the Arabic al-Rūm, literally "the Romans," but often meaning the culturally Greek inhabitants of the Eastern Roman or Byzantine Empire and by extension (if anachronistically, as here) "Greeks" in general.

15 The belief that vermin and other animals could be spontaneously generated was only finally debunked by Pasteur in the mid-nineteenth century.

16 "Stinking, crawling bugs" must be bedbugs.

17 Presumably the idea is that if the naturally hot south wind blows long enough, its heat eventually neutralizes the cooling effect of the southern pools. An earlier reporter on Egypt warned in the mid-first/late eighth century of the Marīsī's pestilential effect, "If it keeps on blowing, the Egyptians buy their winding sheets" (al-Ḥimyarī, *Al-Rawḍ al-miʿṭār fī khabar al-aqṭār*, s.v. "al-Marīs").

18 The strength of qualities characterizing a particular temperament was measured in degrees, on ascending scales of one to four for heat and cold, and of one to two for moisture and dryness (Dozy, *Supplément aux dictionnaires arabes*, s.v. *d-r-j*).

19 Perhaps not an impossibility, given that certain kinds of sawdust contain allergens.

20 The spider, here *ratīlā[ʾ]* but usually *rutaylāʾ*, is usually (but unconvincingly) glossed as a "tarantula" (e.g. Dozy, *Supplément*, s.v. *r-t-l*). Al-Damīrī's eighth/fourteenth-century zoological encyclopedia, which has the spelling *ruthaylā*, says that the term is used for up to eight different spiders, of which "the largest and nastiest is the Egyptian" (*Ḥayāt al-ḥayawān al-kubrā*, 2:455). Alternatively, the word could signify a plant of the same name that supposedly contains the antidote to the spider's venom (al-Baghdādī, *Riḥlat ʿAbd al-Laṭīf*, 64 n. 18).

21 Elsewhere, *Ficus sycomorus* has a symbiotic relationship with a specialized pollinating wasp. In Egypt, the wasp is absent and the unpollinated figs need help to ripen: scoring or gashing the fruit makes them produce ethylene, which acts as a ripening hormone. (Miller, Morris and Stuart-Smith, *Plants of Dhofar*, 206.) The operation is termed *khatn*, "circumcision" (Habiba Al-Sayfi, personal communication).

22 A "plaster," that is, in its original sense of a bandage spread with curative substances.

23 The midsummer heliacal rising of Sirius marked the beginning of the season when the raw gum could be collected. Some other authorities, however, put the start of the harvest later: according to al-Maqrīzī, it was as late as the seventeenth day of the Coptic month of Thoout, or September 14th (al-Maqrīzī, *Khiṭaṭ*, 1:270). (On Coptic and other months, see Appendix, "The Egyptian Calendar.")

24 This idea is perhaps suggested or reinforced by the fact that the Arabic for "gum," *lathā*, can also mean "dew." Strictly speaking, the gum of balsam would have been a gum resin.

25 Does he mean the amount of gum, or of oil? Below, he implies that twenty *riṭl*s is a *normal* annual crop of oil, and that it would need

two hundred *riṭl*s of crude gum to produce it. Here, twenty *riṭl*s of oil would thus seem rather too much; but twenty *riṭl*s of gum would seem much too little. Then again, 596/1200 was, as we shall see (in §2.1.8, below), an exceptionally dry year.

26 According to ʿAbd al-Laṭīf's contemporary, Yāqūt, who also visited the balsam gardens, heating the oil further purified it. The person in charge was a Copt; in answer to repeated demands from the rulers of Egypt to divulge the details of the process, he said, "As long as I have offspring [to whom I can pass them on], I would not teach my secrets to anyone else, not even under threat of death" (Yāqūt, *Muʿjam al-buldān*, s.v. "al-Maṭariyyah").

27 "The ruler's treasury," *khizānat al-malik*, is followed by the illegible traces of a word, which looks as if it may have been deliberately erased. It may have been the honorific name of a particular Ayyubid prince. It is possible that ʿAbd al-Laṭīf had mistakenly written the name of al-Malik al-Afḍal, claimant of the throne of Egypt in the period 595–96/1198–1200.

28 Figures given by al-Maqrīzī suggest that the raw gum yielded between a seventh and an eighth of its weight in oil (al-Maqrīzī, *Khiṭaṭ*, 1:272).

29 The famous balsam of Palestine was the balm of Gilead, mentioned in the Book of Jeremiah (8:22).

30 The sentence is confused. It would make better sense if it said that the raw gum is harvested at the rising of Sirius (actually in midsummer), and the oil extracted from it in Shubāṭ [February]. Cf. al-Maqrīzī, who says that the "cooking" of the oil—the final stage of its extraction—took place in the month of Paremhat, which begins at the end of February (al-Maqrīzī, *Khiṭaṭ*, 1:272).

31 The bark of *Commiphora gileadensis* has been used in recent times in southern Arabia as a disinfectant (Miller, Morris, and Stuart-Smith, *Plants of Dhofar*, 84).

32 Strictly speaking, *Colocasia esculenta* has corms rather than roots.

33 "Ulceration of the intestines" is, more literally, "abrasion of the skin of the intestines." Would "ulcerative colitis" be the modern English diagnosis?

34 Today, taro is usually washed thoroughly before frying (Habiba Al-Sayfi, personal communication).

35 The reading of the interlinear addition "and a palm spathe" is tentative.

36 The "broad beans" can only be cormels, miniature corms that "bud" out at the top of the corm proper and can be used to grow new plants (as described below in the text); they are vaguely comparable to beans in shape, but more so in the way rootlets sprout from them. Dioscorides's original text goes: "When it has flowered, it bears tiny bladders like beggars' bags in miniature, in which is a 'bean' that grows up above the cover in the form of a bubble" (quoted in al-Baghdādī, *Relation*, 101 n. 68). ʿAbd al-Laṭīf may have been confused about where these "beans" appeared, hence the obscurity of his paraphrase. At any rate, it seems that he is not relying here on personal observation.

37 I.e., Yemenis use ginger as a vegetable, not only as a flavoring.

38 He probably means that he has seen bananas growing (as they do) in al-Ghawr, but only the fruit on sale in Damascus.

39 Strictly speaking, as it does not have a woody stem, the banana "tree" is a very large herb.

40 "Lush with fragrance and freshness": *tarifu*, "being lush, luxuriant, bosky," might also be read as *tariffu*, "fluttering," and thus, here, "wafting fragrance."

41 This seems to mean that the fibrous "grain" of *Colocasia* corms becomes more noticeable when they are fried. The banana plant also grows from a corm.

42 The "mother" banana (not to be confused with the "mother" tree) is really the plant's bud; its concentric layers are, botanically speaking, bracts.

43 It is now thought that bananas originated in SE Asia.

44 "Its parent": literally, "its mother."

45 This timescale seems much too short when compared with that of present-day bananas.

46 The point is that rushes of normal length (seldom much more than 40 inches) would not be long enough, used transversely, to produce a mat with a seamless width of 2.5 cubits, or ca. 50 inches.

47 A basic version of these mats is still produced in Tamil Nadu, modern-day al-Maʿbar. Today the region is more famous for its high-quality figured mats of *korai* grass, a kind of reed.

48 Some varieties of citron (*Citrus medica*) do indeed lack pulp, and contain only albedo (edible white "pith"). Regarding large citrons, al-Maqrīzī (*Khiṭaṭ*, 1:28) mentions one so enormous that it made a whole load for a camel.

49 These marks may resemble those of today's "navel" oranges. Regarding the color, the Arabic says, "intensely *red* . . . deeper *red* than an orange," but, at least in older texts, "red" is used for the color orange too. A marginal note gives *mufarṭaḥ*, "broad," as a correction or alternative for *mufalṭaḥ*, "flattened."

50 Green gram, *Vigna radiata*, is also known as mung. Regarding its being sold by the apothecaries, Yule and Burnell (*Hobson-Jobson*, s.v. "Moong") mention its use in diets for fever sufferers.

51 *Aqāqiyā*, under the name *qaraẓ*, tends today to be used externally, mixed with henna, to treat foot pains (Habiba Al-Sayfi, personal communication).

52 The point is that the *qathad* is a similar size to the *faqqūṣ*, but comes from a different genus of Cucurbitaceae. The *faqqūṣ* and the common cucumber (*khiyār*) appear together in proverbs, e.g., "There's neither a *khiyār* in it, nor a *faqqūṣ*" (Habiba Al-Sayfi, personal communication)—that is, there's little or nothing to choose between two options, two groups of people, etc. But because *al-khiyār* happens, by coincidence, to mean also "the (better) choice, option, the chosen ones," the sense is the Orwellian one of all being equal, but some being more equal than others.

53 Violet "conserve" (here *maʿjūn*, "something kneaded, dough, paste") is technically known as *khamīrah*. It was produced by pounding the flowers, then thickening the resulting liquid with sugar (Dozy, *Supplément*, s.v. *kh-m-r*).

54 The word translated as "cherries" is *qarāsiyā* (also spelled *qarāṣiyā*), cognate with Greek *kerasos*. Today in Egypt, the dried plums called *qarāsiyā* are used, together with other dried fruits and nuts, to make

a Ramadan beverage (Habiba Al-Sayfi, personal communication). Cherries, plums, and sloes are all produced by the genus *Prunus*, so perhaps the confusion of names is to be expected; in any case, the wider Arabic nomenclature of fruit is—as the end of the paragraph shows—a mixed fruit salad.

55 Many visitors to Egypt mentioned the chicken industry, an early example of factory farming, though none in such detail as ʿAbd al-Laṭīf. Lane, however, explains an important point omitted in our text—why it was worth going through the rigmarole. The reason was that the factory owners got the eggs from backyard poultry keepers, but only gave them one chick for every two eggs received; even allowing for eggs that failed to hatch (up to a third), they would still make a profit in chicks. E.g., from every six eggs received, the factory could expect four to hatch, but would only give the egg producer three, thus earning a chick. The poultry keepers would benefit, too, as their hens would continue laying, rather than periodically spending three weeks incubating a full clutch. (The only losers were the overworked hens.) By Lane's time, a few refinements had been made to the process, but the essentials were the same, and business was still flourishing, with 164 factories throughout Egypt producing ca. 17.4 million chicks in the year 1830–31 (Lane, *An Account of the Manners and Customs of the Modern Egyptians*, 309–11).

56 Sacy (al-Baghdādī, *Relation*, 135 and 150–51 n. 3) reads *ʿaqd*, "arch, arched top" (clearly voweled as such in the manuscript) as if it were the plural of *ʿuqdah*, "knot, knuckle," and thus makes the width two spans and a few knuckles by the same in height. Admittedly, the dimensions of the chamber and its door do seem small: were children employed to perform the operations to be described?

57 This seems to suggest that the two *ṭājan*s sat in rectangular depressions, where the roof was not insulated with reeds, flax, clay, and bricks (as described above).

58 "Fiber . . . mats": conceivably, "rag rugs."

59 I.e., (1 turn × 1 egg × 2000) × 3, rather than simply (3 turns × 1 egg) × 2000. The total of turns is the same, but the first method would take a lot

longer. Henry David Thoreau, baking hoe-cakes by Walden Pond, used a nice simile when he recalled "tending and turning them as carefully as an Egyptian his hatching eggs." (*Walden; or, Life in the Woods*, 40.)

60 I have not been able to establish whether hens really do test the heat of eggs with their eyes.

61 Dictionaries do not seem to elucidate this term, but the sense may be akin to that of a judicial "hearing" in English.

62 "Glimming" is a neologism in English; but, as a "glim" has the triple meaning of a light given off, a lamp, and (colloquially) an eye, it is appropriate. The English-speaking poultry keeper's equivalent of glimming is "candling," but there seems to be no cognate equivalent of "glimmery"—hence my coinage.

63 "Becoming downy and filling out": Sacy's (al-Baghdādī, *Relation*, 139) and Zand and Videan's (al-Baghdādī, *Eastern Key*, 87) interpretations of the verbs as "moving" and "breathing" are possible, given a dearth of dots and vowels, but strain meaning.

64 The first three names are of Coptic months, the second three of Syriac months. See Appendix, "The Egyptian Calendar."

65 A normal price for the humbler sort of donkey was around three dinars (Goitein, *Mediterranean Society*, 1:270). Jews and Christians avoided (and occasionally, under Muslim rule, were banned from) riding horses, always regarded as more ostentatious than other mounts; speaking of the Geniza, the vast collection of documents spanning many centuries that he studied, Goitein writes, "Nowhere in the Geniza have I come upon a horse owned by a Jew" (*Mediterranean Society*, 4:263).

66 Sc., "and it is the father that provides the form." Strictly speaking, in English, the offspring of donkey mothers and horse fathers are not mules but hinnies.

67 This seems too large. The maximum of "ten cubits and more" claimed in the quotation ascribed to Aristotle, below, is about the length of large individuals today—up to ca. 16.5 feet.

68 The true musk pod is a gland, situated between the navel and genitalia of the males of the family Moschidae, and containing a highly

scented secretion long prized by perfumiers (see al-Sīrāfī and Ibn Faḍlān, *Two Travel Books*, 105–7). The crocodilian equivalent is situated in the reptile's cloaca.

69 Cf. al-Damīrī (*Ḥayawān*, 1:536), who quotes the less incredible claim that crocodiles can get stuck upside down because their legs are short and their backs are stiff.

70 "Blood vessels": Arabic *ʿirq* can also mean nerve, duct, etc.

71 The Arabic is not very clear here, but a passage by al-Qazwīnī (*ʿAjāʾib al-makhlūqāt wa-gharāʾib al-mawjūdāt*, 134) elucidates it: "[The skink] results when the offspring of the crocodile are taken out of the water: those that head back for the water become crocodiles, while those that head inland become skinks."

72 Again, the sense is not altogether clear. It seems, however, to be this: although it is thought that the skink is a dry-land version of the crocodile, the fact that it is anatomically distinct, and that female skinks lay their own eggs, shows it to be a separate genus.

73 Al-Muẓaffar (*Al-Muʿtamad fī l-adwiyah al-mufradah*, 230) clarifies: only the end of the tail should be cut off, because the flesh around its base has a particularly potent aphrodisiac effect.

74 The "cockerel's testes" in this case are perhaps not the actual testes, as above, but a kind of round white berry said to resemble them (Dozy, *Supplément*, s.v. *kh-ṣ-y*, quoting Ibn al-Bayṭār). To administer skink "on its own" means not adding any other *active* ingredients. Of the inactive ingredients mentioned, honey water is prepared by dissolving one part of honey in three of water (al-Muẓaffar, *Muʿtamad*, 484).

75 "A simple": a medicine with only one (active) constituent. At least as late as the early nineteenth century, dried skinks were being exported in large numbers to Europe (al-Baghdādī, *Relation*, 164 n. 42). They are still sold as an aphrodisiac by traditional druggists in Cairo and elsewhere.

76 I.e., the hippopotamus. The Arabic may be a calque on the Greek *hippos ho potamios*, "river horse." Literally, ʿAbd al-Laṭīf calls the animal a "sea horse," but since the Nile is often called "a sea" in Arabic (see n. 8, above), the translation is allowable.

77 Hippopotami were classed until quite recently in the suborder Suina, which includes pigs.

78 "Just skin and bone": the Arabic says, more literally, "stripped [of flesh], as if it were bone."

79 In weight, hippos are little more than half as heavy as even small "forest" elephants. Their "hoof"-like feet actually have four webbed toes.

80 The "water snake" is not a snake but an eel.

81 Literally, "the bone of its back." Sacy suggested (al-Baghdādī, *Relation*, 170 n. 61) that the turtle here described is a soft-shelled Nilotic turtle, *Trionyx triunguis*. However, in view of its size and its prominent "flanges," the description better fits the much larger green turtle, *Chelonia mydas*.

82 Cf. the English terms calipash and calipee, denoting two kinds of turtle meat, respectively green and yellow.

83 I.e., the clams are sold by volume, not weight.

84 "Most of them taper": strictly, the adjective *makhrūṭ* means "conical," but it was used in most descriptions of the pyramids (e.g. Ibn Baṭṭūṭa, *The Travels of Ibn Baṭṭūṭa*, 1:51).

85 The arches were part of a great causeway that led to Giza from the Nile (al-Baghdādī, *Relation*, 212–13 n. 6). They underwent a major restoration in 708/1308–9 (al-Maqrīzī, *Khiṭaṭ*, 2:151–52); two spans are still extant, and bear inscriptions in Qarāqūsh's name (*Encyclopaedia of Islam*, 4:430). The witless official presumably meant, by blocking the arches, to convert them into a dam at the time of the Nile's flood.

86 The pyramid of Khufu (slightly truncated, as it was in ʿAbd al-Laṭīf's time) and that of Khafre currently measure 455 feet and 448 feet in height, respectively.

87 E.g., "High as some lofty peak above the land,/ Like breasts that swell upon a chest they stand" (quoted without attribution in al-Maqrīzī, *Khiṭaṭ*, 1:118).

88 The pyramid of Menkaure, originally 215 feet tall, is in fact less than half the height of the other two.

89 The same sentiment had earlier inspired a verse by the sixth/twelfth-century poet ʿUmārah al-Yamanī: "All that man builds is doomed to

fear Time's passing years;/ Alone on earth, these are the monuments Time fears" (quoted in al-Maqrīzī, *Khiṭaṭ*, 1:121).

90 Four hundred black cubits = ca. 709 feet, which is not far short of the current measurement of ca. 755 feet for the sides of the Great Pyramid's base. ʿAbd al-Laṭīf's "vertical height," however, seems to be a mistake for (or misunderstanding of) "diagonal height," i.e. the distance from each corner of the Pyramid's base up to its apex.

91 Lane (*An Arabic-English Lexicon*, s.v. *gh-l-w*) gives the length of a *ghalwah*, or bowshot, as between two hundred and four hundred cubits, which hardly helps precise measurement.

92 I.e., he didn't go barefoot or gird up his loins, which would have made the ascent easier.

93 ʿAbd al-Laṭīf's reservations about the expert's figures may be due to a misunderstanding. If the expert was using the shorter "legal cubit" (see "cubit" in the Glossary), and if his "vertical height" means what it says, then his measurements are not far off. If ʿAbd al-Laṭīf's own "vertical height" actually means "diagonal height in black cubits" (cf. n. 90, above), he too is quite near the mark.

94 The expression is a little elliptical in the Arabic, but implies that it was by luck that the tunnel coincided with one of the passages inside the pyramid. There is some doubt about whether it really was al-Maʾmūn who, as the following sentence says, opened up this tunnel, or whether much earlier tomb robbers had made a way in from the same spot (cf. al-Baghdādī, *Relation*, 219–20 n. 21). The ascription of the tunnel to al-Maʾmūn, however, is at least as old as the fourth/tenth century (al-Masʿūdī, quoted in al-Maqrīzī, *Khiṭaṭ*, 1:113).

95 One is reminded of the famous Pyramid Texts, inscribed on the pyramids at Saqqara. The pyramid of Khufu at Giza still retained its outer casing in ʿAbd al-Laṭīf's time, on which the texts he refers to were presumably inscribed. They may, however, have consisted largely or entirely of graffiti in various scripts (cf. Cooperson, "Al-Maʾmūn, the Pyramids and the Hieroglyphs," 118).

96 An old idiom goes, "Allah threw at him the third stone under the cooking-pot." The explanation (al-Zabīdī, *Tāj al-ʿarūs fī jawāhir al-qāmūs*,

s.v. *th-f-w*) is that people cooking *al fresco* often don't bother to find an actual third stone to form a "trivet" for their pot, and make do with the mountainside as a third support. The first two proverbial stones thrown are thus divine warning shots, the third an unregarded but mountainous calamity. Quoting a passage now otherwise lost from ʿAbd al-Laṭīf's partially preserved autobiography, al-Maqrīzī (*Khiṭaṭ*, 1:115) is more specific about al-ʿAzīz's "foolish friends": the culprit was apparently "a foolish *ʿajamī* man," i.e. a non-Arab, most likely of Iranian origin.

97 In the wording of the phrase, "with their cavalry and foot soldiers," there is a small but cutting allusion to diabolic forces mentioned in Q Isrāʾ 17:64.

98 The vertical scar inflicted by al-ʿAzīz is still clearly visible on the pyramid's north face.

99 These grottos must be the underground limestone quarries at Ṭurah, south of Maadi.

100 The Aswan area was the most famous source of red granite in Egypt. In referring to al-Qulzum, ʿAbd al-Laṭīf may be thinking of the ancient porphyry quarry at Jabal Abū Dukhān, near the Red Sea coastal town of al-Ghurdaqah/Hurghada.

101 The gigantic buildings and grottos are the remains of temples and subterranean tombs.

102 Abū l-Hawl, literally "the Father of Dread/the Terrifying One." This, the conventional Arabic name for the Sphinx of Giza, may in fact be an arabicized version of an earlier Coptic name.

103 The head of the Sphinx is ca. 490 yards—more like two long bowshots—from the corner of the pyramid of Khufu. Its length, including its outstretched paws, is ca. 240 feet, or about double ʿAbd al-Laṭīf's estimate; however, the monument was not fully revealed until the twentieth century. ʿAbd al-Laṭīf was probably unaware that the Sphinx's body is that of a couchant lion, and may have imagined it to be that of a standing human. Traces of the red pigment still survive, despite the vandalism perpetrated in the eighth/fourteenth century (see following note).

104 The Sphinx's beautiful face assumed its now familiar punch-drunk form in ca. 780/1378–79, when it was vandalized by a zealot called Shaykh Muḥammad Ṣā'im al-Dahr ("the Eternal Faster"). He considered it a manifestation of idolatry. (Al-Maqrīzī, *Khiṭaṭ*, 1:123.)

105 Regarding the word "idol," which will appear often, ʿAbd al-Laṭīf does not use the Arabic term for "statue" current today, *timthāl*; occasionally he uses *ṣūrah*, "image, picture, likeness," but more often *ṣanam*—"image, representation" and, especially, "idol." In English, the latter word perhaps has a more pejorative coloring than in Arabic; but "statue" is too neutral.

106 The classical sense of *misallah*, obelisk, is "large needle" (cf., in the following note, the English "Cleopatra's Needles"). The two obelisks at ʿAyn Shams were erected by the Twelfth Dynasty pharaoh Senusret I in the twentieth century BC. ʿAbd al-Laṭīf overestimates the height, actually about 69 feet.

107 These are "Cleopatra's Needles": one is now in London on the Embankment of the Thames, the other in New York's Central Park. Originally, they too stood at Heliopolis; they were taken to Alexandria in Roman times.

108 Perhaps a disingenuous way of saying that he hadn't seen them in person.

109 On the subject of raising of heavy masses, ʿAbd al-Laṭīf may have in mind the Arabic translation of the first-century AD Alexandrian inventor Heron's *Mechanica*, which deals with this topic.

110 In defense of Qarājā's motives (if not his vandalism), it should be noted that, at the beginning of Saladin's rise to power in Egypt, the Crusaders had besieged and come near to capturing the neighboring coastal city of Damietta.

111 The surrounding pillars were in fact part of the Serapeum, the temple of Serapis. Aristotle taught in his famous colonnade, or *peripatos*, in Athens. Benjamin of Tudela (who visited Egypt a generation before ʿAbd al-Laṭīf) says, rightly, that Aristotle's philosophy was taught here in Alexandria, but not that Aristotle visited in person (al-Tuṭīlī, *Riḥlat ibn Yūnah al-Andalusī ilā bilād al-sharq al-Islāmī*, 177). Cecilia

Martini Bonadeo comments aptly on ʿAbd al-Laṭīf's wishful thinking here that it "is paradigmatic of the distance [of scholars like him] . . . from their Greek sources and, at the same time, of their intent to reconnect themselves to this [Greek] tradition" (Martini Bonadeo, *Philosophical Journey*, 211).

112 The Library of Alexandria, developed from the third century BC onwards by the Ptolemies, was of legendary fame in the Hellenistic world. ʿAbd al-Laṭīf appears to be the first writer to claim that it was burned on the Arab takeover of the city; subsequently, the story is elaborated by other Arabic sources. It seems clear, however, that the famous old collection(s) of books had been destroyed or dispersed long before the Arabs appeared. (See e.g.: al-Baghdādī, *Kitāb al-Ifādah* (1403/1983), 169–74; Manguel, *Library at Night*, 32–33 and 339 n. 144; al-Tuṭīlī, *Riḥlat ibn Yūnah*, 177 n. 1; al-Baghdādī, *Relation*, 240–44 n. 55.) ʿAbd al-Laṭīf's "may God be pleased with him" is formulaic, and not a particular expression of approval of the alleged burning.

113 62 1/6 ("legal") cubits is ca. 101.6 feet. Present-day measurement gives a height, including base and capital, of 88.09 feet.

114 There is a slight discrepancy: these latter figures add up to 234, not 233. The rooftop mosque mentioned in the following sentence seems to have been a wooden prayer pavilion built (or first built) by Aḥmad ibn Ṭūlūn (d. 270/884). It was eventually blown away by the wind. (Al-Maqrīzī, *Khiṭaṭ*, 1:158.)

115 Q Qaṣaṣ 28:15 and 28:21.

116 "And before that for a period known only to God the Exalted": *wa-qablahum bi-mā shā'a llāhu taʿālā*, literally, "and before them for what [time] God the Exalted willed." Similar expressions will recur, each calling for a slightly different translation according to its context.

117 The time span is about right, if legend is correct in dating the foundation of Memphis to the First Dynasty, i.e. probably before 3000 BC.

118 Pharaonic builders used braces—or, to give the technical term, swallow-tail cramps—to stabilize ashlar masonry (Wright, *Ancient Building Technology*, 3:166).

119 This might be the granite statue of Ramesses II, re-erected in Cairo's Ramesses Square in the 1950s, although that is rather smaller than ʿAbd al-Laṭīf's figure of thirty cubits. A less likely candidate is the larger statue of Ramesses II, still *in situ* at Saqqara though now lying on its back. It bears traces of red pigment, but is made of limestone, not granite.

120 "Compound" (more literally, "instrumental") parts are particular bodily members or organs, such as eyes, ears, hands, lungs, hearts, and so on. "Simple parts" (literally, those "mutually similar [in material or function]") include bones, flesh, cartilage, blood vessels, and skin. (Cf. al-Qazwīnī, *ʿAjāʾib*, 277 ff.)

121 Arabic *zirr al-qalb*, "button of the heart," is explained in the dictionaries as a small bone under the heart, resembling half a walnut. Probably the metasternum is meant—a lump of cartilage at the lower end of the sternum that usually ossifies in middle age.

122 "The groin and the inguinal ligaments": again, the anatomy is hazy, and the translation tentative.

123 I.e., the two lateral extremities of the wrist.

124 "Grooves": Arabic *nahray* is more literally "channels," and could conceivably refer to blood vessels; Sacy (al-Baghdādī, *Relation*, 258 n. 87) amends to *nahday*, and understands the term as "condyles." I prefer to leave the sense open.

125 Many pharaonic statues (e.g., the limestone figure of Ramesses II at Saqqara mentioned in n. 119, above) are shown gripping cylindrical objects.

126 Naturalistic statues of lions have survived, e.g. one from Saqqara now in the Louvre (smaller, however, than life size).

127 "Engineering": *handasah* is also mensuration, geometry, and architecture.

128 "Trunk": *tannūr*, literally a tandoor oven, cylindrical in form.

129 I.e., the median cubital vein.

130 Aristotle's text, reworked by ʿAbd al-Laṭīf below, is in fact from the first book of *De partibus animalium*. Sacy (al-Baghdādī, *Relation*, 261–63 n. 98) quotes the Greek original.

131 As in the old story of the men who, either blind(folded) or in a darkened room, examined an elephant by touch and came away with contrasting ideas about its nature (e.g. al-Rūmī's version in *Tales from the Masnavi*, 16), the elephant was an emblem of something not only vast and powerful, but also incomprehensible to the unenlightened: it stood for the multiform, inscrutable world of nature. The ant, in contrast, was a well-known metaphor for the puniness of human endeavor (e.g. al-Damīrī, *Ḥayawān*, 4:119).

132 The English title customarily given to Galen's famous work. The Arabic title translates, perhaps more descriptively, as *Useful Functions of the Organs*.

133 Q Nisā' 4:28.

134 Q Ṣāffāt 37:96. Shawkat Toorawa points out that, ironically—given the subject of discussion—the preceding verse of the same chapter concerns idols: «He said, "Do you worship that which you [yourselves] carve?"» (Q Ṣāffāt 37:95).

135 "The invisible and the visible" is an allusion to several Qur'anic verses, e.g. Q Raʿd 13:9.

136 Q Dhāriyāt 51:21. I.e., God's sovereignty also pervades human beings.

137 Q Ghāfir 40:19.

138 Q Isrā' 17:44.

139 Literally, "the days have left . . . them as fragments, and left them as old ropes." The unusual word for "fragments," *judhādh*, appears in a Qur'anic verse about Abraham breaking idols into pieces (Q Anbiyā' 21:58). "Old rope" is, as in English, a metaphor for something worthless.

140 Perhaps the hole left by the "millstone" was in fact a socket for a missing crown or other piece of headgear.

141 An example (though probably not the one seen by ʿAbd al-Laṭīf) is the statue, at Karnak, of Ramesses II with his daughter standing between his feet.

142 Q Naḥl 16:120.

143 Some see the Arabic *ummah*, usually "a nation," as an alternative to the cognate *imam*, and thus meaning in this context "a [righteous] leader" (Lane, *Lexicon*, s.v. *'-m-m*).

144 Q Aʿrāf 7:138. This is from the story of the Golden Calf, shared with the Book of Exodus.

145 The "human being" is Jesus, who to Muslims is a prophet but, ultimately, a mortal man. The assertion that Christian iconography is an extension of pagan practice is also found in a comment by the fourth-century AD bishop Eusebios, who noted that Christian icons developed from painted images of pagan deities used for domestic worship (Mathews, *Byzantium: From Antiquity to the Renaissance*, 45–47).

146 Three "treatises in response to the Jews and the Christians" are mentioned in Ibn Abī Uṣaybiʿah's list of ʿAbd al-Laṭīf's works (al-Baghdādī, *Kitāb al-Ifādah* (1403/1983), 163).

147 "Masters" is a little ambiguous. It probably means "the monuments' founders," but it could also mean "the divinities to whom the monuments were dedicated."

148 Pharaoh and his people appear often in the Qurʾan. A particular mention of an ancient Egyptian monument is that, in Q Ghāfir 40:36, of a tower that Pharaoh ordered to be built.

149 "Left to their own devices" is perhaps an allusion to Q Qiyāmah 75:36, which implies that such a state of liberty can lead to a neglect of one's obligations to God.

150 By the poet Abū Nuwās (d. ca. 200/815). The generally accepted version goes, "Every *hand* he saw, he thought to be a cup;/ Every *human being*, the boy who tops it up" (Abū Nuwās, *Dīwān*, 204).

151 The idea that curses threaten those who disturb the relics of ancient Egyptians antiquities is still current. A recent case concerned the opening of a huge sarcophagus in Alexandria.

152 "Country folk": the people of the *rīf*, the cultivated land as opposed to the uncultivated *bādiyah*, the lands of the *badw* or Bedouins.

153 The relative was most probably a relative by marriage.

154 The antiquarian judge of Abusir may have been al-Qāḍī Ibn al-Shahrazūrī who, in 579/1183–84, carried out excavations there at the so-called "House of Hermes" (al-Maqrīzī, *Khiṭaṭ*, 1:119–20).

155 "Mineral pitch," *qufr* (also spelled *qafr*), exudes from rocks or is found on water. The lighter-colored sort is said to be superior,

but it is sometimes adulterated with darker asphalt (al-Muẓaffar, *Muʿtamad*, 393).

156 Various substances, including bitumen, wood pitch, wood tar, frankincense, and myrrh, are known to have been used in the mummification process.

157 Sacy (al-Baghdādī, *Relation*, 271–72 n. 133) was unable to find this text in Galen's works, and suggests that ʿAbd al-Laṭīf misattributed the quotation.

158 The mummified insects would have been scarab beetles, *Scarabaeus sacer*. A painstakingly interred cache of them was found in 2018 at the Saqqara necropolis.

159 "Mummies": literally, "wrapped bones, remains." The English word derives, of course, from Arabic *mūmiyā*; but ʿAbd al-Laṭīf only ever uses that term to mean the substance used in embalming, not the embalmed corpses themselves.

160 These fibers protect the immature leaf of the date palm.

161 Recent excavations at the animal necropolis at Saqqara have continued to reveal mummified animals, including birds and dogs, in their millions.

162 Mummified horses and donkeys are uncommon but not unknown.

163 Regarding the name "albino lizard," there is an old belief that the (innocent) gecko is responsible for the sort of localized albinism called leucoderma or vitiligo. Al-Damīrī, for example, says that if a gecko finds table salt in a house, it will wallow in it; eating the tainted salt causes the discoloration in humans (*Ḥayawān*, 2:500).

164 This is an exaggeration. The largest pyramid in the area appears to have been the Fifth Dynasty pyramid of Neferirkare. With an estimated original height of 239 feet, it would have been a little larger than the pyramid of Menkaure at Giza, but considerably smaller than those of Khufu and Khafre.

165 This might seem, at first sight, to contradict what ʿAbd al-Laṭīf said earlier (in §1.4.57) about the monuments being mentioned in the scriptures. Here, though, he means that pyramids, as such, do not appear in Holy Writ.

166 In the fifth book of his *Treatise on Hygiene*, Galen mentions a dubious etymology for the Greek term for decrepit old age (*pempelos*), deriving it from a phrase meaning "[about to be] sent down," (from *pempein*, to send) sc. to the underworld. The Arabic translation of Galen slyly substitutes "sent into the Pyramids" (al-Baghdādī, *Relation*, 292–93 n. 151). As for the etymology of Arabic *haram*, "pyramid," itself, there are several fanciful ideas but no consensus.

167 The customary English rendering of Galen's title is *Commentary on Airs, Waters, Places.*

168 The quotation is from book 1, chapter 2 of Galen's *Anatomical Procedures* (cf. al-Baghdādī, *Relation*, 294 n. 154).

169 "The Romans": *al-rūm* could equally include the Greeks of Ptolemaic times (which is what it clearly means on its first appearance, in §1.1.10, above).

170 "The mission": Arabic *daʿwah.* Here, in effect, it means that authority *tout court*; but the term also harks back to the Abbasids' revolutionary origins in the second/eighth century. This concluding paragraph is a sweeping, elegant, and beautifully pointed gesture of obeisance to the dedicatee of the book, the Abbasid caliph, for it places him at the apex of a lot of history and geography.

171 "Wind tower": ʿAbd al-Laṭīf uses a Persian-origin term, *bādhāhanj.* The more recent term in Egypt is *malqaf.* The expensive sort were lined with marble and furnished with elaborately carved doors (Goitein, *Mediterranean Society*, 4:65); they were even celebrated in verse (*ibid.*, 4: 365–66 n. 97). The surprisingly cheap downmarket versions may have been similar to the form prevalent in the thirteenth/nineteenth century: a sloping, shed-like structure of plastered wood, placed on the roof, that channeled breezes down into the house via a simple aperture (Lane, *Manners*, 19; illustration, 10).

172 "Drainage channels": probably not drain *pipes* as such, but open vertical channels carrying liquid waste down the external wall, made from a durable, waterproof material such as lime-based cement.

173 At least some parts of the Cairo conurbation were furnished with sewers in the present-day sense. Excavations at Fustat have revealed

sophisticated systems, using underground clay pipes that carried waste water to cesspools or to the Nile (Goitein, *Mediterranean Society*, 4:36 and 4:54).

174 These could contain more than fifty independent dwellings (see §2.2.29, below). Later, Mamluk-period complexes could be enormous: the eighth/fourteenth-century Wikālat Qawṣūn consisted of a shopping center and, above it, flats housing about four thousand people (al-Maqrīzī, *Khiṭaṭ*, 2:93).

175 A *qaysāriyyah*, "bazaar," usually has covered galleries surrounding an open courtyard.

176 The first term, *musannāh*, usually refers to a diversion dam. The precise meaning of the second, *zarbiyyah*, is not given in the dictionaries. As used by al-Maqrīzī, it seems to mean an embankment wall (*Khiṭaṭ*, 2:185 and 2:283) and sometimes, by extension, the land protected by the wall (*ibid.*, 2:186).

177 At the end of the eighth/fourteenth century, there were thirty working bathhouses in Cairo (Goitein, *Mediterranean Society*, 5:96). In ʿAbd al-Laṭīf's time, people tended to go to the bath weekly; bathhouses were important social centers, particularly for women (Goitein, *Mediterranean Society*, 5:96–98).

178 *Mufawwaf*, "striped," probably refers to the Ayyubid/Mamluk fashion for jazzy, zebra-striped masonry using courses of dark and light stone, often called *ablaq*. Such masonry would be used as a dado in a bathhouse.

179 I.e., the stained glass roundels are set into the vaults, domes, etc. to provide illumination.

180 Arabic psychiatric texts prescribe the contemplation of fine decorations in the bathhouse as a remedy for melancholy (cf. Goitein, *Mediterranean Society*, 4:406 n. 183).

181 "Tin": Arabic *raṣāṣ* means both lead ("black *raṣāṣ* ") and tin ("white *raṣāṣ*"). The word was also used for pewter, originally an alloy of the two metals, and that is perhaps what is meant here.

182 "Concoction" in the older, etymological sense of the word, "[digestion by] cooking together"; the Arabic, *nuḍj*, means something like

"cookedness." ʿAbd al-Laṭīf may have been prompted to make this comparison with the digestive system by the old (but inverse) analogy, in which bodily organs are compared with interconnecting vessels; it appears as early as the Hippocratic texts (Hornblower and Spawforth, *Classical Dictionary*, s.v. "experiment").

183 "A physical cause": Arabic *ʿillah ṭabīʿiyyah* might equally be translated, "a natural cause." The Arabic adjective is used to cover both meanings, rather as "natural philosophy" in English used to encompass what we now call physics, chemistry, and biology. Similarly, "a physical property of salt," in the last sentence of the paragraph, might also be translated, "a natural property . . . ."

184 Before rope making was mechanized, its practitioners would work in a long, alley-like space called a "rope walk," walking backwards as they twisted the strands of cord together. Their swivelling motion is a good analogy for the Egyptian style of rowing, similar to the sculling style of Venetian gondoliers.

185 Given the rather nebulous palette of Arabic, "black" in this context probably means "dark brown."

186 The best known of the vinegar-flavored dishes was a stew called *sikbāj* (see section §2.2.13, below, and the Glossary).

187 The rose water, *jullāb* (origin of English "julep"), was presumably sweetened.

188 Sweet-and-savory stews were still in vogue in the 1830s (Lane, *Manners*, 146). They now seem to have disappeared from the cuisine of Cairo (Habiba Al-Sayfi, personal communication).

189 Presumably pumpkins.

190 "To get 'a scent of the fire'": i.e. to be fried very lightly.

191 The spices are "hot" in the sense employed by Graeco-Arab dietetics, which classifies comestibles according to the qualities of the elements (see "humoral temperament" in the Glossary)—i.e., as hot, cold, dry, or moist. Compare the surviving usage, "*hot* chillis, curries," etc., in English today.

192 "Squabs": pigeon squabs may be meant.

193 "Triangular and flask-shaped pastries": Arabic (from Persian) *sambūsak* are the same as the snacks called, in Anglo-Indian, "samosas." The

flask-shaped sort, *qamāqim*, are literally "scent sprinklers"—i.e. they are shaped like bulbous miniature bottles with tapering necks; in English, one might call them "teardrop-shaped."

194 What would be most shocking to most Muslim readers is the fact that the animals in question have not been properly slaughtered.

195 I.e., from latter part of June until mid-September.

196 The land tax was levied, more often in kind than in cash, on cultivated land. When the Nile's rise reached the sixteen-cubit mark at which the tax became payable, the sultan would be rowed in state to the Nilometer (the gauge showing the river's level), which he would ritually scent (al-Maqrīzī, *Khiṭaṭ*, 1:61). Sixteen cubits remained the crucial level into early modern times (Lane, *Manners*, 490–99, including an account of latter-day customs associated with the rise).

197 Down to ʿAbd al-Laṭīf 's day, it was said that if the rise reached seventeen cubits, the extra cubit above the Sultan's Water would generate an extra 100,000 dinars in tax; however, a rise to nineteen cubits—one cubit more than "the maximum of necessity"—would generate 100,000 dinars *less* than would the Sultan's Water (al-Maqrīzī, *Khiṭaṭ*, 1:60).

198 "The Days of Sun-drying," *ayyām al-tashrīq*, are the three days following the Festival of Sacrifice (Lane, *Lexicon*, s.v. *sh-r-q*).

199 All the words under discussion in this paragraph share a triliteral root, *sh-r-q*. They are, in order of appearance: *sharraqa*, to dry (transitive and intransitive) in the sun; *sharaqa*, to rise (the sun); *tashrīq*, sun-drying (a noun derived from *sharraqa*); *shariqa*, to gag or choke.

200 "The south": more accurately, the south-east.

201 So-called "broken" plurals are a distinctive feature of Arabic; they come in dozens of patterns. Perhaps the nearest things in English are irregular verb paradigms in which the root consonants stay the same while the other letters change (e.g. **wr**i**t**e–**wr**o**t**e–**wr**i**tt**en). As for words derived from the root *sh-r-q*, they are still current in Egypt: e.g., when the land is parched, it is said to be *sharqānah* (Habiba Al-Sayfi, personal communication).

202 This is the usual way to present an Arabic verb paradigm. *Nāla-yanūlu-nawlan*, for example, means literally, "he gave—he gives—a giving."

203 The (somewhat labored) point here is that *raʿy* and *riʿy* are from the same root, but while the first has the vowel *a*, the second has *i*; similarly, *nawl* (with an *a*) and *nīl* (with an *i*) are also from the same root. Despite all these musings, Yāqūt (*Muʿjam*, s.v. "al-Nīl") is almost certainly right in saying that the river's name is an arabicization of the Latin/Greek "Nilus." The latter, in the form "Neilos," is known as far back as Hesiod's time, ca. 700 BC (Hornblower and Spawforth, *Classical Dictionary*, s.v. "Nile").

204 I.e., from 1/622 to 597/1200–1 or 598/1201–2.

205 The potentially dire consequences of that "insufficiency" of 356/967 seem to have been contained by the able slave ruler of Egypt, Kāfūr.

206 A pair of Arabic jingles incorporated some important Nile lore. Using the standard transliterations of the first two Coptic months mentioned here, they go, roughly, "In the month of Epep,/ The Nile goes up with lumbering step," and, "If in Mesōrē no rise should appear,/ Then look for none until the following year" (al-Maqrīzī, *Khiṭaṭ*, 1:273).

207 "Algal" refers to the green algae still to be found seasonally in the waters of the Nile.

208 "To combine": perhaps, "to form a new elemental mixture." The equivalent in terms of later science might be, "to form a new chemical compound."

209 Until 1959, archbishops of Ethiopia were still supplied by the Coptic Orthodox pope in Alexandria. The king of Abyssinia in ʿAbd al-Laṭīf's time was Gebre Mesqel Lalibela (r. 1181–1221).

210 "The stars": Sacy (al-Baghdādī, *Relation*, 335) and, following him, Zand and Videan (al-Baghdādī, *Eastern Key*, 211) say "the air." That is not only less literal, but it also misses the point—that the supposed influence comes from heavenly bodies.

211 Al-Maqrīzī gives more detail. The mud must have had Nile water flowing over it; exactly sixteen dirhams' weight is placed in a covered

pot on the eve of the Coptic feast of Mīkā'īl (St Michael the Archangel, whose feast is celebrated on the twelfth of every month—in this case, the night of 11–12 Paōne is meant). In the morning, the increase in weight is measured, using carob seeds as the unit: the number of seeds predicts the number of cubits of the Nile's coming rise (al-Maqrīzī, *Khiṭaṭ*, 1:68). An alternative was to perform the operation with dough kneaded with Nile water. The custom was still widespread in early modern times (Lane, *Manners*, 489–90).

212 There were several other such methods. One involved taking the Hijri date that coincided with the first day of the Coptic month of Parmoute, adding it to 85, and dividing the total by six: the result predicted the rise in cubits for that year (al-Maqrīzī, *Khiṭaṭ*, 1:68). E.g., if 1 Parmoute fell on 5 Rajab, (85 + 5) ÷ 6 = 15, so the expected rise would be fifteen cubits. Rustic Nilologists said that you should see how far the hippos graze when they come out of the river: the water would rise to that point (al-Maqrīzī, *Khiṭaṭ*, 1:67).

213 By "the quantity of water in it," 'Abd al-Laṭīf means the quantity in the bottom of the Nilometer pit *before* the season of the rise.

214 The "basin," Arabic *birkah* (cf., in English, big geographical features like the Amazon Basin), may be a misty representation of Lake Victoria.

215 *Al-aḥkām al-nujūmiyyah*, "astral decrees," is a usual term for astrology/astromancy.

216 The cosmically holistic thinking behind this goes: (a) heavenly bodies and constellations have individual temperaments, just as living creatures do; (b) places, as well as people, have "ascendant stars" (i.e., they are all subject to the influence or governance of heavenly bodies); (c) by working out the temperaments of all the heavenly bodies concerned, at the times of historic high and low rises, recurrent patterns will emerge; (d) these patterns can suggest when future problems with the Nile's rise might occur. The "experimental model" is literally an "experimental picture."

217 Astrological means of predicting the Nile's rises did exist. Al-Maqrīzī quotes two authorities on how to make forecasts by observing Venus, Mercury, and the Moon; one of these authorities, however, was

following Ptolemy, while the other was the third/ninth-century Abū Maʿshar (*Khiṭaṭ*, 1:68). ʿAbd al-Laṭīf's point is that no one has bothered to add any new data to this antiquated body of astrological lore.

218 Ṭūlūnid rule finally ended in 292/905.

219 The "disturbances" may allude to the fact that soon after this date, in 301/913, the burgeoning Fatimid dynasty launched a series of damaging but (as yet) unsuccessful assaults on Egypt from their base in present-day Tunisia.

220 After the death in 595/1198 of Saladin's son al-Malik al-ʿAzīz, ruler of Egypt, his brother al-Malik al-Afḍal tried to seize control of the country. He was opposed and defeated by his paternal uncle, al-Malik al-ʿĀdil, who was proclaimed ruler of both Egypt and Syria in 596/1200 (cf. al-Maqrīzī, *Khiṭaṭ*, 2:235).

221 At face value, the sentence that opens this chapter goes, "And then the year seven entered, preying upon the reasons for life." But it is charged with secondary meanings: there are shades of "snapping the [spinal] cords of life," "cutting short the lengths of lives," "severing the connections between lives," and "seizing livelihoods." Most striking, though, is the fact that "seven," *sabʿ*, short for "[59]7," is an alternative vocalization for *sabuʿ*, "beast of prey." Seven is thus, in one literal sense, the number of the beast. The English translation uses another monstrous wordplay: the year "seven" is the year that "pre-dates"—both seizes prey and brings forward the date of death.

222 "They dispersed . . . like the people of Sabā" is a proverbial phrase for a cataclysmic diaspora. The story of Sabā/Sabaʾ, as told in the Qurʾan, also provides the scriptural quote here (Q Sabaʾ 34:19).

223 I.e., in the latter part of March.

224 By "the paupers," *al-fuqarāʾ* (singular *al-faqīr*), ʿAbd al-Laṭīf designates not just poor people in general, but a fairly distinct social group. In Egypt at this time, the term probably means those with neither property nor professions (cf. *Encyclopaedia of Islam*, s.v. "Faḳīr"). Two centuries later, al-Maqrīzī identified seven major social groups in Egypt, the last of which comprised the paupers, the indigent, and beggars ("Famines," 72).

225 "The prefect" is *al-wālī* in the Arabic. Before, in a provincial setting, the word has been translated as "governor." In Cairo, it almost certainly means the same as *ṣāḥib al-shurṭah*, "chief of police" (cf. Goitein, *Mediterranean Society*, 2:368).

226 *Qafaṣ* can mean "[rib]cage" (and, not inconceivably here, "crown of lamb"). However, the context suggests that the whole skeleton is intended, hence the less specific "lattice." The term may refer to a method of carving that leaves a roasted animal's skeleton intact and articulated, perhaps as a centerpiece for a banquet.

227 In book 1 of his *Anatomical Procedures*, Galen does however say that he had been able to study the skeleton of a highwayman, left on a gibbet and pecked clean by birds (cf. al-Baghdādī, *Relation*, 382–83 n. 8).

228 *Al-nās*, "people," here, as often (still) in Arabic, means "['decent'] people" with at least a modicum of money and property, as opposed to the paupers (on whom see n. 224, above).

229 "The novel . . . experience": from at least as early as the second/ninth century, there had been an appetite among the cultivated literate milieu for low-life doings (cf. *Encyclopaedia of Islam*, s.v. "Sāsān, Banū"). Rarely can the appetite have been indulged as literally as described here.

230 Bread was, and is, used to scoop up and eat many cooked dishes; if meat was served at all, helpings were usually very small. To eat a meal without bread, particularly one featuring large quantities of meat, was a rare indulgence.

231 "Scraps of bread": Arabic *kisar*, "fragments," could also mean "small change" (cf. the colloquial use of English "bits" for small coins). Then again, al-Maqrīzī says that, in Alexandria, he once saw bits of bread actually being used as "cash" to buy inexpensive provisions (cf. al-Baghdādī, *Relation*, 387 n. 22).

232 Q Ṣāffāt 37:61. The quotation is appropriate to almsgiving but, bearing in mind the coming scene, the man's words are more sinister.

233 The rhymed Arabic phrase goes, more literally, "thinking the best [of the man] overcame him, and the power of covetousness drew him on."

234 I.e., and therefore not be worth eating.

235 The absence or removal of the veil can be a powerful statement of protest against an injustice. Here, though, it may just show that she was in an almighty hurry.

236 The Arabic expression says that he got away "by a sip of the chin"; this apparently comes to mean "with the last bit of his soul in his mouth," i.e. as the soul is on its way out (al-Zabīdī, *Tāj*, s.v. *j-r-ʿ*). It might be thought of as a combination of a close shave, the skin of the teeth, the nick of time, the heart in the mouth, and the last gasp.

237 The text has the alternative name, "the Mosque of Miṣr." Originally built in the first/seventh century, it is still extant.

238 "Those who led the most cloistered lives": *arbāb al-zawāyā*, literally, "people who were [customarily] in corners/in mosque study groups/in monks' cells/in oratories." The phrase could refer to actual religious recluses, but probably has a more general sense, perhaps even that of "the housebound."

239 Sacy (al-Baghdādī, *Relation*, 369) and, following him, Zand and Videan (al-Baghdādī, *Eastern Key*, 239) take the "scourge" to refer to cannibalism in general. Looking at ʿAbd al-Laṭīf's paragraph breaks, I see it as applying specifically to grave robbing, and thus interpolate "newly interred" later in the sentence.

240 Mountain passes are hardly common in Egypt, and certainly not on the routes to Faiyum and Alexandria. But the expression is a proverbial one originating in Q Ḥajj 22:27, which says that pilgrims will come to Mecca "from every deep/far-penetrating mountain pass," i.e. from every remote spot on Earth.

241 This and a later passage (§2.3.9, below) suggest that ʿAbd al-Laṭīf interviewed officials or looked at records. By "the public place of ablution," Arabic *mīḍaʾah*, a general "place for obsequies" may be intended. The comparable *fisqiyyat al-mawtā*, literally "the water tank of the dead," is said to mean, simply, a cemetery (Dozy, *Supplément*, s.v. *f-s-q*).

242 "A token number": the Arabic phrase means, literally, "[just enough] for discharging an oath." The idea is that when you say, e.g., "If X happens, I swear I'll eat my hat," and then X *does* happen, you can get

away with pulling the smallest token bit of straw off your second-best panama and nibbling at that. (Cf. al-Zabīdī, *Tāj*, s.v. *ḥ-l-l.*)

243 "A living, breathing soul": the Arabic phrase says, "a blower on coals"—perhaps akin to someone who, in the words of the old English song, can "keep the Home-fires burning."

244 Q Anbiyā' 21:15. The verse describes divine punishment inflicted on evildoers.

245 A pit loom is designed so that the warps are stretched not far above the ground, while the weaver sits at ground level with his feet operating the pedals of the loom in a sunken pit.

246 Q Yā Sīn 36:29. Once more, the verse describes the divine punishment of wrongdoers.

247 Wolves and hyenas appear together in poetry, the first as a scourge of the living, the second as a bane of the dead (cf. Lane, *Lexicon*, s.v. *ḍ-b-ʿ*). The word translated as "wolves," *dhi'āb*, covers both wolves and jackals; as it happens, the Egyptian sort (*Canis anthus lupaster*), formerly considered to be jackals, have lately been reclassified wolves. ʿAbd al-Laṭīf's informant may have been a manager overseeing the cultivation of an estate allotted to one of the ruling elite.

248 "All the other waterways": Sacy (al-Baghdādī, *Relation*, 371–72) and Zand and Videan (al-Baghdādī, *Eastern Key*, 245) take it as "all the banks [of the waterways]." Arabic *shuṭūṭ* has both senses.

249 The simile comes at the end of the most famous of all pre-Islamic odes, in a description of the aftermath of a flood: "And at even the drowned beasts lay where the torrent had borne them, dead,/ high up on the valley sides, like earth-stained roots of squills." (Lyall's slightly free translation, quoted in Irwin, *Night*, 15; cf. Imru' al-Qays, *Dīwān*, 122).

250 As above (§2.2.1 and n. 222), the quotation is from Q Saba' 34:19.

251 The sale by or to Muslims of their freeborn coreligionists is prohibited by Islam, and would thus incur divine wrath. The repetition in "common practice . . . common law" reflects a small but intentional visual pun in the Arabic script, where two words repeat the same graphic form, but with different letter dots.

252 “Despite all these portents . . . devoted to the idols of their lusts”: “devoted to the idols” is an allusion to Q A‘rāf 7:138 and the story of the Golden Calf (see above, §1.4.55 and n. 144). The allusion is itself nicely signalled by the word *āyāt*, which means both “portents” and “verses,” i.e. of the Qur’an; the portents are, of course, the suitably apocalyptic ones of drought, famine, pestilence, and cannibalism, which ‘Abd al-Laṭīf believes might be expected to inspire piety rather than lust. The dangers of ignoring *āyāt* are themselves mentioned in Q A‘rāf 7:146–7.

253 As above (n. 231), *kisar*, “scraps of bread,” could also mean “small change.”

254 A marginal note explains “folds” as “animal pens.”

255 Q Aḥqāf 46:25. The verse describes the aftermath of the destruction of the ancient ‘Ādite people of Arabia, who ignored prophetic warnings about their impiety.

256 In more normal times, a pair of oxen is on record as being bought for fifteen dinars (Goitein, *Mediterranean Society*, 4:263).

257 “Due amount . . . due time”: water from the Nile flood was channeled over as wide an area as possible; individual farms and plots received fixed amounts, allotted by time. The whole complex operation needed people to open and close floodgates and dykes, and to build bunds to retain water in fields. Detail on irrigation practices is given by al-Maqrīzī (*Khiṭaṭ*, 1:61).

258 A marginal note here says, “‘Strengthenings,’ *taqāwin*, the plural of *taqwiyyah*, are the grain that is sown.” More precisely, *taqāwin* are supplies of seed advanced for the following season, when none is left because it has all been paid in tax (*Encyclopaedia of Islam*, s.v. “Kharādj”).

259 A marginal note here says, “The Egyptian *irdabb* is the equivalent of the *kārah* in Baghdad; *fūl* are broad beans.” An *irdabb* of wheat was roughly what a “middle-class” household might consume in a month (Goitein, *Mediterranean Society*, 4:235). According to al-Maqrīzī (“Famines,” 31), its price went as high as eight dinars. Under more normal circumstances, the ideal price was one dinar (Goitein, *Mediterranean Society*, 4:244).

260 "A natural temperament": a medical metaphor for "the normal state of affairs."

261 "Poultry breeders" translates a problematic word, *qammāṭīn*. Al-Zabīdī (*Tāj*, s.v. *q-m-ṭ*) has the verbal noun *qimāṭ* as a technical term for "the mating of birds," hence my suggestion. Today, the word seems unknown in any Cairene context to do with birds (Habiba Al-Sayfi, personal communication).

262 Normal egg prices are hard to ascertain, but they were relatively cheap: 1½ dirhams would buy "a huge amount" (Goitein, *Mediterranean Society*, 4:250). A full-sized chicken might usually cost two dirhams (*ibid.*, 4:250).

263 Presumably, the sense is that landlords would sell off the timbers of properties for which they could find no tenants.

264 A phrase from Q Baqarah 2:259 and Q Ḥajj 22:45. The usual explanation is that the roofs have collapsed first, then the walls have fallen in on top of the debris from the roofs (e.g. Lane, *Lexicon*, s.v. *ʿ-r-sh*).

265 "City center": *qaṣabat al-madīnah*. Cairo's *qaṣabah* (cf. the anglicized "kasbah") was considered to extend from Bab Zuwaylah northward to Bāb al-Futūḥ (al-Maqrīzī, *Khiṭaṭ*, 1: 373 and 1:376).

266 The population of the Cairo conurbation at this time has been estimated at 60,000 (Shatzmiller, *Labour in the Medieval Islamic World*, 57–60); the seemingly high figure of 111,000 must be due to the huge number of migrants who had fled to the city because of famine. The provision of shrouds for the deceased poor was a pious act of charity; al-Maqrīzī puts the number donated by the sultan, al-ʿĀdil, during the famine and pestilence, at 220,000 "in [only] a short period" (al-Maqrīzī, *Khiṭaṭ*, 2:235; "Famines," 31). Some recipients were clearly put on record; the Dīwān in which their names appeared may have been *dīwān al-māl*, the finance "ministry," which included a department dealing with alms disbursed by the Ayyubid court (cf. *Encyclopaedia of Islam*, s.v. "Dīwān," especially 2:329). On "the place of ablution," see n. 241, above.

267 "The two cities": Cairo and Old Fustat.

268 I.e., each team completed one job, but died before they could go on to the next one.

269 The officer presumably had an *iqṭāʿ*. At this period, the state retained control of much land, but assigned to high-ranking officers certain revenues from specific holdings, known as *iqṭāʿāt*. It is not entirely clear whom "We" refers to here. It could of course be ʿAbd al-Laṭīf, who often refers to himself in the plural; but I suspect it is his anonymous informant who mentioned undertaking an agricultural project a little earlier (in §2.2.23, above)—hence my presenting these lines as direct speech.

270 That is, for seven hundred people who had died that day or during the preceding night. Funeral prayers, conducted in the presence of the deceased, often in a mosque, are performed just before burial. Such a mortality rate reveals the severity of the epidemic: even at the height of the first wave of the notorious "Black Death" in 1348, the maximum figure for daily deaths in Alexandria was only a little over one thousand (Ibn Baṭṭūṭa, *Travels*, 4:920).

271 I.e., fourteen *successive* heirs: they died one after another, each leaving the property to the next in a macabre version of pass-the-parcel.

272 The slightly gnomic phrase may imply, "a settling of the score in [the demographic] nature [of the region]," rather than some more metaphorical "natural settling of the score."

273 For the stories of the three other physicians, see §2.2.9, above. Earlier in the sentence, the physician might be "an elderly Jewish physician from Miṣr." However, many Jewish physicians were also community leaders—famously, ʿAbd al-Laṭīf 's acquaintance Moses Maimonides (cf. Goitein, *Mediterranean Society*, 2: 243–45). It thus seems best here to call this physician an "elder," which reflects the ambiguity of age and eminence implicit in the Arabic word "shaykh."

274 The epicenter seems to have been somewhere in southwest Syria; the quake was cataclysmic enough to shake sense into the parties of the ongoing Crusader wars and force them into a temporary truce (cf. *Encyclopaedia of Islam*, s.v. "Zalzala"). Huge (but almost certainly exaggerated) numbers of victims are claimed by some contemporary sources—30,000 dead in Nābulus alone, for example (al-Baghdādī, *Riḥlat ʿAbd al-Laṭīf*, 11). The quake also seems to have triggered a

tsunami in the Mediterranean, as is shown by the coming mention of ships and fishes cast on dry land.

275 "And the wave crests rose up like great mountains," an addition from the margin, alludes to Q Shuʿarāʾ 26:63, which describes the parting of the sea for Moses.

276 The Last Hour marks the end of the world; it is followed by the Resurrection and the Day of Judgement. Q Zalzalah ("The Earthquake") 99:1–2 refers to the apocalyptic tremor.

277 An hour in the strict sense sounds like exaggeration—unless the apparently singular "shockwave" was in fact a series of tremors that only seemed continuous. That said, the duration of the incident does seem to have been extraordinarily long, as the second letter will reveal.

278 *Sūrat al-kahf*, the eighteenth chapter of the Qur'an, has 110 verses and takes about twenty minutes to recite aloud, swiftly. One might, however, whisper it to oneself in half that time, but a ten-minute tremor still seems exceptionally long.

279 The great lead-covered dome and adjoining parts of the Umayyad Mosque were likened to an eagle: the dome itself was seen as the bird's head, the façade (overlooking the courtyard) below it as the breast, and the arcades bordering the courtyard on either side as the wings (Ibn Jubayr, *Riḥlah*, 237–38).

280 "The Muslim towns": i.e. as opposed to those of the Crusaders. *Bilād*, here "towns," can also mean settlements/villages/cities, and/or the regions dependent on them, and by extension "country" in its different English senses.

281 "The children" could equally be "the son" (Arabic *walad*, like English "offspring," can refer to both singular and plural). At this time, Ṣafad was held as an *iqṭāʿ* (see n. 269, above) by a high Ayyubid officer (*Encyclopaedia of Islam*, s.v. "Ṣafad").

282 More succinctly, the villages had been wiped off the map.

283 The rhubarb is *Rheum ribes*, or "Syrian rhubarb," which had various medicinal uses.

284 The quotation is from Q Āl ʿImrān 3:173. It is often recited, sometimes many times in succession, in times of fear, disaster, and so on.

285 ʿAbd al-Laṭīf probably means Galen's *Anatomical Procedures.*

286 Among ʿAbd al-Laṭīf's many medical works, none of the known titles suggests that he got round to fulfilling this specific wish (al-Baghdādī, *Kitāb al-Ifādah* (1403/1983), 160–65; Martini Bonadeo, *Philosophical Journey*, 198–206); he may, however, have addressed the question in his lost (but probably wide-ranging) work on anatomy, *Kitāb al-Kifāyah fī l-tashrīḥ* (al-Baghdādī, *Kitāb al-Ifādah* (1403/1983), 162). The lower jawbone or mandible does in fact consist of two segments at the fetal stage, but these fuse in the first year after birth, leaving a faint ridge in the center.

287 ʿAbd al-Laṭīf is referring to the five sacral vertebrae at the lower end of the spine, plus the first segment of the coccyx (which resembles the lowest sacral vertebra in form). The sacral vertebrae fuse in adulthood to form the sacrum; the unfused examples ʿAbd al-Laṭīf found must have belonged to adolescents or children.

288 There are echoes of early Arabic poetry here. E.g. al-Khansāʾ (d. ca. 23/643–44) begins a lament for her brother by asking, "A mote in your eye, dust blown on the wind? / Or a place deserted, its people gone?" (Quoted in Irwin, *Night*, 25).

289 Regarding colors, precise shades of meaning are always hard to translate. Could the baby have been a "strawberry blond"?

290 Mules are normally infertile, but females have been known very occasionally to give birth. Al-Damīrī, who assiduously collected references to animals, mentions only one such case, in 444/1052–53 (*Ḥayawān*, 1:456). From early times, such births were considered to be portents of catastrophe. Herodotus (*Histories*, 7:57), for example, mentions a mule giving birth as heralding the Persian invasion of Greece.

291 The lamb might have been a kid; the Arabic word covers both. In newborn humans, such milk is traditionally known as "witch's milk."

292 "Gentile" translates *ummī*, a much-discussed word often glossed as "illiterate." "Gentile" *may* be preferable: in other words, Muḥammad, before he received the Qurʾan, came from a community—Arabic *ummah*, Latin *gens* (whence "gentile")—who, unlike the Jews and the Christians, did not have a scripture.

Glossary of Names and Terms

Abbasids dynasty of caliphs, descended from the Prophet Muḥammad's paternal uncle al-ʿAbbās ibn ʿAbd al-Muṭṭalib. They came to power in the middle of the second/eighth century and founded Baghdad soon after. From there they ruled—latterly in theory more than in reality—until the Mongols' destruction of the city in 656/1258.

ʿAbd Allāh ibn Ṭāhir (d. 230/844) a member of a virtually independent dynasty in Khurasan, he governed Egypt on behalf of al-Maʾmūn (q.v.) from 211/826–27 onwards.

Abū Ḥanīfah al-Dīnawarī see *al-Dīnawarī, Abū Ḥanīfah.*

Abusir also Abu Sir, properly Būṣīr and, in full, Būṣīr al-Sidr (to distinguish it from other sites of the same name), a place in the province of Giza (q.v.). The name derives ultimately from that of the god Osiris.

Abyssinia the alternative name for Ethiopia.

Acre (Ar. ʿAkkah) a town on the coast of Palestine, northeast of present-day Haifa. At the time of the 598/1202 earthquake, it was in Crusader hands.

agama lizard *Agama stellio.*

Agathodaimon (Ar. Aghādhīmūn) in full, Agathos Daimon, or "good god/destiny," a deity of good fortune popular as a guardian of houses in Greek-ruled Egypt.

al-Akhfash the surname, or rather nickname, of a number of grammarians and philologists (meaning "weak-sighted"; the attribute seems to have been an occupational hazard). The dates of the three most famous bearers of the name span the second/eighth to fourth/tenth centuries.

Akhlāṭ alternatively Khilāṭ, a major city of Armenia at the western end of Lake Van.

Alexander of Aphrodisias Peripatetic philosopher known for his commentaries on Aristotle, fl. ca. AD 200. There seems to be no work of history, as such, among the titles usually ascribed to him.

Alexandria (Ar. al-Iskandariyyah) city on the Mediterranean coast of Egypt, located at the westernmost corner of the Nile Delta. It was founded in 331 BC by Alexander III ("the Great") of Macedon.

ʿAlī ibn Riḍwān (d. ca. 453/1061) Egyptian physician and medical writer, a close follower of Galen (q.v.).

ʿAmr ibn al-ʿĀṣ (d. ca. 42/663) a contemporary of the Prophet Muḥammad and fellow member of the tribe of Quraysh. He conquered Egypt for the Muslims between 19/640 and 21/642, and governed it (though not continuously) up to his death at an advanced age.

Anatolius in the text, "Nīṭwālīs," which Silvestre de Sacy believed to be a deformation of the name of a little-known writer on veterinary matters, already corrupted in one Greek source to *Νεπουάλιο[ς]* (Nepualio[s]) (al-Baghdādī, *Relation*, 165 n. 46). A small extra deformation would, indeed, produce *Νετουάλιο[ς]* (Netualio[s]), almost identical to ʿAbd al-Laṭīf's rendering. The Anatolius in question, apparently of the fourth century AD (Hornblower and Spawforth, *Classical Dictionary*, s.v. "veterinary medicine"), might be the same as the fourth-century Anatolius of Berytus (Beirut), a writer on agriculture whose work appeared in Arabic (*Encyclopaedia of Islam*, s.v. "Filāḥa").

Ancient Miṣr an alternative name for Memphis (q.v.).

aqāqiyā the juice of the leaves and fruit of the *qaraẓ* (q.v.) tree.

Aristotle (d. 322 BC) Greek philosopher and scientist. A work on plants was attributed to him. The book was lost, but not before Nicolaus of Damascus (q.v.) had produced a reworked version in the first century BC. This reworking was eventually translated into Arabic.

Ashʿab (d. ca. 154/771) an inhabitant of Medina, famous for his wit and his greed.

al-Aṣmaʿī (d. ca. 213/828) philologist and collector of anecdotes from Basra, Iraq. He was much in demand at the Abbasid court in Baghdad.

Ashqelon (Ar. ʿAsqalān) also spelled Ashkelon, a coastal town northeast of Gaza.

Aswan (Ar. Uswān) a town on the Nile in the far south of Upper Egypt.

ath'ab identified by the dictionaries as a kind of fig tree that grows in wadis. Al-Dīnawarī (q.v.) said that it bears white figs, and that the biggest specimens are large enough to shade "thousands" of people (al-Zabīdī, *Tāj*, s.v. *th-ʾ-b*). Allowing for doubts about al-Dīnawarī's accuracy (§1.2.4), this suggests that it is a name for the aptly termed *Ficus vasta*.

ʿAyn Shams ancient Ōn, Greek Heliopolis, now a northern part of the Cairo conurbation. Coptic Christian tradition said that the water which irrigated the famous balsam (q.v.) garden came from the same source in which Mary washed Jesus's clothes during the Holy Family's flight to Egypt. With the exception of the one obelisk that still stands, most of the remains described by ʿAbd al-Laṭīf have disappeared or been overlaid by suburban sprawl.

Ayyubids a dynasty of Kurdish origin, founded by Saladin (q.v.), that ruled large parts of the Middle East in the sixth and seventh/twelfth and thirteenth centuries.

ʿaẓāʾ lizards if the term refers to a particular species, its scientific name is hard to determine. The lexica assert that its urine is proverbially hard to find.

Baalbek (Ar. Baʿlabakk), a town in present-day Lebanon on the edge of the Bekaa (Biqāʿ) Valley. The remains of the fortifications ruined by the 598/1202 earthquake have since been removed, but they incorporated the extant structures of the two great first- to second-century AD Syro-Hellenistic temples for which the place is still famous.

Bāb Jayrūn a gate of Damascus dating from the third century AD. According to Arabic tradition, it is named for the (legendary) builder of the city, Jayrūn ibn Saʿd ibn ʿĀd.

Babylon the ruins of the ancient city lie about fifty miles south of Baghdad. An important place since early in the second millennium BC, it was at its most splendid under the Neo-Babylonian empire in the sixth century BC, but continued to flourish for several centuries thereafter.

balsam (Ar. *balasān*) the Egyptian balsam probably came from a cultivated version of *Commiphora gileadensis*, although this is not certain: the mystique that surrounded it was cultivated as carefully as the plant itself. In the early ninth/fifteenth century, al-Maqrīzī noted that balsam oil was used in the public hospital, especially in the treatment of rheumatism, and that the Copts would add a little to their baptismal water (al-Baghdādī, *Relation*, 91 n. 49).

Bāniyās a town on the coast of Syria, about thirty miles south of Latakia (al-Lādhiqiyyah). Despite its inclusion by ʿAbd al-Laṭīf among the Muslim towns, it was held in his day by the Crusaders.

Bārīn a small town a day's journey from Ḥamāh (q.v.), its castle was still in ruins more than a century later (Abū l-Fidāʾ, *Kitāb Taqwīm al-buldān*, 259).

Barqah the old name of the town of al-Marj in northeastern Libya, and of the adjacent coastal strip and inland plateau that together make up the region of Cyrenaica; Benghazi is now the largest settlement of the region. At the time of which ʿAbd al-Laṭīf speaks, Barqah had long been known as a self-contained province.

bashām probably (but not certainly) the wild *Commiphora gileadensis*. ʿAbd al-Laṭīf's contemporary, Yāqūt, was told by an informant who had seen both plants that the Egyptian balsam (q.v.) was "precisely the same as the *bashām* bush, but we have never known anyone to extract oil from the latter" (Yāqūt, *Muʿjam*, s.v. "al-Maṭariyyah").

Bayt Jinn Sacy (al-Baghdādī, *Relation*, 446 n. 47) mentions three settlements called Bayt Jann (probably a better spelling). Of these, the one situated a little west of Ṣafad (q.v.) seems the most likely to be that mentioned in our text.

Bedouin Arabs used to translate the single word *al-ʿarab*. The meaning of this word has proved slippery over the millennia (see Mackintosh-Smith, *Arabs*, *passim*); ʿAbd al-Laṭīf uses it in the sense of tribal and/or nomadic groups of the *bādiyah*, the uncultivated lands, whence comes the plural adjective *badawiyyīn*, giving "Bedouin."

Biʾr al-Balsam the name of a water source in the neighborhood of the Dead Sea.

biṭṭīkh see *melon*.

black cubit see *cubit*.

black poppy see *opium*.

Bukhtī as applied to a camel, a crossbreed born from the union of a two-humped Bactrian sire with an Arabian one-humped dam.

Bustān al-Qiṭʿah an unidentified garden in Alexandria (q.v.).

Cairo (Ar. al-Qāhirah, "The Victorious") the capital city of Egypt, founded after the Fatimid takeover of the country (358/969) on behalf of al-Muʿizz (q.v.). Situated a little to the north of the old Islamic capital, Fustat (q.v.), it has given its name to the entire conurbation. ʿAbd al-Laṭīf always uses it in its proper sense, to denote the Fatimid "new" town.

the Cataracts five shallow, rocky, and unnavigable stretches of the Nile, situated between Aswan (q.v.) and Atbara, far to the south in the Sudan. The First and Second Cataracts are now submerged in Lake Nasser, formed by the Aswan High Dam.

Children of Israel a Qurʾanic term most often used of the Jews in the time of Moses.

the Citadel the great Ayyubid fortress built, on a spur of the al-Muqaṭṭam range, for Saladin by the emir Qarāqūsh (qq.v.). A date of 579/1183–84 is attested for some of the work. The celebrated well, often called "the Well of Joseph" (supposedly from Saladin's given name, Ar. Yūsuf) or "the Spiral Well," is still extant. ʿAbd al-Laṭīf writes correctly of *two* well shafts: there is an upper one for access, furnished with a spiral ramp, and a lower one hewn down to the water. As al-Maqrīzī explains (*Khiṭaṭ*, 2:204), the water was drawn up by two teams of oxen working two sets of gears, one partway down and one at the well head.

Clime (Ar. *iqlīm*) Greek geographers divided what they saw as the inhabited world into seven "climes": regional bands parallel with and beginning at the Equator, numbered from south to north. On the world map described in *Kitāb Nuzhat al-mushtāq* by al-Idrīsī, the major geographer of the generation before ʿAbd al-Laṭīf, the division between the First and Second Climes runs, roughly, along the modern border between Egypt and the Sudan.

Copts (Ar. Qibṭ, Aqbāṭ), native Egyptian Christians; also used in Arabic for ancient Egyptians in general. Etymologically, Copts are "Gypts"; the name "Egypt" derives, in turn, from ancient Egyptian Ha-Ka-Ptah, or "the Sanctuary of Ptah," a name of Memphis (q.v.).

costus *Saussurea costus*. The fragrant roots of the plant, which grows in the Himalayan foothills, have been widely exported since ancient times.

cubit the length of a cubit has always varied according to time, place, and what is being measured. In Egypt, a "cubit of the hand" or "legal cubit" of 19.61 inches was long in use. The cubits on the extant Nilometer (q.v.), however, average 21.28 inches (*Encyclopaedia of Islam*, s.v. "Dhirāʿ"); this is the "black cubit," so called (supposedly) from its having been measured from the forearm of a well-built black bodyguard of the second/eighth-century caliph Hārūn al-Rashīd (al-Maqrīzī, *Khiṭaṭ*, 1:59). As a rule, 20 inches is a round figure to keep in mind. Cubits (of whatever sort) were subdivided into 24 finger-breadths.

cupper cupping is a medical treatment which involves placing a cup-shaped receptacle on the skin and creating a partial vacuum inside it, in order to suck the tissue outwards. Sometimes an incision is also made in the skin, so that blood will be drawn out.

ḍaghābīs see *melon*.

Damietta (Ar. Dimyāṭ) a city at the easternmost mouth of the Nile Delta.

Damīrah the name of two neighboring villages near Damietta (q.v.).

Damūh perhaps "Dammūh" (the spelling has never been decided). The Jewish "monastery" here was a synagogue, apparently a genuinely ancient one associated with Memphis, and long the focus of an annual visitation (Goitein, *Mediterranean Society*, 3:211 and 5:20–24). According to al-Maqrīzī, it was the most revered place of worship for Jews in Egypt; the building extant in al-Maqrīzī's time supposedly dated to about AD 110, and its attractions included an ancient tree said to have grown from a staff planted in the ground by Moses (*Khiṭaṭ*, 2:464–65). ʿAbd al-Laṭīf's "monastery" may result from a belief among the Copts that they had sold a monastery there to the Jews (al-Maqrīzī, *Khiṭaṭ*, 2: 504).

dand plants of the genus *Croton*. The three species ʿAbd al-Laṭīf had in mind were probably Ṣīnī, Shiḥrī and Hindī, i.e. Chinese, South

Arabian, and Indian (cf. Dozy, *Supplément*, s.v. *d-n-d*; Shiḥrī is an emendation for Dozy's *shajarī*). Some *Crotons* are powerful and poisonous purgatives.

dillīnus from the Greek *telline*, a small bivalve shellfish; cf. the family Tellinidae, genus *Tellina*, and English "tellin."

dinar the standard gold coin, for many centuries, of much of the Islamic world. Its official weight was about 0.137 troy ounces.

al-Dīnawarī, Abū Ḥanīfah third/ninth-century scholar of Iranian origin. Botany was only one of his many fields of study. His *Kitāb al-Nabāt* (*Book of Plants*) survives in part.

Dioscorides (d. AD 90) scientist from Cilicia, Asia Minor. The definitive Arabic translation of his famous work, *De Materia Medica*, was made in Baghdad in the third/ninth century.

dirham the standard silver coin, for many centuries, of much of the Islamic world. Its weight varied between 0.080 and 0.096 troy ounces. Two grades of dirham were known, "true" high-silver *nuqrah* dirhams, and low-silver (but actually more common) *waraq* dirhams. The exchange rate of the former—which we can assume ʿAbd al-Laṭīf always has in mind—against the gold dinar (q.v.) was notionally 13⅓:1, that of the latter 40:1. In practice, the rates fluctuated (cf. Goitein, *Mediterranean Society*,1:390).

Dīwān originally simply a register, the term expanded to mean the place where the register was kept, and by extension a government department or ministry.

dullāʿ see *melon*.

emir (Ar. *amīr*) a commander or, in later usage, prince. Under the Ayyubids and their successors, the Mamluks, the title was given to military officers in general.

Esna (Ar. Isnā) a town on the Nile in Upper Egypt, between Luxor and Edfu.

Euphrates one of the great rivers of the Fertile Crescent, it rises in eastern Turkey and flows through Syria and Iraq to join the Tigris (q.v.) and debouch into the Arabian/Persian Gulf.

faddān a pair of bulls used for plowing and, by extension, the notional area of land they can plow in a day. Now considered equal to an acre, the *faddān* was probably larger in ʿAbd al-Laṭīf's time: its official area in ninth/fifteenth-century Egypt was the equivalent of 1.57 acres.

Faiyum (Ar. al-Fayyūm) a rich and fertile region in Middle Egypt west of the Nile Valley, to which it is connected by a channel called Baḥr Yūsuf.

faqqūṣ see *melon.*

farsakh a linear measure (Persian *parasang*) of about 3.59 miles, but varying according to local usage.

"fishlet of Sidon" as one would assume from the comparison with reptiles, not a fish as such; al-Ḥimyarī (*Rawḍ*, s.v. "Ṣaydāʾ") confirms that it has four legs. Given its small size and the claim of aphrodisiac effects, it is probably a kind of salamander, for which similar claims are still made. A likely candidate would be the fire salamander, *Salamandra salamandra*, which is found on the coastal strip of Lebanon (wildlebanon.org, accessed November 2018).

Franks western European Christians. By their lands, ʿAbd al-Laṭīf means the Crusader states of the Levant.

fūl broad beans.

Fustat (Ar. al-Fusṭāṭ) the garrison city and administrative headquarters for Egypt, founded by the country's Arab conquerors in 20/641. (Cairo (q.v.) would be founded some three centuries later, a little to the north.) In ʿAbd al-Laṭīf's time, Fustat was still built up but had declined in importance. See also Old Fustat.

Galen second-century AD physician and medical writer from Pergamon, Asia Minor. Along with Dioscorides (q.v.), he had an enormous influence on the development of Arabic medical and pharmacological thought.

al-Gharbiyyah "the Western [Province]," situated in Lower Egypt within the Nile Delta. Al-Maḥallah (q.v.) was its former center; for the past two centuries or so, Ṭanṭā has been the provincial capital.

al-Ghawr "the Depression," here meaning the deep-sunk valley through which the River Jordan flows from Lake Tiberias to the Dead Sea.

al-Ghazālī (d. ca. 505/1111) theologian, mystic, and religious reformer from eastern Iran. He led a mobile life divided between teaching, writing, and mystical retreat.

Giza (Ar. al-Jīzah) a town (and, today, a governorate) on the left bank of the Nile across from the main Cairo conurbation. Home to the most famous pyramids, the Sphinx, and other monuments.

golden shower tree *Cassia fistula.*

the Green Chamber a monolithic shrine which dated to the sixth century BC. Abū Ḥāmid (*Tuḥfat al-albāb wa-nukhbat al-aʿjāb*, 104) nicely described the color of the stone as "myrtle green." At some time after 750/1349–50, the Mamluk emir Sayf al-Dīn Shaykhū(n) broke up the monument and built bits of it into his mosque and Sufi hospice, situated a little northeast of the Mosque of Ibn Ṭūlūn (q.v.; al-Maqrīzī, *Khiṭaṭ*, 1:135). At least one piece survives in the hospice, which "One enters beneath a pharaonic cornice (a spolia [*sic*] of the Saite king Amasis, brought to Cairo from Memphis . . .)" (Williams, *Islamic Monuments in Cairo*, 61).

Ḥalab an urban district just south of Cairo (q.v.) proper, outside Bab Zuwaylah, and formerly one of the places where soldiers were settled (al-Maqrīzī, *Khiṭaṭ*, 2:23). The settlers are said to have come from the Syrian city of Aleppo (Ḥalab) in early Fatimid times, hence the name (al-Zabīdī, *Tāj*, s.v. *ḥ-l-b*). See also the Ḥalabiyyah.

the Ḥalabiyyah probably to be translated as "the Aleppan Regiment." Aleppan troops are said to have been deployed in the forefront of assaults on fortifications, acting as engineers or sappers. Cf. also the mention of imported Aleppans in the previous entry above, on Ḥalab.

Ḥamāh sometimes transliterated "Ḥamāt," a city on the Orontes River in central Syria, about ninety miles south of Aleppo.

ḥanīf Qurʾanic term for an adherent of a primitive, pre-Muḥammadan monotheism, free of later Jewish and Christian accretions.

haram the Arabic word for "pyramid"; see also n. 166 on the text. Among the "fanciful ideas" about its etymology mentioned in that note, a supposed link with the name Hermes (q.v.) is one of the more picturesque. The other explanations are hardly more convincing.

Ḥārat al-Sāsah an unidentified district in or near Cairo (q.v.). The name, which might mean "the Quarter of the Grooms," does not seem to be mentioned in any other sources.

harīsah Goitein calls it the hamburger of the time (*Mediterranean Society*, 1:115); but, as is made clear in the chapter on food, it is really a deconstructed hamburger, or hash. Today, the word is used for various sweets whose main ingredient is nuts (Habiba Al-Sayfi, personal communication). Perhaps these are culinary descendants of the pistachio *harīsah* for which ʿAbd al-Laṭīf gives the recipe (§1.6.5). The verb *harasa* means, *inter alia*, "to mash, crush, blend," hence the additional application of the name *harīsah* (anglicized to "harissa") to a paste of spices and oil used in North African cuisine.

al-Ḥawf the region east of the Nile Delta and north of the Sinai Peninsula.

Ḥawrān a region in southern Syria, east of the Golan, of which the major settlement is Bosra. In ʿAbd al-Laṭīf's time, as now, it was a rich agricultural region producing cereals.

Hermes (Ar. Hurmīs/Hirmīs) surnamed Trismegistus ("the Thrice-Great"), a complex figure identified variously with the Egyptian deity Thoth, the Biblical patriarch Enoch, and others. According to some accounts he was the builder of the pyramids.

Hijaz (Ar. al-Ḥijāz) the northwestern part of the Arabian Peninsula, now belonging to the Kingdom of Saudi Arabia, in which the holy cities of Mecca and Medina are situated.

Hijrah the Prophet Muḥammad's *hijrah* or migration (from Mecca to Medina) in AD 622 provides the name of and a starting date for the Islamic era.

al-Hilāliyyah a street or district just to the south of Cairo (q.v.), "on the left, outside the New Gate of al-Ḥākim" (al-Maqrīzī, *Khiṭaṭ*, 2:20). This gate seems to have stood to the east or southeast of the still extant Bāb Zuwaylah (cf. al-Baghdādī, *Relation*, 428 n. 10).

Hippocrates fifth-century BC physician of Cos, and the most famous medical name in antiquity. A large corpus of medical works is attributed to him; how many are actually by him has been much debated.

the Hospital the *bīmāristān* or hospital of Damascus had been founded not many decades before by the city's then ruler, Nūr al-Dīn ibn Zangī. It is claimed that building costs were covered by a ransom—five castles and half a million dinars—received for a captured Crusader ruler (al-Maqrīzī, *Khiṭaṭ*, 2:408). The building was repaired, and remained in use as a hospital until the thirteenth/nineteenth century. It is now a museum of science and medicine (Mackintosh-Smith, *Travels with a Tangerine*, 155).

humoral temperament in the science of ʿAbd al-Laṭīf's time, developed out of Hellenistic ideas, four elements made up all created things—earth, water, air, and fire. Each element was characterized by a pair of qualities: earth was cold and dry, water cold and moist, air hot and moist, fire hot and dry. Sharing these same pairs of qualities were the four liquid "humors" present in animals—black bile, phlegm, blood, and yellow bile. "Temperament" (Arabic *mizāj*) was the mixture and balance of the humors; it varied from species to species, from individual to individual, and over time. Disturbances in the balance of the humors were what caused disease.

iblīz Sacy (al-Baghdādī, *Relation*, 8 n. 4) notes a similarity to the usual Greek word for mud, *pelos*, but adds that Greek writers also use the term *ilys* for Nile mud. The Arabic lexicographers observe that the common people pronounce the word "*iblīs*," literally, "devil" (al-Zabīdī, *Tāj*, s.v. *b-l-z*).

Ibn Abī l-Raddād overseer of the Nilometer (q.v.) when ʿAbd al-Laṭīf was in Egypt. At the time of its construction in the third/ninth century, the Nilometer was placed under the management of one Abū Raddād (al-Maqrīzī, *Khiṭaṭ*, 1:58) and in the 1830s an "Aboo-Raddád" was still in charge of it (Lane, *Manners*, 499)—a remarkable case of a job staying in the family, unless it is a case of the name going with the job.

Ibn Samajūn (d. early fifth/eleventh century) physician of Córdoba, Spain and an author of pharmacological works.

Ibn Wahb the text suggests that he was an authority on agriculture, or perhaps philology. If history remembers him, it probably does so under a different part of his name.

Ikhmīm also spelled Akhmīm, a town on the Nile in Upper Egypt, about 300 miles south of Cairo. It was a provincial capital.

Imruʾ al-Qays the celebrated sixth-century AD Arabian poet Ḥunduj ibn Ḥujr.

irdabb a measure of volume, equal to about 2.55 US bushels (Goitein, *Mediterranean Society*, 1:361), in use in Egypt since Ptolemaic times. An *irdabb* of wheat weighed about 154 pounds (Goitein, *Mediterranean Society*, 4:235).

ʿIrqah a place in the region of Lebanese Tripoli, situated near the sea.

al-Isrāʾīlī probably Abū Yaʿqūb Isḥāq ibn Sulaymān, physician and medical writer born in Egypt. He worked latterly for the Fatimid ruler al-Mahdī in Tunisia, and died in the early fourth/tenth century.

Iṭfīḥ (also spelled Aṭfīḥ) a town on the east bank of the Nile in the northernmost part of Upper Egypt. It belongs today to the governorate of Giza (q.v.).

Jabal Lubnān "Mount Lebanon": in ʿAbd al-Laṭīf's time the name was often applied to the more northerly ranges of Lebanon, from Baalbek (q.v.) to Tripoli. The region is known today as Kasrawān.

Jabal al-Qamar the idea that the waters of the Nile originate in a mountain range of this name—"the Mountain(s) of the Moon"—goes back at least to the second-century AD geographer Ptolemy (q.v.). They have been variously (but never conclusively) identified on the modern map of East Africa.

"jolter" a literal translation of the Arabic *raʿʿād*. The creatures so called are electric catfish of the genus *Malapterurus*. Various authorities claimed that its shocks cure headaches and rectal prolapses, and that if you hang a piece of it about your person, your spouse will never leave you (al-Maqrīzī, *Khiṭaṭ*, 1:66).

jujube the fruit of the lote tree (q.v.).

jummayz *Ficus sycomorus*, the sycamore fig.

Kalb al-Jabbār "the Giant's Dog," here an alternative name for the star Sirius. The "Giant" is the constellation Orion and his "Dog" is the neighboring constellation of Canis Major, in which Sirius is the main feature.

al-Kallāsah "the Lime Kiln," the name of a college abutting the northern wall of the Umayyad Mosque in Damascus. It was built on the site of the kiln that produced the lime for the mosque (Al-Nuʿaymī, *Al-Dāris fī tārīkh al-madāris*, 1:340).

kārah a measure of weight. If Dozy is right (*Supplément*, s.v. *k-w-r*), a *kārah* in Iraq weighed 240 Iraqi *riṭl*s, or nearly 220 pounds: this would make it almost 40% heavier than the Egyptian *irdabb* (q.v.), of which ʿAbd al-Laṭīf says it is the equivalent.

Kasrawī an adjective derived from Kisrā (q.v.); Kisrawī is the more usual spelling. The large bricks thus designated at Ctesiphon, part of the Sasanid metropolis southeast of Baghdad, are about 12 inches square by about 3 inches thick (al-Baghdādī, *Relation*, 259 n. 91).

khabīṣ a sweet made of pitted dates mashed with clarified butter and starch.

al-Khalīj a canal dug in ancient times from the Nile to the Red Sea. In ʿAbd al-Laṭīf's day most of the waterway had long been blocked, but a short initial section opening off the Nile still existed. It seems to have run roughly north–northeast, skirting the western side of Fatimid Cairo (q.v.).

Khaysī "of Khays," a place in the west of al-Ḥawf (q.v.).

khirbiz see *melon*.

Khurasan a large province in northeastern Iran that in earlier times included parts of Afghanistan and Central Asia.

khushkanān a Persian-origin word (sometimes rendered in Arabic *khashkanānij*). Literally "dry bread," it was used for a kind of pastry made of wheat kneaded with sesame oil, stuffed with sugar and nuts, and finally fried (al-Baghdādī, *Riḥlat ʿAbd al-Laṭīf*, 120 n. 7, quoting a tenth/sixteenth-century source). By coincidence, it appears as a vehicle for a sectarian jibe in a verse by ʿAbd al-Laṭīf's plagiarist, Shāfiʿ ibn ʿAlī (see p. xxx): "They say of Ḥanbalīs, just turn away / when they persist in their huff-puffing. // It's nothing but a *khushkanān*, I say, / and I'm not going in the stuffing" (Ibn Ḥajar, *Durar*, 2:185).

Kisrā arabicized form of the Persian name Khusraw, borne by two important kings of the late pre-Islamic Sasanid dynasty of Persia. It was used in

Arabic as a title for Sasanid rulers in general (cf. the way "Caesar" became a title, and was further adapted into the forms "Kaiser," "Tsar," etc.).

labakh a botanical puzzle. Even in ʿAbd al-Laṭīf's time, there was confusion over its identity: his contemporary, Yāqūt, says that, far from being rare, the tree grew all over Egypt (*Muʿjam*, s.v. "Anṣinā"). And yet a later, local authority says that the tree had completely or almost completely disappeared from Egypt by ca. 700/1300—that is, within a century of our text (al-Maqrīzī, quoted in al-Baghdādī, *Relation*, 65–66 n. 15). Since then, the name *labakh* has grafted itself on to trees that are clearly not the one described here (e.g. *Albizia lebbeck*, which also has rattling seeds, but forming in long pods rather than in date-shaped fruit). Sacy's laboriously reached (al-Baghdādī, *Relation*, 47–72 n. 15) conclusion still stands: that the tree is what Classical authors called *persea*; the problem is, we do not know for certain what the *persea* was. Of the various possibilities, perhaps the best fit with ʿAbd al-Laṭīf's description might be found in some species of *Cordia*.

Levant the lands at the eastern end of the Mediterranean, including present-day Israel, Jordan, Lebanon, Palestine, and Syria.

the Lighthouse the famous "Pharos" of Alexandria, constructed in the early third century BC on Pharos Island (which gave its name to the building). After ʿAbd al-Laṭīf's time, it suffered neglect and was further damaged in earthquakes. A fortress, still extant, was built on the site in the ninth/fifteenth century.

lobia (Ar. *lūbiyāʾ*) usually the kidney bean, but some other bean may be intended in the text.

lote tree *Ziziphus spina-christi*. Its fruit is often known as the jujube.

Lower Egypt the region from Cairo northwards to the Mediterranean, including the Nile Delta.

al-Maʿbar usually indefinite ("Maʿbar"), the Arabic name for the east coast of southern India. Roughly the same as the Coromandel Coast of Tamil Nadu and Andhra Pradesh.

al-Madāʾin a pre-Islamic imperial metropolis or conurbation about twenty miles southeast of Baghdad, including the city of Ctesiphon and monuments of the Sasanid dynasty.

the Maghrib "the West," usually in the sense of North Africa west of Cyrenaica (see Barqah, above), and sometimes including the Iberian peninsula.

Magians (Ar. Majūs) a name usually designating adherents of the Zoroastrian faith.

al-Maḥallah often al-Maḥallah al-Kubrā, "Great Maḥallah," to distinguish it from other places of the same name. A town in the Nile Delta about sixty miles east of Alexandria (q.v.), and until early modern times provincial capital of al-Gharbiyyah (q.v.).

al-Malik al-ʿĀdil (d. ca. 615/1218) the Ayyubid prince Abū Bakr Muḥammad ibn Ayyūb, also entitled Sayf al-Dīn (the Crusaders' "Saphadin"). Younger brother of Saladin (q.v.), he became ruler of Egypt and Syria in 596/1200.

al-Malik al-ʿAzīz ʿUthmān ibn Yūsuf (d. ca. 595/1198) Ayyubid prince, son of Saladin (q.v.). He ruled Egypt from his father's death in 589/1193 until his own death.

al-Maʾmūn (r. 198–218/813–33) seventh Abbasid caliph, patron of translation, science, and philosophy. He was in Egypt in 217/832 and is said to have explored the interior of the pyramid of Khufu.

al-Maqs the river port of Cairo (q.v.).

al-Marīs usually the name for the northernmost part of Nubia, i.e., the lands beginning south of Aswan (q.v.), and for its inhabitants. For al-Maqrīzī, however, the name seems to cover regions further south as well (*Khiṭaṭ*, 1:191).

marsh mallow *Althaea officinalis.*

mastic usually designating the gum-yielding *Pistacia lentiscus*, ʿAbd al-Laṭīf may mean by it the aromatic "herb mastic," *Thymus mastichina*, used as a flavoring.

melon ʿAbd al-Laṭīf mentions several varieties: *biṭṭīkh*, the usual name for sweet, scented varieties of melon, of which *ṭibbīkh* is a variant and *khirbiz* (a word of Persian origin) a synonym; *ḍaghābīs*, which denotes miniature serpent melons as well as edible, asparagus-like shoots that grow at the base of certain thorn trees and of other plants; *faqqūṣ* which, as explained in the text, is also a small serpent melon;

and *shilinq*, which Sacy explains is the term for a melon in the form of a cucumber (al-Baghdādī, *Relation*, 127 n. 133). As for the watermelon, the various names mentioned in the text (*dullāʿ*, Raqqī, etc.) are attested elsewhere, except for *zabash*, which may be a version of *dbshī* (voweling uncertain), noted by Dozy (*Supplément*, s.v. *b-ṭ-kh*).

Memphis (Ar. Manf, probably to be pronounced "Mamf"), capital of the Egyptian Old Kingdom situated on the left bank of the Nile upstream of the present Cairo conurbation. Whether Nebuchadnezzar attacked it is unclear, but it was undoubtedly sacked by Assyrian forces before his time, in the seventh century BC.

miasmata the plural of "miasma," an effusion produced by putrescent matter and stagnant water. Along with the resulting corrupt air—"malaria"—miasmata were long held to be agents of disease.

mithqāl a unit of weight, theoretically 0.14 troy ounces. In practice, its weight was the same as that of a dinar (q.v.).

mizr a kind of weak beer, probably akin to "small beer," the northern European staple before safe water supplies became general.

Mosque of ʿAmr ibn al-ʿĀṣ originally built by ʿAmr ibn al-ʿĀṣ (q.v.) in the first/seventh century, north of the pre-Islamic fortress of Babylon (see Old Fustat), and still extant.

Mosque of Ibn Ṭulūn extant third/ninth-century mosque built by Aḥmad ibn Ṭūlūn (see Ṭūlūnids) in the al-Qaṭāʾiʿ district.

Mosul (Ar. al-Mawṣil) a city on the Tigris River in the north of present-day Iraq.

mountain fig a wild variety of the cultivated fig.

al-Muʿizz (r. 341–65/953–75) fourth caliph of the Fatimid dynasty (297–567/909–1171). His seat was in Ifrīqiyah (present-day Tunisia), but he spent the last three years of his life in Cairo (q.v.), which was founded on his orders after the Fatimid takeover of Egypt in 358/969.

mulūkhiyyah *Corchorus olitorius*, garden mallow. The Arabic name is from Greek *molokhe*. According to surviving shopping lists from ʿAbd al-Laṭīf's era, half a dirham's (q.v.) worth would buy enough for a feast (Goitein, *Mediterranean Society*, 4:230).

mulūkhiyyah of the Blacks see *shūshandībā*.

mulūkiyyah this alternative name for *mulūkhiyyah* has a grandiose ring: it looks like an adjective meaning "royal."

mūmiyā also *mūmiyā'*, cf. English "mummy," from Persian *mūm*, "wax." As ʿAbd al-Laṭīf emphasizes, *mūmiyā* proper is a naturally occurring bituminous substance; the substance found in ancient corpses is a man-made composite. The extension of the word, to mean an embalmed corpse stuffed with the substance, is relatively recent.

al-Muqaṭṭam usually applied today to the escarpment and plateau east of Cairo, for earlier geographers the name denoted the whole range of uplands east of the Egyptian Nile. Some saw this range as part of an intercontinental chain that extended from China to West Africa.

Nabataeans a rather loose term for various peoples of Iraq, it was most often applied to the indigenous Eastern Aramaic-speaking peasants, to distinguish them from the Arabic-speaking incomers of the first/seventh century. (The same term was also used for the Nabataeans of the Jordan region, whose capital was Petra, although they were regarded as a distinct people.)

Nābulus a town about twenty-eight miles north of Jerusalem, it has long been a center of the Samaritans (q.v.).

Najd an "upland." As a proper name it denotes the central plateau of the Arabian Peninsula.

al-Nāṣir li-dīn Allāh (r. 575–622/1180–1225) thirty-fourth Abbasid caliph. After some 250 years during which the Abbasid dynasty, based in Baghdad, had been largely impotent figureheads and real power had belonged to non-Arab interlopers, al-Nāṣir did much to restore the prestige of the caliphate. (See also pp. xxviii–xxx.)

naydat al-bawsh *naydah* is the general term for the dish. The second element, *al-bawsh*, is puzzling. Its usual meaning is "the common herd, the riff-raff"; the cognate verb is to do with being mixed in a disorderly fashion. However, al-Zabīdī, compiling his lexicon nearly six centuries on from our text, also gives *bawsh* (on its own) as the name of an Egyptian food, namely wheat and lentils baked in a sealed pot (*Tāj*, s.v. *b-w-sh*)—conceivably a descendant of ʿAbd al-Laṭīf's dish.

Nebuchadnezzar (II) (Ar. Bukht Naṣṣar) Neo-Babylonian king who reigned 604–562 BC. He sacked Jerusalem in 587 BC, and may have campaigned in Egypt after that.

Nicolaus (Ar. Nīqūlāwus) Nicolaus of Damascus, a scholar of wide interests, b. 64 BC. Arabic botany and pharmacology knew him for his commentary on a work on plants attributed to Aristotle.

Nilometer a gauge for measuring the Nile's annual rise, the amount of which had a bearing on whether agricultural taxes were levied (§2.1.3). The Nilometer ʿAbd al-Laṭīf knew was completed in 247/861–62 and is still extant on Roda Island. It consists of an octagonal column with graduated markings, standing in a pit or cistern, into which water flows through three tunnels.

Nubians a somewhat vague term for the peoples dwelling along the Nile upstream from the First Cataract (see Cataracts, above). Nubia has sometimes been regarded as extending to the Fifth Cataract, and occasionally as far as the confluence of the White and Blue Niles. (See also al-Marīs, above.)

okra (Ar. *bāmiyah*) *Abelmoschus esculentus.* The Latin name, from the Arabic epithet *abū l-misk*, "the father of musk," is due to the sweet smell and taste of the seeds (Miller, Morris and Stuart-Smith, *Plants of Dhofar*, 198).

Old Fustat (Ar. Miṣr) the urban area on the right bank of the Nile south of Cairo (q.v.) proper, including the site of the pre-Islamic fortress known as Babylon, early Islamic Fustat (q.v.), and areas developed under the Ṭūlūnids (q.v.). It had declined greatly in late Fatimid times; the Ayyubids tried to regenerate it, only for it to be devastated by the famine and plague described by ʿAbd al-Laṭīf (al-Maqrīzī, *Khiṭaṭ*, 1:339).

opium the best opium was said to come from a place called Abū Tīj, south of Asyūt in Upper Egypt. Some authorities mention adulteration with various resins, including sandarac.

Pillar of Columns (Ar. ʿAmūd al-Sawārī) often called in European accounts "Pompey's Pillar," but actually erected by the Roman emperor Diocletian to commemorate the suppression in AD 298 of a revolt. The Arabic name is curious. Sacy (al-Baghdādī, *Relation*, 234 n. 53) is possibly right in saying that it derives from the lesser columns that surrounded it until the time of Qarājā (q.v.). Other origins have been proposed for the name. The present writer would add that, at least as far back as the fourth/tenth century, the Egyptians called red granite columns *uswānī* (i.e. of Aswan; al-Masʿūdī quoted in al-Maqrīzī, *Khiṭaṭ*, 1:159), which suggests that the name might be a version of *al-*ʿAmūd al-*Uswānī*. For that matter, it could also be a version of *al-*ʿAmūd al-*Ṣawwānī*, "the Column of Hard Stone, sc. Granite."

Ptolemy Alexandrian writer on science, especially astronomy and geography, fl. in the second century AD. The *Karpos* (*Fruit*) ascribed to him is an evidently spurious collection of one hundred astrological aphorisms (Hornblower and Spawforth, *Classical Dictionary*, s.v. "Ptolemy (4) . . . (Claudius Ptolemaeus)").

purslane common purslane, *Portulaca oleracea*.

qadaḥ a container or measure. The term is not normally used to denote a particular capacity but, going by the information given on amounts of fuel, the *qadaḥ* in question should contain eight handfuls.

al-Qarāfah the great cemetery south of Cairo (q.v.), in use since the foundation of Fustat (q.v.).

Qarājā little or nothing seems to be known about him beyond the information given in the text—that he was Saladin's governor of Alexandria.

Qarāqūsh Bahāʾ al-Dīn Qarāqūsh al-Asadī, Saladin's (q.v.) chief of public works in Egypt. He was not universally popular: a satirical book appeared, entitled *Chief of Jerks: Collected "Wisdom" of the Minister of Works* (to imitate the cruel rhyme of the Ar. title, *Al-Fāshūsh fī aḥkām qarāqūsh*) (al-Maqrīzī, *Khiṭaṭ*, 2:151). The biographical encyclopedist Ibn Khallikān (who, incidentally, spent a brief time as a student of ʿAbd al-Laṭīf) thought the book's contents were probably a fabrication (*Wafayāt al-aʿyān*, 2:280).

qaraẓ properly speaking, the leaves and the fruit of the *sanṭ* tree, *Acacia nilotica*. *Aqāqiyā*, as stated in the text, is the term for their juice.

al-Qulzum an ancient port on the Red Sea near Suez. It had been abandoned by the time of ʿAbd al-Laṭīf, but geographers long continued to call the Red Sea the "Sea of al-Qulzum."

Qūṣ a town in Upper Egypt, about nineteen miles north of Luxor.

Raqqī melon see *melon.*

rāwiyah a very large leather bag used for transporting water, or alternatively a pair of such bags, slung either side of a camel's hump (Lane, *Lexicon*, s.v. *r-w-y*).

al-Rāzī (d. ca. 313/925) celebrated physician, philosopher, and alchemist of Rayy (Iran) and Baghdad, known in Latin as Rhazes.

riṭl the standard Egyptian *riṭl* of ʿAbd al-Laṭīf's time weighed the equivalent of 0.98 pounds. Also spelled *raṭl*, the Arabic word comes ultimately, like "liter," from Greek *litron*.

Roda Island (Ar. Jazīrat al-Rawḍah) an island in the Nile, separated from Fustat (q.v.) by a narrow channel.

Sabā also spelled Saba', the Biblical Sheba. A powerful pre-Islamic people of South Arabia.

Sabians on its first appearance (§1.4.13), apropos the pyramids, the name denotes a group of gnostic astrolators centered on Ḥarrān in northern Mesopotamia (now eastern Turkey). A later mention of Sabians (§1.4.56), along with the Copts, refers to a sect of disputed identity, possibly Judaeo-Christian, in southern Iraq. The last appearance of the name could denote either group.

Ṣafad a hilltop town in Galilee, overlooking the Sea of Galilee.

safflower *Carthamus tinctoria*, a plant used for dyeing.

Ṣāfīthā now spelled Ṣāfītā, in Syria, southeast of Ṭarṭūs and northwest of Krak des Chevaliers. Chastel Blanc, built by the Knights Templar and still extant in Ṣāfītā, is the castle mentioned as partially destroyed in the earthquake of 598/1202; it was subsequently rebuilt.

Saladin Ṣalāḥ al-Dīn Yūsuf ibn Ayyūb (d. ca. 589/1193), Kurdish founder of the Ayyubid dynasty and celebrated warrior in the wars against the Crusaders. In 564/1169 he was appointed vizier to the enfeebled Fatimid caliph in Cairo; two years later, he deposed his nominal master and restored Egypt's allegiance to the Abbasid caliphate of Baghdad, though with himself as *de facto* ruler.

samār the rush *Juncus rigidus* and other similar species.

Samaritans adherents of a religion that shares the Israelite origins, but rejects the later accretions, of Judaism. They hold as sacred the Pentateuch (though with variations from the text as preserved by the Jews). Their major center has always been Nābulus (q.v.).

sanṭ *Acacia nilotica*. See *qaraẓ*.

sarb *Sarpa salpa*, a type of sea bream. ʿAbd al-Laṭīf's near-contemporary al-Qazwīnī also mentions the effects here described (*Āthār al-bilād wa-akhbār al-ʿibād*, 193–94). Anecdotes are still told today of hallucinations and nightmares brought on by eating the fish. The hallucinogens may be produced by the particular plankton that form the fish's diet.

sās the coarser fibers of flax heads and stems, not suitable for making linen cloth. Sacy (al-Baghdādī, *Relation*, 151 n. 4), following Wahl, says it derives from a Coptic word.

Sea of Pitch (Ar. Baḥr al-Zift) this and similar names are usually given to the Circumambient Ocean that surrounds the Afro-Eurasian landmass. Here, however, it is a name for the Dead Sea. Similarly, Sir John Mandeville, the alleged eighth/fourteenth-century writer of a French travel book that draws on earlier European sources, called the Dead Sea "Lake Asfaltit," the Asphalt Lake (Mandeville, *The Travels of Sir John Mandeville*, 89).

shabbārah a boat or barge with a free-standing cabin constructed on the upper deck. Ibn Baṭṭūṭah describes the Mongol ruler in Baghdad traveling on the Tigris in one, accompanied by two more containing musicians and dancers. (Ibn Baṭṭūṭa, *Travels*, 2:336–37 and n. 216.).

shilinq see *melon*.

shūshandībā Sacy's reading of the word, which he explains as a Syriac term, literally "lily of the wolf," for a (probably wild) variety of edible mallow (al-Baghdādī, *Relation*, 45 n. 14).

Sidon (Ar. Ṣaydā) a city on the Lebanese coast, important since Phoenician times.

ṣiḥnāh salted sprats. See *ṣīr*.

sikbāj a meat stew, thickened with flour and flavored with spices and, most importantly, vinegar.

ṣīr salted sprats. *Ṣiḥnāh/ṣaḥnāh* seems to mean the same, or something very similar. The fondness of Egyptians for *ṣīr* was well known: the Prophet Muḥammad's daughter Zaynab is said to have offered an Egyptian visitor fried locusts, then (perhaps sensing his reluctance) to have commented, "Or perhaps *ṣīr* are more to your taste . . ." (al-Damīrī, *Ḥayawān*, 2:696).

Sirius the brightest star in the sky (after the sun), situated in the constellation of Canis Major.

skink *pace* ʿAbd al-Laṭīf's opening comments on it, the skink is related neither to the crocodile nor to the varanus (q.v.). The allegedly aphrodisiac sort referred to in the text is probably the wedge-snouted skink, *Sphenops sepsoides*.

soap cakes Ibn Baṭṭūṭah mentions a sweet of the same name in India; it was made from starch, almonds, honey, and sesame oil (Ibn Baṭṭūṭa, *Travels*, 3:607). Sacy remarks (al-Baghdādī, *Relation*, 316–17 n. 8) that it has, "*sans doute, quelque ressemblance avec notre nougat.*"

spadix the "spike" of flowers within a spathe.

sumac shrubs or trees of the genus *Rhus*, bearing small red berries used as a spice.

ṭājan also spelled *ṭājin* and anglicized as "tagine/tajine," usually a frying pan, saucepan, or other similar utensil. Ultimately from Greek *teganon*.

ṭalḥ the name seems to be used for more than one species of *Acacia*. The one intended here might be *A. senegal* (cf. Miller, Morris and Stuart-Smith, *Plants of Dhofar*, 180–81).

tannūr a cylindrical or barrel-shaped oven, open at the top. Cf. Anglo-Indian "tandoor."

taro (Ar. *qulqās*) *Colocasia esculenta*. According to shopping lists of the time, a household might spend ⅝ dirham on it in one day (Goitein, *Mediterranean Society*, 4:232).

temperament see *humoral temperament*.

ṭibbīkh see *melon*.

Tibnīn a Syrian town in the hills overlooking Bāniyās (q.v.).

Tigris one of the great rivers of the Fertile Crescent, it rises in eastern Turkey and flows through Iraq to join the Euphrates (q.v.) and debouch into the Arabian/Persian Gulf.

Tihāmah a "lowland," and in particular that running along the Red Sea coast of Arabia.

Tinnīs once a major port town of the eastern part of the Nile Delta, most of its civilian population had been evacuated before ʿAbd al-Laṭīf's arrival in Egypt, owing to repeated assaults by European forces. Not long after his departure, the town was largely destroyed in order to deter a Crusader occupation.

Torah strictly speaking, the five books of the Pentateuch, but in Arabic usage "al-Tawrāh" generally means the Jewish scriptures as a whole.

Ṭūlūnids (254–92/868–905) a short-lived (three generations) but important dynasty in Egypt. Their founder, Aḥmad ibn Ṭūlūn, whose father was of Central Asian Turkic origin, became governor of Egypt on behalf of the Abbasids in 256/870, but gained effective independence from Baghdad.

Tyre (Ar. Ṣūr) a southern Lebanese coastal city, like Sidon (q.v.) important since Phoenician times.

ʿUmar the caliph ʿUmar ibn al-Khaṭṭāb, second successor of the Prophet Muḥammad as head of the Muslim community. He ruled from Medina, 13–23/634–44.

Upper Egypt roughly, the Nile Valley region of Egypt south of Cairo.

ūqiyyah a unit of weight equal to 1.2 troy ounces.

ʿushayrī usually spelled *ʿushārī*. In addition to the description of the vessel in the text (§1.5.10), it is worth remarking that some examples were very lavish indeed. One, built for the Fatimid caliph al-Mustanṣir's mother in the fifth/eleventh century, was named al-Fiḍḍī, "The Silver [Barge]/The Argentine," as its decoration included 130,000 dirhams' worth of silver; the paintwork alone cost another 2,400 dinars. At the time, the caliphal flotilla numbered three dozen pleasure-*ʿushārī*s (al-Maqrīzī, *Khiṭaṭ*, 1:475–76 and 478).

al-Ushmūnayn a settlement on the Nile in Upper Egypt, about 140 miles south of Cairo. Formerly important, it is now much diminished.

Uskurjat Firʿawn the first element of the name, variously spelled, signifies a small bowl for condiments etc., so perhaps "Pharaoh's Pickle Bowl" would be a suitable translation (cf. such English names as "the Devil's Punch-Bowl"). None of the usual sources, including al-Maqrīzī's indispensable *Khiṭaṭ*, appears to mention either the name or the feature; but then, names change and disappear, and holes in the ground get filled in. The Pickle Bowl might have been situated somewhere in the al-Raṣad Hills south of al-Fusṭāṭ; more than that this writer cannot say. Such an ill-omened place is best forgotten.

varanus Arabic *waral*, a variant of which, *waran*, is the origin of the Latin/English name. The species in the text is *Varanus griseus*, the desert monitor.

waybah a measure of volume, the equivalent of about 0.43 US bushels (Goitein, *Mediterranean Society*, 1:361).

Yaḥyā possibly the Andalusian Abū Zakariyyā Yaḥyā ibn Muḥammad Ibn al-ʿAwwām of Seville, active in the latter part of the sixth/twelfth century, who compiled a substantial *Book of Agriculture*. He may be too late, however, to be the Yaḥyā intended here; if so, another agricultural authority or philologist is meant.

al-Yāzūrī Abū Muḥammad al-Ḥasan (or al-Ḥusayn) ibn ʿAlī, Fatimid vizier (in office 440–50/1048–58). It is alleged that he encouraged the nomadic Arab tribes of Banū Hilāl and Banū Sulaym to migrate across North Africa. Whether the claim is true or not, it was at this time that their depradations affected the agricultural economy of Barqah.

zabash see *melon*.

zanbaq as well as meaning jasmine oil, the word is used as a name for various flowering plants, principally lilies.

Zuqāq al-Birkah "the Lane of the Pool." Sacy (al-Baghdādī, *Relation*, 400 n. 66) takes it as leading to Birkat al-Ḥabash, a large pool or cistern southeast of Fustat.

Bibliography

Abū l-Fidā', al-Malik al-Mu'ayyad Ismā'īl ibn 'Alī. *Kitāb Taqwīm al-buldān.* Edited by Joseph Toussaint Reinaud and William Mac Guckin de Slane. Beirut: Dār Ṣādir, n.d. Originally published Paris: Imprimerie Royale, 1840.

Abū Ḥāmid al-Gharnāṭī, Muḥammad ibn 'Abd al-Raḥīm. *Tuḥfat al-albāb wa-nukhbat al-a'jāb.* Edited by Ismā'īl al-'Arabī. [Casablanca]: Dār al-Āfāq al-Jadīdah, 1413/1993.

Abū Nuwās, al-Ḥasan ibn Hāni'. *Dīwān.* Edited by Aḥmad 'Abd al-Majīd al-Ghazālī. Beirut: Dār al-Kitāb al-'Arabī, 1404/1984.

Al-Baghdādī, 'Abd al-Laṭīf ibn Yūsuf. *Abdollatiphi Historiæ Ægypti Compendium.* Partially translated by E. Pococke the Younger. [Oxford]: [Oxford University Press], n.d. [ca. 1691].

———. *Abdollatiphi Compendium Memorabilium Aegypti.* Edited by J. White, introduced by H.E.G. Paulus. Tübingen: J.G. Cotta, 1789.

———. *Abd-allatif's, eines arabischen Arztes: Denkwürdigkeiten Egyptens.* Translated by S.F.G. Wahl. Halle: Waisenhaus, 1790.

———. *Abdollatiphi Historiæ Ægypti Compendium.* Edited and translation completed by J. White. Oxford: Oxford University Press, 1800.

———. *Relation de l'Égypte.* Translated and annotated by A.I. Silvestre de Sacy. Paris: Imprimerie Impériale, 1810.

———. *Kitāb al-Ifādah wa-l-i'tibār.* Cairo: Maṭba'at Wādī al-Nīl, 1286/1869–70.

———. *The Eastern Key: Kitāb al-Ifādah wa-l-i'tibār of 'Abd al-Laṭīf al-Baghdādī.* Translated by Kamal Hafuth Zand, John A. Videan, and Ivy E. Videan. London: George Allen and Unwin, 1965.

———. *Kitāb al-Ifādah wa-l-iʿtibār*. Edited by Aḥmad Ghassān Sabānū. Damascus: Dār Quṭaybah, 1403/1983.

———. *Riḥlat ʿAbd al-Laṭīf al-Baghdādī fī Miṣr*. Edited by ʿAbd al-Raḥmān ʿAbdallāh al-Shaykh. 2nd ed. Cairo: al-Hayʾah al-Miṣriyyah al-ʿĀmmah li-l-Kitāb, 1998.

Browne, Sir Thomas. *The Voyce of the World: Selected Writings of Sir Thomas Browne*. Edited by Geoffrey Keynes, preface by Tim Mackintosh-Smith. London: The Folio Society, 2007.

Cooperson, Michael. "Al-Maʾmūn, the Pyramids and the Hieroglyphs." In *ʿAbbasid Studies II*, edited by John Nawas, 165–90. Leuven, Paris, and Walpole MA: Uitgeverij Peeters en Departement Oosterse Studies, 2010.

Al-Damīrī, Muḥammad ibn Mūsā. *Ḥayāt al-ḥayawān al-kubrā*. Edited by Ibrāhīm Ṣāliḥ. 4 vols. Damascus: Dār al-Bashāʾir, 1426/2005.

Dictionary of National Biography. 22 vols. London: Smith, Elder and Co., 1908–9.

Dozy, Reinhart P. *Takmilat al-maʿājim al-ʿarabiyyah*. Translated and annotated by Muḥammad Salīm al-Nuʿaymī and Jamāl al-Khayyāṭ. 10 vols. Baghdad: Dār al-Rashīd and Dār al-Shuʾūn al-Thaqāfiyyah al-ʿĀmmah, 1980–2000. [= *Supplément aux dictionnaires arabes*. 2 vols. Leiden: Brill, 1881.]

Encyclopaedia of Islam. 2nd ed. 11 vols. plus supplement vol. and index vol. Leiden: Brill, 1960–2009.

Goitein, S. D. *A Mediterranean Society: The Jewish Communities of the World as Portrayed in the Documents of the Cairo Geniza*. 5 vols. Berkeley, Los Angeles, and London: University of California Press, 1999.

Al-Harawī, ʿAlī ibn Abī Bakr. *Kitāb al-Ishārāt ilā maʿrifat al-ziyārāt*. Edited by Janine Sourdel-Thomine. Damascus: Institut Français de Damas, 1953.

Herodotus. *Herodotus: The Histories*. Translated by Aubrey de Selincourt. 2nd ed. Harmondsworth: Penguin Books, 1972.

Al-Ḥimyarī, Muḥammad ibn ʿAbd al-Munʿim. *Al-Rawḍ al-miʿṭār fī khabar al-aqṭār*. Edited by Iḥsān ʿAbbās. 2nd ed. Beirut: Maktabat Lubnān, 1984.

Hornblower, Simon and Antony Spawforth, eds. *The Oxford Classical Dictionary*. 3rd ed. (revised). Oxford: Oxford University Press, 2003.

Ibn Abī Uṣaybiʿah. *ʿUyūn al-anbāʾ fī ṭabaqāt al-aṭibbāʾ*. Edited by Nizār Riḍā. Beirut: Dār Maktabat al-Ḥayāh, 1965.

Ibn Baṭṭūṭa, Muḥammad ibn ʿAbd Allāh. *The Travels of Ibn Baṭṭūṭa: A.D. 1325–1354*, translated by H.A.R. Gibb and C.F. Beckingham. 4 vols. London: The Hakluyt Society, 1958–94.

Ibn Ḥajar al-ʿAsqalānī, Aḥmad ibn ʿAlī. *Al-Durar al-kāminah*. 4 vols. Beirut: Dār al-Jīl, 1414/1993.

Ibn Jubayr, Muḥammad ibn Aḥmad. *Riḥlah*. Beirut: Dār Ṣādir, 1400/1980.

Ibn Khaldūn, ʿAbd al-Raḥmān ibn Muḥammad. *The Muqaddimah: An Introduction to History*. Translated by Franz Rosenthal, edited and abridged by N.J. Dawood. Princeton: Princeton University Press, 1989.

Ibn Khallikān, Aḥmad ibn Muḥammad. *Wafayāt al-aʿyān*. 4 vols. Beirut: Dār Iḥyāʾ al-Turāth al-ʿArabī, 1417/1997.

Al-Idrīsī, Muḥammad ibn Muḥammad. *Kitāb Nuzhat al-mushtāq fī ikhtirāq al-āfāq*. 2 vols. Cairo: Maṭbaʿat al-Thaqāfah al-Dīniyyah, n.d.

Imruʾ al-Qays. *Dīwān*. Beirut: Dār al-Kutub al-ʿIlmiyyah, 1403/1983.

Irwin, Robert. *Night and Horses and the Desert: The Penguin Anthology of Classical Arabic Literature*. London: Penguin Books, 2000.

———. *The Alhambra*. London: Profile Books, 2005.

———. *For Lust of Knowing: The Orientalists and their Enemies*. London: Allen Lane, 2006.

Kratchkovsky, I. Y. *Al-Adab al-jughrāfī al-ʿArabī*. Translated by Ṣalāḥ al-Dīn ʿUthmān Hāshim. Cairo: Lajnat al-Taʾlīf wa-l-Tarjamah wa-l-Nashr, 1963. [= *Istoria Arabskoi Geograficheskoi Literatury*. Moscow and Leningrad: Institute of Oriental Studies, 1957.]

Lane, Edward William. *Madd al-qāmūs: An Arabic-English Lexicon*. 8 vols. New Delhi: Asian Educational Services, 1985. Originally published London: Williams and Norgate, 1863–93.

———. *An Account of the Manners and Customs of the Modern Egyptians*. 5th ed. Introduced by Jason Thompson. Cairo and New York: The American University in Cairo Press, 2003. Originally published London: John Murray, 1860.

Mackintosh-Smith, Tim. *Travels with a Tangerine: A Journey in the Footnotes of Ibn Battutah*. London: John Murray, 2001.

———. *Ghost Writer*. London: Slightly Foxed, 2005.

———. *Arabs: A 3,000-Year History of Peoples, Tribes and Empires*. New Haven and London: Yale University Press, 2019.

Mandeville, Sir John. *The Travels of Sir John Mandeville*. Translated by C.W.R.D. Moseley. London: Penguin Books, 1983.

Manguel, Alberto. *The Library at Night*. New Haven and London: Yale University Press, 2008.

———. *A Reader on Reading*. New Haven and London: Yale University Press, 2010.

Al-Maqrīzī, Aḥmad ibn ʿAlī. *Kitāb al-Mawāʿiẓ wa-l-iʿtibār bi-dhikr al-khiṭaṭ wa-l-āthār* [also known as "Al-Khiṭaṭ al-Maqrīziyyah"]. Cairo: Maktabat al-Thaqāfah al-Dīniyyah, n.d. Originally published Bulāq: al-Maṭbaʿah al-Amīriyyah, 1270/1853–54.

———. "Le Traité des famines de Maqrīzī." Translated by Gaston Wiet. *Journal of the Economic and Social History of the Orient*, 5, no. 1 (February 1962): 1–90.

Martini Bonadeo, Cecilia. *ʿAbd al-Laṭīf al-Baġdādī's Philosophical Journey: From Aristotle's Metaphysics to the "Metaphysical Science"*. Leiden and Boston: Brill, 2013.

Mathews, Thomas. *Byzantium: From Antiquity to the Renaissance*. New Haven and London: Yale University Press, 1998.

Miller, Anthony G., Miranda Morris, and Susanna Stuart-Smith. *Plants of Dhofar*. Muscat: Office of the Adviser for Conservation of the Environment, Diwan of Royal Court, 1988.

Miquel, André. *La géographie humaine du monde musulman jusqu'au milieu du 11è siècle*, Vol. I: *Géographie et géographie humaine dans la littérature arabe des origines à 1050*. Paris and the Hague: Mouton, 1973.

Al-Muẓaffar al-Ghassānī, Yūsuf ibn ʿUmar ibn ʿAlī ibn Rasūl, al-Malik. *Al-Muʿtamad fī l-adwiyah al-mufradah*. Edited by Muṣṭafā al-Saqqā. Beirut: Dār al-Maʿrifah, n.d.

Al-Nuʿaymī, ʿAbd al-Qādir ibn Muḥammad. *Al-Dāris fī tārīkh al-madāris*. 2 vols. Beirut: Dār al-Kutub al-ʿIlmiyyah, 1410/1990.

Popper, Karl. *The Logic of Scientific Discovery*. London: Hutchinson, 1959.

Al-Qazwīnī, Zakariyyā' ibn Muḥammad. *Āthār al-bilād wa-akhbār al-ʿibād*. Beirut: Dār Ṣādir, n.d.

———. *ʿAjā'ib al-makhlūqāt wa-gharā'ib al-mawjūdāt*. Aleppo: Dār al-Sharq al-ʿArabī, n.d.

[Rūmī, Jalāl al-Dīn]. *Tales from the Masnavi*. Translated by Arthur J. Arberry. Richmond, Surrey: Curzon Press, 1993.

Saunders, R. H. *Healing Through the Spirit Agency: by the great Persian [sic] physician Abduhl Latif, "the man of Baghdad", and information concerning the life hereafter of the deepest interest to all inquirers and students of psychic phenomena*. London: Hutchinson, 1928.

Schnurrer, Christianus Fridericus de. *Bibliotheca Arabica*. Halle: J.C. Hendel, 1811.

Shatzmiller, Maya. *Labour in the Medieval Islamic World*. Leiden: Brill, 1993.

Al-Sīrāfī, Abū Zayd and Aḥmad ibn Faḍlān. *Two Arabic Travel Books (Accounts of China and India and Mission to the Volga)*. Edited and translated by Tim Mackintosh-Smith and James E. Montgomery. New York and London: New York University Press, 2014.

Stern, S. M. "A Collection of Treatises by ʿAbd al-Laṭīf al-Baghdādī." *Islamic Studies*, 1, no. 1 (March 1962): 53–70.

Thoreau, Henry David. *Walden; or, Life in the Woods*. New York: Dover, 1995.

Toorawa, Shawkat M. "A Portrait of ʿAbd al-Laṭīf al-Baghdādī's Education and Instruction." In *Law and Education in Medieval Islam: Studies in Memory of George Makdisi*, edited by Joseph E. Lowry, Devin J. Stewart, and Shawkat M. Toorawa, 91–109. Oxford: E.J.W. Gibb Memorial Trust Series, 2004.

———. "Travel in the medieval Islamic world: the importance of patronage, as illustrated by ʿAbd al-Latif al-Baghdadi (d. 629/1231) (and other littérateurs)." In *Eastward Bound: Travel and travellers 1050–1550*, edited by Rosamund Allen, 53–70. Manchester and New York: Manchester University Press, 2004.

Al-Tuṭīlī, Binyāmīn ibn Yūnah [Benjamin of Tudela]. *Riḥlat ibn Yūnah al-Andalusī ilā bilād al-sharq al-Islāmī*. Translated and annotated by ʿAzrā Ḥaddād. Beirut: Dār Ibn Zaydūn, 1416/1996.

Twells, Leonard. *The Lives of Dr Edward Pocock [*sic*], the Celebrated Orientalist [. . . et al.]*. 2 vols. London: F.C. and J. Rivington, 1816.

Williams, Caroline. *Islamic Monuments in Cairo: The Practical Guide*. Cairo: American University in Cairo Press, 2008.

Wright, G. R. H. *Ancient Building Technology*. Vol. 3. Leiden: Brill, 2009.

Yāqūt al-Ḥamawī. *Muʿjam al-buldān*. Edited by Farīd ʿAbd al-ʿAzīz al-Jundī. 7 vols. Beirut: Dār al-Kutub al-ʿIlmiyyah, n.d.

Yule, Henry. *The Travels of Marco Polo*. 3rd ed. Revised with notes and addenda by Henri Cordier. 2 vols. New York: Dover Publications, 1993. Originally published London: John Murray, 1920 and 1929.

Yule, Henry and A. C. Burnell. *Hobson-Jobson: The Anglo-Indian Dictionary*. Edited by W. Crooke. 2nd ed. Ware: Wordsworth Editions, 1996. Originally published London: John Murray, 1903.

Al-Zabīdī, Muḥammad Murtaḍā al-Ḥusaynī. *Tāj al-ʿarūs fī jawāhir al-qāmūs*. Edited by ʿAbd al-Sattār Aḥmad Farrāj et al. 40 vols. Kuwait: Maṭbaʿat Ḥukūmat al-Kuwayt, 1385–1422/1965–2001.

Index

Abbasid caliphs and caliphate, xi, xii, xxi, xxv, xxvii, xxviii, xxix, §1.4.77, 115n5, 133n170

ʿAbd Allāh ibn Ṭāhir, §1.2.41

ʿAbd al-Laṭīf ibn Yūsuf ibn Muḥammad al-Baghdādī, Muwaffaq al-Dīn, xi–xivi, xvii, xix–xx, xxi–xlvii, lii–liii, livn1, livn4, livn6, livn8, lvn24, lvin38, lvin47, lvin49, lvin57, lvin59, lviin78, §0.1, §2.3.41, 115n1, 115n7, 116n9, 117n20, 118n26, 118n27, 119n36, 121n55, 123n76, 124n86, 125n90, 125n93, 125n95, 126n96, 126n100, 126n103, 127n105, 127n106, 127n109, 127n111, 128n112, 129n119, 129n130, 130n141, 130n146, 132n157, 132n159, 132n165, 133n171, 134n177, 135n182, 136n197, 137n209, 138n213, 139n217, 139n224, 141n239, 141n241, 141n247, 143n252, 145n269, 145n273, 145n274, 147n285, 147n286, 147n287; arrival in Egypt, xxiv; as anatomist, xxxiv, lii; as autopsist, xxxiv; as conservationist, xxi; as empiricist, xxxiv; as grammarian, xxxv; as humorist, xxxvii; as "Ibn al-Labbād," xxiii; as "al-Muṭajjin," xxvi, lvn14; as scientist, xxxiv; birth, xxiii; character, xxvi; criticism of, xxvi; death, xxvi; early life and education, xxiii; historical thinking, xxix–xxx; in Ayyubid court circles, xxiii–xxiv; lost large book on Egypt, xxiv–xxv, xxvii; memoirs, xxiii, xxvii; old age, xxv; postmortem communications via spiritualist mediums, xlv–xlvi, lviin78; return to Baghdad, xxvii; studies, xxi–xxv, xxxiv; teaching, xxiv–xxv; travels, xxiii–xxvi; work on palm trees, xl. *See* also Kitāb al-Ifādah, works

Abraham, §1.4.34, §1.4.55, 130n139

Abū Ḥanīfah al-Dīnawarī. *See* al-Dīnawarī, Abū Ḥanīfah

Abū Maʿshar, 139n217

Abū Nuwās, 131n150

Abusir, xxxi, §1.4.2, §1.4.65, §1.4.71, §§1.4.73–75, §2.3.31, 131n154

Abyssinia, §1.3.20, §1.4.64, §2.1.14, 137n209

acacia, §1.2.39. *See* also aqāqiyā, qaraẓ

Acre, xxiii, §2.3.23

accounts, xi, xxx, xxxvii, xxxviii, of cannibalism, §2.2.19; of earthquakes, §2.3.25; of Egypt, xii, xv, xxii, xxxii, xxxvi, §§0.1–2, §1.4.1, §1.4.8, §1.4.11, §1.4.14, §1.4.26, §1.4.76, 121n55, 136n196; of famine, xii, xxii, §§2.2.23–25; of the Nile, §2.1.9, §2.1.15, §2.1.25, §2.3.37
ʿĀdite people, 143n255
agama, §1.3.16, §1.3.18
Agathodaimon, §1.4.14
Aḥmad ibn Ṭūlūn, 128n114. *See* also Ṭūlūnids
al-Akhfash (surname of several grammarians), §1.2.41
Akhlāṭ, §2.3.15
Akhmīm. *See* Ikhmīm
alchemy, xxiii
alcoholic drink, §1.2.6. *See* also beer, drink
Aleppo, xix, xxv, xliii, li
Alexander III ("the Great"), §1.4.29, §1.4.34
Alexander of Aphrodisias, xxxi, §1.4.76
Alexandria, xii, xxix, xxxviii, xlix, l, §1.1.4, §1.1.10, §1.2.32, §§1.3.28–30, §1.4.25, §§1.4.27–28, §1.4.34, §§1.4.76–77, §2.2.18, §2.2.20, §2.2.35, §2.3.7, §§2.3.10–11, §2.3.14, 127n107, 127n109, 127n111, 128n112, 131n151, 137n209, 140n231, 141n240, 145n270; Bustān al-Qiṭʿah, §1.2.32; library, §1.4.29, 128n112; Lighthouse, §1.4.30, §1.4.32; Pillar of Columns, §§1.4.27–29, §1.4.31; Serapeum, 127n111
algae, §§2.1.10–11, §2.1.13, §2.1.17, §§2.1.21–23, §2.2.31, 137n207
ʿAlī ibn Riḍwān, §1.2.21
almond, §1.2.3, §1.6.5; almond trees, §1.2.46
ʿAmr ibn al-ʿĀṣ, xxxii, §1.4.29, §1.4.34, §2.2.16
Anatolia, xxv, §2.2.25. *See* also Asia Minor
Anatolius (writer on agriculture), xxxi, §1.3.24
anatomical proportion, xxxi, xxxiii, §§1.4.21–23, §§1.4.40–42, §§1.4.44–45, §§1.4.46–47, §1.4.49, §2.3.27. *See* also art, figure, idol, sculpture
anatomy, human, xxi, xxxiv, xxxvi, lii, §1.4.46, §1.4.48, §2.2.2, §§2.3.28–29, 129n122, 147n286; Book of, §2.3.26
Ancient Miṣr, §1.4.33, §1.4.35. *See* also Memphis
animals, xiii, xiv, xv, xxi, §0.4, §1.2.26, §1.3.8, §1.3.12, §1.3.15, §§1.3.17–18, §§1.3.24–26, §1.4.45, §1.4.69, §1.4.73, §2.1.4, §2.2.2, §2.3.37, 116n15, 123n76, 132n161, 136n194, 140n226, 143n254, 147n290; Book of Animals, §1.4.49. *See* also agama, cattle, chicken, clam, crocodile, donkey, dolphins, eel, fish, "fishlet of Sidon," hippopotamus, horse, "jolter," livestock, mule, oxen, poultry, scarab beetles, skink, spider, turtle, varanus, vermin
antiquities, xiv, xxi, xxxii, xxxiii, 131n151; vandalism and theft of, xiv, xxxii, §1.4.28, 126n103, 127n104, 127n110
aphrodisiac, §1.3.18, §§1.3.21–22, 123n73, 123n75

brick, xiv, §1.3.2, §1.4.2, §1.4.46, §1.5.2, §1.5.4, 121n57. *See* also masonry
Browne, Sir Thomas, xxxvi, lvin42
building, xxi, xxx, xxxiv, §0.4, §1.4.20, §1.4.35, §1.4.39, §1.4.76, §§1.5.1–2, §2.2.17, §2.2.31, §2.3.13, 126n101, 128n118. *See* also architecture, bathhouse, bazaar, dam, market, palace, pyramid, residential compounds, temple, wind tower
burial, §§1.4.61–63, §2.2.21, 145n270; burial grounds, §1.4.69, §1.4.71, §1.4.75, §2.3.31. *See* also mūmiyā/mūmiyāʾ, mummies and mummification, pyramid, sarcophagus
"burned out," §2.1.17, §2.1.19, §2.1.24, §2.1.31, §2.3.37
Bursa, xli
Bustān al-Qiṭʿah, §1.2.32

Caesars, xii, xxix, §1.4.77
Cairo, xv, xx, xxiv–xxv, xxxviii, xlviii, xlix, l, §1.3.25, §1.4.3, §1.4.34, §2.2.1, §2.2.21, §2.2.29, §2.3.4, §2.3.6,§2.3.41, 116n10, 123n75, 129n119, 133n173, 134n177, 135n188, 140n225, 144n265, 144n266, 144n267; bathhouses, §§1.5.6–8, 134n177, 134n178, 134n180; bazaars, §1.5.3, 134n175; Citadel, §1.4.3; Dīwān, §2.3.9, 144n266, 144n268; mosque, xx, xxiv, xlviii, §1.4.32, 128n114, 141n237; of ʿAmr ibn al-ʿĀṣ, xlviii, §2.2.16; of Ibn Ṭulūn, xlviii, §2.2.16; population statistics, xxxviii, §2.2.21, §2.3.2, §2.3.6, §2.3.11, 144n266; prefect (chief of police), §2.2.2, §2.2.7, §2.2.13, §2.2.15, §2.3.12, §2.3.36, 140n225; property rents, §2.3.8; residential compound, §1.5.3, §2.2.29, §2.3.8; sewers, §1.5.2, 133n173. *See* also Old Cairo
calendar, liii, §1.1.9, 116n13, 117n23, 122n64. *See* also Coptic calendar, Syro-Macedonian calendar
cannibalism, xiii, xxii, xxxvi, xxxvii, xxxix, xli, §2.2.3, §2.2.8, §2.2.15, §2.2.19, §2.3.1, §2.3.35, 141n239, 143n252; execution of cannibals, xli, §2.2.2, §2.2.7, §2.3.35; stays of execution, §2.2.13–14
Cataracts, §1.3.15
catfish, electric. *See* "jolter"
cattle, §1.3.13, §1.3.25, §§1.4.71–72; dung, §1.3.1, §1.3.5. *See* also livestock, oxen
cheese, xx, §1.6.6, §1.6.9
"chick factories." *See* egg, artificial incubation
chicken, xxxix, §2.3.4, 121n55; prices, §2.3.4, 144n262; recipes, §1.6.3, §§1.6.5–8. *See* also egg, poultry
Children of Israel, §1.4.55
Christians, §1.3.12, §1.4.56, 122n65, 131n145, 131n146, 147n292
citrons, §§1.2.29–30, 120n48
citrus fruits, §1.2.29, §1.2.31
clam, §1.3.31, §1.6.9, 124n83
"Cleopatra's Needles," §1.4.25, 127n106, 127n107
climate, xxxiv, xlvii. *See* also dry/dryness, humidity, rain, wind
Climes, §1.1.3, §1.1.5, §2.1.29
cold, §1.1.11, §1.5.6, §2.2.25, §2.3.13; as humoral quality, §1.2.2, §1.2.7, 117n18, 135n191

cooking, §§1.2.1–2, §§1.2.15–16, §1.2.18, §1.2.20, §1.4.15, §1.5.8, §1.6.3, §1.6.5, §1.6.7, §2.1.12, 118n30, 125n96, 134n182, 140n230. *See* also diet, drink, food, sweet; of human flesh, §2.2.7, §2.2.13, §2.2.15
Coptic calendar, liii, §2.1.9, §2.2.32, 117n23, 122n64, 137n206, 138n212
Copts, xii, xxix, §§1.4.55–56, §1.4.76–77, §2.1.16, §2.1.27, 118n26, 126n102, 137n209, 138n211. *See* also Christians
crocodile, xiii, §§1.3.15–16, §1.3.18, 123n69, 123n71
crops, §1.1.5, §1.2.6, §1.2.10, §1.2.22, §1.2.36, §1.2.40, §1.3.25, §§2.1.1–2, §2.1.16, §2.2.34, §2.3.33, 117n25. *See* also cultivation
Crusaders. *See* Franks
Ctesiphon. *See* al-Madāʾin
cucumber, §1.2.40, 120n52; as comparison §1.2.1, §1.2.15, §1.2.25
cuisine, 135n188. *See* also cooking, diet, drink, food, sweet
cultivation, §1.1.5, §1.2.2, §§2.1.2–3, §2.2.23, §2.2.34, §2.3.10, 131n152, 136n196, 142n247; uncultivated, §2.2.34, 131n152. *See* also crops
Cyprus, §2.3.15
Cyrenaica. *See* Barqah

Damascus, xxiii–xxv, xxxi, l, li, §1.2.16, §1.2.22, §1.2.45, §2.3.16, §§2.3.20–22, 119n38; Bāb Jayrūn, §2.3.22; Hospital, §2.3.20; al-Kallāsah, §2.3.20, §2.3.22; Umayyad Mosque, §2.3.20, 146n279
Damietta, §1.1.2, §1.1.4, §1.1.8, §1.2.44, §1.3.17, §1.3.23, §1.3.25, §1.6.9, §2.2.18, §2.3.7, §2.3.10, §2.3.14, 127n110
Damīrah, §1.2.41
al-Damīrī, Muḥammad ibn Mūsā, 117n20, 123n69, 130n131, 132n163, 147n290
dam, 124n85, 134n176; construction of, §1.5.5. *See* also Aswan High Dam
Damūh, §1.4.33
date (fruit), §1.2.34, §2.1.16; palms, §§1.2.22–24, §1.2.27, §1.2.34, §1.4.71, 132n160; relationship to bananas, §§1.2.3–4, §§1.2.24–26; stone, xiii, §1.2.23. *See* also hybridity
Dāwud ibn Bahrām, xxv
desert, §1.6.9
destruction, §2.2.32, 143n255; of antiquities, §1.4.15, §§1.4.34–35, §1.4.59, 128n112
diet, §1.6.4, §1.6.9, 120n50; dietary, §2.1.11. *See* also cooking, cuisine, drink, food, sweet
al-Dīnawarī, Abū Ḥanīfah, §1.2.4, §1.2.8, §1.2.27, §1.2.39
Dioscorides, xxxi, §§1.2.18–20, §1.3.20, 119n36
disfigurement, §1.4.22; of antiquities, §1.4.35, §1.4.59. *See* also antiquities, destruction
donkey, §1.3.12, §1.3.14, §1.4.73, §1.6.9, 122n65, 122n66, 132n162; prices, 122n65
dolphins, §1.3.17
drainage, §1.5.2, 133n172. *See* also sewers
drink, §1.2.4, §1.2.6, §1.2.37, §1.3.24, §1.6.9, §2.1.4, §2.1.11; alcoholic

Greek, xx, xxxi, §1.1.10, 116n14, 120n54, 123n76, 128n111, 129n130, 133n166, 133n169, 137n203
Green Chamber, xxxiii, lvn35, §1.4.36
green gram, §1.2.35, 120n50

Habiba Ahmed Mohamed Al-Sayfi, vii, xx, 117n21, 119n34, 120n51, 120n52, 121n54, 135n188, 136n201, 144n261
Ḥalab, §2.2.29
Ḥalabiyyah (military unit), §1.4.15
Ḥamāh/Ḥamāt, §§2.3.16–18
Ḥārat al-Sāsah, §2.3.6
al-Harawī, ʿAlī ibn Abī Bakr, lvn33, lvin38
harīsah (hash), §1.5.8, §1.6.5
al-Ḥawf, §2.2.25
Ḥawrān, §2.3.23
Hecataeus of Abdera, xxxi–xxxii
Heliopolis. *See* ʿAyn Shams
Hermes "Trismegistus," §1.4.14, 131n154
Herodotus, xxxi–xxxii, lvn31, lvn32, 147n290
Heron of Alexandria, 127n109
hieroglyphic characters, xlvi, 125n95
highland, §1.1.5
Hijaz, §2.2.1
al-Hilāliyyah, §2.3.6
hill, §1.1.1, §1.4.16, §1.4.59; hillock, xxxix, §1.4.31, §1.4.73, §2.3.26, §§2.3.33–34
Hippocrates, xxxi, 135n182; in book title, §1.4.76
hippopotamus, §1.3.25, 123n76, 124n77, 124n79, 138n212; as "river horse," §1.3.23, 123n76
horse, §1.3.12, §1.3.14, §1.3.23, §1.4.73, 122n65, 122n66, 132n162; horseman, §1.4.19, §2.2.5
hot, §1.3.9, §1.5.6, §§1.5.8–9, §2.3.13, 116n17; as humoral quality, §1.1.7, §1.2.16, §1.2.26, §1.6.6, 116n12, 135n191
Hulagu, xli, xliii
humidity, §§1.1.6–8, §1.1.10, §2.1.1, §2.1.19
humor/humoral, §§1.1.7–8, 135n191. *See* also cold, dry, hot, moist, temperament
hunt, §§1.3.24–25, §2.2.6; grounds, §1.6.8
Hunt, Thomas, xliv
hybridity, §1.2.23, §1.2.26, §1.2.29, §1.2.41
Hyde, Thomas, xliv

Ibn Abī l-Raddād, §2.2.32, §2.3.38
Ibn Abī Uṣaybiʿah, xxii, xxv–xxvi, xxxvi, xl, livn4, 131n146
Ibn Jubayr, xxvii, 146n279
Ibn al-Qifṭī, xxvi
Ibn Samajūn, §1.2.5, §1.2.12
Ibn al-Shahrazūrī, al-Qāḍī, 131n154
Ibn Taghrībirdī, xxxviii, lvin59
Ibn Wahb, §1.2.41
idol, xxxiii, §1.4.23, §§1.4.40–41, §1.4.44, §1.4.50, §§1.4.54–55, §1.4.59, §2.2.27, 127n104, 127n105, 130n134, 130n139, 143n252. *See* also anatomical proportion, art, figure (in art), sculpture
Ikhmīm, §2.3.7
Imruʾ al-Qays, §2.2.24, 142n249
increase (of river depth), §1.1.6, §§2.1.16–18, §2.1.20, §2.2.32, §§2.3.38–39. *See* also flood, inundation, rise (of river)
India/Indian, §1.2.20, §1.2.22, §1.2.28, §1.2.43, §1.2.46, §1.3.20, 135n193
indigo, §1.2.46

mosque, xx, xxiv, §1.4.32, 128n114, 141n237, 141n238, 145n270, 146n279; of ʿAmr ibn al-ʿĀṣ, xlviii, §2.2.16; of Ibn Ṭulūn, xlviii, §2.2.16
Mosul, xxiii, l, §2.2.25
mountain, §1.1.2, §1.2.39, §1.4.68, §2.2.20, §2.3.15, §2.3.18, §2.3.24, 116n9, 126n96, 141n240; mountain fig §1.2.4, §1.2.6; of water, §2.3.39, 146n275
mouse. *See* vermin
mud, §1.1.5, §1.1.10, §1.2.18, §1.4.2, §1.5.4, §2.1.16, §2.1.21, §2.2.31, 137n211. *See* also sediment; huts, §2.2.12
Muḥammad, Prophet, xxxii, §§0.2–3, §1.6.10, §2.3.40, 115n5, 147n292
Muḥammad Ṣāʾim al-Dahr, Shaykh, 127n104
al-Muʿizz, Fatimid caliph, §1.4.34
mule, §1.3.12, §1.3.14, §§1.3.23–24, §2.3.36, 122n66, 147n290
mulūkhiyyah (garden mallow), §1.2.2
mūmiyā/mūmiyāʾ (substance used in mummification), §1.4.66–68, 132n159
mummies and mummification, xxi, xlvi, §1.4.66, 132n156, 132n158, 132n159; animal, §§1.4.71–72, 132n158, 132n161, 132n162; human, §§1.4.71–72
mung. *See* gram, green
al-Muqaṭṭam, §1.1.10, §1.4.3
Mūsā ibn Maymūn. *See* Maimonides, Moses
musk, §1.2.32, §§1.6.5–7; from crocodiles, §1.3.15, 122n68
al-Mustanṣir, Abbasid caliph, xxv, livn12
al-Mutanabbī, xxxix
al-Muʿtaṣim, Abbasid caliph, xxviii, xxx

Nabataeans, xxix, §1.4.77
Nābulus, li, §2.3.23, 145n274
al-Nāʾilī/Ibn Nāʾilī, ʿAbd Allāh, xxiii
Najd, §1.2.13
Napoleon I, xx, xliv
al-Nāṣir, Abbasid caliph, xi–xii, xxviii–xxx, livn12, lvn25, §0.2; revival of caliphate, xxviii
naydah (food), §1.6.1, §1.6.9
Nebuchadnezzar II, §1.4.34
Nicolaus of Damascus, xiv, xxxi
Nile River, xxxi–xxxii, xxxiv, xxxix, xlvii, xlviii, xlix, l, lii, liii, lviin72, §0.4, §§1.1.1–6, §1.1.9, §1.3.15, §1.3.17, §§1.3.19–20, §1.3.29, §1.4.2, §1.4.5, §1.4.19, §1.4.33, §1.6.9, §§2.1.1–2, §§2.1.4–6, §§2.1.8–10, §§2.1.13–17, §2.1.19, §§2.1.21–25, §2.1.28, §2.2.1, §§2.2.23–24, §2.2.31, §§2.3.37–38, 115n8, 116n9, 116n10, 123n76, 124n85, 134n173, 136n196, 137n206, 137n211, 138n216, 138n217, 143n257; annual inundation, §1.1.3, §1.1.6, §1.6.9 §2.1.1. *See* also flood, increase (of river depth), rise (of river); "burned out," §2.1.17, §2.1.19, §2.1.24, §2.1.31, §2.3.37; forecasting, §2.1.16, §2.1.28, 138n217; name, §2.1.6, 137n203; records, §2.1.8, §§2.1.14–15; presence of algae, §§2.1.10–11, §2.1.13, §2.1.17, §§2.1.21–23, §2.2.31, 137n207; sediment, §1.1.5, §2.1.21. *See* also mud; "Sultan's Water,"

poultry, §2.3.4, 121n55, 122n62, 144n261. *See* also egg, chicken
prefect (chief of police), §2.2.2, §2.2.7, §2.2.13, §2.2.15, §2.3.12, §2.3.36, 140n225
prostitutes, §2.2.27
Ptolemy, Claudius, xxxi, §2.1.28, 139n217
pumpkin, §1.2.43, 135n189
pyramid, xxvii, xxix–xxx, xxxi, xxxii, xxxv, xxxvi, xlii, xlviii, xlix, §§1.4.2–15, §§1.4.17–21, §1.4.62, §§1.4.75–76, 124n84, 125n94, 125n95, 126n98, 132n165, 133n166; attempt to demolish, §1.4.15; of Giza, §§1.4.3–5, §1.4.75, 125n90, 132n164; of Khafre, 124n86, 132n164; of Khufu, 124n86, 125n95, 126n103, 132n164; of Menkaure, §1.4.5, §1.4.75, 124n88, 132n164; of Neferirkare, 132n164
Pyramid Texts, 125n95
Pythagoreans, xxxi

Qā'it Bāy, xx
al-Qarāfah, §2.2.16
Qarājā, §1.4.28, 127n110
Qarāqūsh al-Asadī, Bahā' al-Dīn, §§1.4.3–4, 124n85
qaraẓ, §§1.2.37–39, 120n51. *See* also acacia, aqāqiyā
quarries, §1.4.19, 126n99, 126n100
quinces, §1.2.45
al-Qulzum, xlix, §1.3.20, §1.4.19, 126n100
Qur'an, xi, xxiv, xxxi, xxxiv, lii, §1.4.57, §2.2.23, §2.2.33, 115n3, 115n6, 130n135, 130n139, 131n148, 139n222, 143n252, 146n278, 147n292
Qūṣ, §1.1.10, §1.4.70, §2.2.18, §2.2.22, §2.2.35, §2.3.7, §2.3.14

radish, §1.2.12, §1.6.2, §2.1.12
rain, lviin72, §§1.1.3–5, §1.4.24, §§2.1.18–19, §§2.1.21–22; rainfall, §2.1.14, §§2.1.18–19, §§2.1.21–22
Ramesses II, 129n119, 129n125, 130n141
rat. *See* vermin
al-Rāzī, xxiii, §1.2.12
recipe, xxi, §1.6.3, §1.6.6, §2.2.14. *See* also ingredient
remedy, §§1.2.14–15, §1.2.18, §1.2.36, 134n180. *See* also medicine
rhubarb, xxvii, §2.3.24, 146n283
rise (of river), xxxi–xxxii, xlvii, lii, liii, §0.4, §1.1.3, §§1.1.5–6, §1.1.9, §§2.1.1–5, §§2.1.7–10, §§2.1.14–15, §§2.1.17–21, §2.1.23, §§2.1.25–26, §2.1.28, §2.2.1, §§2.2.32–33, §2.3.1, §§2.3.38–40, 136n196, 136n197, 137n206, 138n211, 138n212, 138n213, 138n216, 138n217. *See* also flood, increase (of river depth), inundation
river, xxxi–xxxii, xxxix, xlvii, xlviii, xlix, l, li, lii, §§1.1.2–4, §1.3.19, §§1.3.23–25, §1.5.10, §2.1.1, §2.1.14, §§2.1.22–24, §2.2.24, §§2.2.31–32, §§2.3.37–39, 116n10, 123n76, 136n196, 137n203, 138n212. *See* also Nile River
robbers/robbery, xxi, xxvi, 125n94
Roda Island, §2.2.12
Romans, xii, xxix, §1.4.77, 116n14, 127n107, 133n169
rose, §§1.2.18–19, §1.2.44, §§1.6.3–4; rose water, §1.6.3, §§1.6.5–7, 135n187
rowing, §§1.5.11–12, 135n184

Sabā/Saba', people of, §2.2.1, 139n222
Sabians, §1.4.14, §1.4.56, §1.4.76
Sacy, Antoine Isaac Silvestre, Baron de. *See* Silvestre, Baron de Sacy, Antoine Isaac
Ṣafad, §2.3.23, 146n281
Ṣāfīthā, §2.3.23
Saladin (Ṣalāḥ al-Dīn Yūsuf ibn Ayyūb), xxiii–xxiv, xxvii, §1.4.3, §1.4.15, §1.4.28, 127n110, 139n220
Ṣalāḥ al-Dīn Yūsuf ibn Ayyūb. *See* Saladin
salamanders. *See* "fishlet of Sidon"
Samaritans, §2.3.23
Sanaa, xix–xx
Saqqara, xlix, 125n95, 129n119, 129n125, 129n126, 132n158, 132n161
sarcophagus, §1.4.11, §1.4.62, §1.4.74, 131n151
al-Sayfi, Habiba. *See* Habiba Ahmed
scarab beetles, 132n158
sculpture, xxi, xxxiii, xxxix, §1.4.22, §1.4.35, 129n125. *See* also anatomical proportion, art, figure (in art), idol
Sea of Pitch, §1.2.12
sediment, §1.1.5, §1.2.11, §2.1.23, 116n11. *See* also mud
Senusret I, 127n106
Serapeum, 127n111. *See* also temple
sewers, §1.5.2, 133n173. *See* also drainage
Shāfi' ibn 'Alī, Nāṣir al-Dīn, xlii; Marvels of Architecture, xlii
al-Shāri', §2.2.10, §2.3.6
al-Shāri'ī, Abū l-Qāsim Hibat Allāh ibn 'Alī, xxiv
Sidon, §1.3.18
sikbāj (stew), §2.2.13, 135n186
Silvestre, Baron de Sacy, Antoine Isaac, xx, xxxvii, xl, xliv–xlvi, lviin71, 121n56, 122n63, 124n81, 129n124, 129n130, 132n157, 137n210, 141n239, 142n248
Sirius, §1.2.10, §1.2.12, 117n23, 118n30
skink, xiii, §§1.3.18–21, 123n71, 123n72, 123n74, 123n75
slave/slavery, §1.5.11, §2.2.26, §2.2.27, 137n205
soap, §1.6.2
Sphinx of Giza, xxxiii, xlii, xlviii, 126n102, 126n103, 127n104
spider, §1.2.5, 117n20
spiritual/spiritualism, xxvii–xxviii, xlv
Stern, S.M., xli, lvin57
"Sultan's Water," §2.1.3, §2.1.18, §2.1.21
sumac, §1.2.15, §1.6.9
al-Ṣūfī, Rashid al-Dīn, xxxiv
sweet (adjective), xiv, xv, xxv, §1.2.1, §1.2.3, §1.2.6, §1.2.8, §1.2.12, §1.2.12, §§1.2.24–25, §1.2.29, §§1.2.40–41, §1.2.43, §§1.2.45–46, §1.6.1, §1.6.4, §2.2.31, 135n188; sweet (noun), §§1.6.1–6. *See* also khabīṣ; sweetness, §1.2.6, §1.2.25, §1.2.34
Syria, xxiii–xxiv, li, 139n220, 145n274
Syro-Macedonian Calendar, liii

Tamil Nadu, 120n47
taro, xiii, xxxv, §§1.2.15–18, §§1.2.20–21, §1.2.23, §§1.2.25–26, 119n34
temperament, xlvii, §§1.1.7–8, §1.2.1, §1.2.7, §1.2.16, §1.2.23, §1.2.26, §1.3.9, §1.3.11, §2.1.26, §2.3.2, 117n18, 135n191, 138n216, 144n260. See also cold, dry, hot, moist, humor/humoral

works, §0.2, §§1.4.3–4, §1.4.22, §1.4.52, §§2.3.29–30, 132n157; by ʿAbd al-Laṭīf xi–xiii, xx, xxi, xxii–xlvi passim,131n146, 147n286. *See* also ʿAbd al-Laṭīf ibn Yūsuf ibn Muḥammad al-Baghdādī, Muwaffaq al-Dīn, Kitāb al-Ifādah

Yaḥyā, §1.2.41
al-Yamānī, ʿUmārah, 124n89
Yāqūt al-Ḥamawī, 118n26, 137n203
al-Yāzūrī, Abū Muḥammad al-Ḥasan/al-Ḥusayn ibn ʿAlī, §2.3.11
Yemen/Yemeni, xix, l, lvn14, §1.2.13, §1.2.20, §1.2.22, §2.2.1, §2.2.25, 119n37
Yule, Sir Henry, xxxvi, lvin44, 120n50
Yūsuf ibn ʿAbd al-Laṭīf al-Baghdādī, Sharaf al-Dīn, xxvi

Zand, Kamal Hafuth, xlv, xlvi, 122n63, 137n210, 141n239, 142n248
Zuqāq al-Birkah, §2.2.29

About the NYU Abu Dhabi Institute

The Library of Arabic Literature is supported by a grant from the NYU Abu Dhabi Institute, a major hub of intellectual and creative activity and advanced research. The Institute hosts academic conferences, workshops, lectures, film series, performances, and other public programs directed both to audiences within the UAE and to the worldwide academic and research community. It is a center of the scholarly community for Abu Dhabi, bringing together faculty and researchers from institutions of higher learning throughout the region.

NYU Abu Dhabi, through the NYU Abu Dhabi Institute, is a world-class center of cutting-edge research, scholarship, and cultural activity. The Institute creates singular opportunities for leading researchers from across the arts, humanities, social sciences, sciences, engineering, and the professions to carry out creative scholarship and conduct research on issues of major disciplinary, multidisciplinary, and global significance.

About the Translator

Tim Mackintosh-Smith is a fan of Arabic travel literature, and the author of several books of his own travels. Of these, a trilogy on Ibn Baṭṭūṭah (*Travels with a Tangerine*, *The Hall of a Thousand Columns*, and *Landfalls*) retraces the Moroccan's wanderings around three continents. Tim's work has gained him the 1998 Thomas Cook/*Daily Telegraph* Travel Book Award and, appropriately, the 2010 Ibn Baṭṭūṭah Prize of Honour. He has also co-written and presented a BBC TV series on Ibn Baṭṭūṭah, and delivered the Hamilton A. R. Gibb Lectures at Harvard. His most recent book, *Arabs: A 3,000 Year History of Peoples, Tribes and Empires* (Yale University Press, 2019), rebalances that history, seeing Islam as part of it, not the start of it.

Tim has been based for more than a third of a century, through thick and thin, in the Yemeni capital Sanaa. Work on this present volume has, however, taken him back more than forty years to a pre-Arabic youth, in which he worked his way through Gardiner's *Egyptian Grammar*, and spent many delightful hours with embalmed Egyptians in the cellars of Bristol City Museum. It has also taken him back to equally happy times with live Egyptians, hence the double dedication—to a dear friend, and to a fondly remembered teacher. For Tim, they personify the present and the past of the marvelous land described in this book.

The Library of Arabic Literature

For more details on individual titles, visit www.libraryofarabicliterature.org

Classical Arabic Literature: A Library of Arabic Literature Anthology
Selected and translated by Geert Jan van Gelder (2012)

A Treasury of Virtues: Sayings, Sermons, and Teachings of ʿAlī, by al-Qāḍī al-Quḍāʿī, with the *One Hundred Proverbs* attributed to al-Jāḥiẓ
Edited and translated by Tahera Qutbuddin (2013)

The Epistle on Legal Theory, by al-Shāfiʿī
Edited and translated by Joseph E. Lowry (2013)

Leg over Leg, by Aḥmad Fāris al-Shidyāq
Edited and translated by Humphrey Davies (4 volumes; 2013–14)

Virtues of the Imām Aḥmad ibn Ḥanbal, by Ibn al-Jawzī
Edited and translated by Michael Cooperson (2 volumes; 2013–15)

The Epistle of Forgiveness, by Abū l-ʿAlāʾ al-Maʿarrī
Edited and translated by Geert Jan van Gelder and Gregor Schoeler (2 volumes; 2013–14)

The Principles of Sufism, by ʿĀʾishah al-Bāʿūniyyah
Edited and translated by Th. Emil Homerin (2014)

The Expeditions: An Early Biography of Muḥammad, by Maʿmar ibn Rāshid
Edited and translated by Sean W. Anthony (2014)

Two Arabic Travel Books
Accounts of China and India, by Abū Zayd al-Sīrāfī
Edited and translated by Tim Mackintosh-Smith (2014)
Mission to the Volga, by Aḥmad ibn Faḍlān
Edited and translated by James Montgomery (2014)

Disagreements of the Jurists: A Manual of Islamic Legal Theory, by al-Qāḍī al-Nuʿmān
Edited and translated by Devin J. Stewart (2015)

Consorts of the Caliphs: Women and the Court of Baghdad, by Ibn al-Sāʿī
Edited by Shawkat M. Toorawa and translated by the Editors of the Library of Arabic Literature (2015)

What ʿĪsā ibn Hishām Told Us, by Muḥammad al-Muwayliḥī
Edited and translated by Roger Allen (2 volumes; 2015)

The Life and Times of Abū Tammām, by Abū Bakr Muḥammad ibn Yaḥyā al-Ṣūlī
Edited and translated by Beatrice Gruendler (2015)

The Sword of Ambition: Bureaucratic Rivalry in Medieval Egypt, by ʿUthmān ibn Ibrāhīm al-Nābulusī
Edited and translated by Luke Yarbrough (2016)

Brains Confounded by the Ode of Abū Shādūf Expounded, by Yūsuf al-Shirbīnī
Edited and translated by Humphrey Davies (2 volumes; 2016)

Light in the Heavens: Sayings of the Prophet Muḥammad, by al-Qāḍī al-Quḍāʿī
Edited and translated by Tahera Qutbuddin (2016)

Risible Rhymes, by Muḥammad ibn Maḥfūẓ al-Sanhūrī
Edited and translated by Humphrey Davies (2016)

A Hundred and One Nights
Edited and translated by Bruce Fudge (2016)

The Excellence of the Arabs, by Ibn Qutaybah
Edited by James E. Montgomery and Peter Webb
Translated by Sarah Bowen Savant and Peter Webb (2017)

Scents and Flavors: A Syrian Cookbook
Edited and translated by Charles Perry (2017)

Arabian Satire: Poetry from 18th-Century Najd, by Ḥmēdān al-Shwēʿir
Edited and translated by Marcel Kurpershoek (2017)

In Darfur: An Account of the Sultanate and Its People, by Muḥammad ibn ʿUmar al-Tūnisī
Edited and translated by Humphrey Davies (2 volumes; 2018)

War Songs, by ʿAntarah ibn Shaddād
Edited by James E. Montgomery
Translated by James E. Montgomery with Richard Sieburth (2018)

Arabian Romantic: Poems on Bedouin Life and Love, by ʿAbdallah ibn Sbayyil
Edited and translated by Marcel Kurpershoek (2018)

Dīwān ʿAntarah ibn Shaddād: A Literary-Historical Study, by James E. Montgomery (2018)

Stories of Piety and Prayer: Deliverance Follows Adversity, by al-Muḥassin ibn ʿAlī al-Tanūkhī
Edited and translated by Julia Bray (2019)

Tajrīd sayf al-himmah li-stikhrāj mā fī dhimmat al-dhimmah: A Scholarly Edition of ʿUthmān ibn Ibrāhīm al-Nābulusī's Text, by Luke Yarbrough (2019)

The Philosopher Responds: An Intellectual Correspondence from the Tenth Century, by Abū Ḥayyān al-Tawḥīdī and Abū ʿAlī Miskawayh
Edited by Bilal Orfali and Maurice A. Pomerantz
Translated by Sophia Vasalou and James E. Montgomery (2 volumes; 2019)

The Discourses: Reflections on History, Sufism, Theology, and Literature—Volume One, by al-Ḥasan al-Yūsī
Edited and translated by Justin Stearns (2020)

Impostures, by al-Ḥarīrī
Translated by Michael Cooperson (2020)

Maqāmāt Abī Zayd al-Sarūjī, by al-Ḥarīrī
Edited by Michael Cooperson (2020)

The Yoga Sutras of Patañjali, by Abū Rayḥān al-Bīrūnī
Edited and translated by Mario Kozah (2020)

The Book of Charlatans, by Jamāl al-Dīn ʿAbd al-Raḥīm al-Jawbarī
Edited by Manuela Dengler
Translated by Humphrey Davies (2020)

A Physician on the Nile: A Description of Egypt and Journal of the Famine Years, by ʿAbd al-Laṭīf al-Baghdādī
Edited and translated by Tim Mackintosh-Smith (2021)

The Book of Travels, by Ḥannā Diyāb
Edited by Johannes Stephan
Translated by Elias Muhanna (2 volumes; 2021)

Kalīlah and Dimnah: Fables of Virtue and Vice, by Ibn al-Muqaffaʿ
Edited by Michael Fishbein
Translated by Michael Fishbein and James E. Montgomery (2021)

Love, Death, Fame: Poetry and Lore from the Emirati Oral Tradition, by al-Māyidī ibn Ẓāhir
Edited and translated by Marcel Kurpershoek (2022)

The Essence of Reality: A Defense of Philosophical Sufism, by ʿAyn al-Quḍāt
Edited and translated by Mohammed Rustom (2022)

The Requirements of the Sufi Path: A Defense of the Mystical Tradition, by Ibn Khaldūn
Edited and translated by Carolyn Baugh (2022)

The Doctors' Dinner Party, by Ibn Buṭlān
Edited and translated by Philip F. Kennedy and Jeremy Farrell (2023)

English-only Paperbacks

Leg over Leg, by Aḥmad Fāris al-Shidyāq (2 volumes; 2015)

The Expeditions: An Early Biography of Muḥammad, by Maʿmar ibn Rāshid (2015)

The Epistle on Legal Theory: A Translation of al-Shāfiʿī's Risālah, by al-Shāfiʿī (2015)

The Epistle of Forgiveness, by Abū l-ʿAlāʾ al-Maʿarrī (2016)

The Principles of Sufism, by ʿĀʾishah al-Bāʿūniyyah (2016)

A Treasury of Virtues: Sayings, Sermons, and Teachings of ʿAlī, by al-Qāḍī al-Quḍāʿī with the *One Hundred Proverbs* attributed to al-Jāḥiẓ (2016)

The Life of Ibn Ḥanbal, by Ibn al-Jawzī (2016)

Mission to the Volga, by Ibn Faḍlān (2017)

Accounts of China and India, by Abū Zayd al-Sīrāfī (2017)

Consorts of the Caliphs: Women and the Court of Baghdad, by Ibn al-Sāʿī (2017)

A Hundred and One Nights (2017)

Disagreements of the Jurists: A Manual of Islamic Legal Theory, by al-Qāḍī al-Nuʿmān (2017)

What ʿĪsā ibn Hishām Told Us, by Muḥammad al-Muwayliḥī (2018)

War Songs, by ʿAntarah ibn Shaddād (2018)

The Life and Times of Abū Tammām, by Abū Bakr Muḥammad ibn Yaḥyā al-Ṣūlī (2018)

The Sword of Ambition, by ʿUthmān ibn Ibrāhīm al-Nābulusī (2019)

Brains Confounded by the Ode of Abū Shādūf Expounded: Volume One, by Yūsuf al-Shirbīnī (2019)

Brains Confounded by the Ode of Abū Shādūf Expounded: Volume Two, by Yūsuf al-Shirbīnī and *Risible Rhymes*, by Muḥammad ibn Maḥfūẓ al-Sanhūrī (2019)

The Excellence of the Arabs, by Ibn Qutaybah (2019)

Light in the Heavens: Sayings of the Prophet Muḥammad, by al-Qāḍī al-Quḍāʿī (2019)

Scents and Flavors: A Syrian Cookbook (2020)

Arabian Satire: Poetry from 18th-Century Najd, by Ḥmēdān al-Shwēʿir (2020)

In Darfur: An Account of the Sultanate and Its People, by Muḥammad al-Tūnisī (2020)

Arabian Romantic: Poems on Bedouin Life and Love, by Ibn Sbayyil (2020)

The Philosopher Responds: An Intellectual Correspondence from the Tenth Century, by Abū Ḥayyān al-Tawḥīdī and Abū ʿAlī Miskawayh (2021)

Impostures, by al-Ḥarīrī (2021)

The Discourses: Reflections on History, Sufism, Theology, and Literature—Volume One, by al-Ḥasan al-Yūsī (2021)

The Yoga Sutras of Patañjali, by Abū Rayḥān al-Bīrūnī (2022)

The Book of Charlatans, by Jamāl al-Dīn ʿAbd al-Raḥīm al-Jawbarī (2022)

The Book of Travels, by Ḥannā Diyāb (2022)

A Physician on the Nile: A Description of Egypt and Journal of the Famine Years, by ʿAbd al-Laṭīf al-Baghdādī (2022)